Asian Port Cities, 1600–1800

Local and Foreign Cultural Interactions

Asian Port Cities, 1600–1800

Local and Foreign Cultural Interactions

Edited by

Haneda Masashi

NUS PRESS

Singapore

in association with

KYOTO UNIVERSITY PRESS

Japan

NUS Press
National University of Singapore
AS3-01-02, 3 Arts Link
Singapore 117569
http://nuspress.nus.edu.sg

ISBN 978-9971-69-463-0 (Paper)

Kyoto University Press
Kyodai-Kaikan (Kyoto University Hall)
15-9 Yoshida-Kawaramachi, Sakyo-ku
Kyoto-city 606-8305
Japan
www.kyoto-up.or.jp

ISBN 978-4-87698-768-9

Institute of Oriental Culture Special Series No. 22

National Library Board Singapore Cataloguing in Publication Data

Asian port cities, 1600–1800: local and foreign cultural interactions / edited by Haneda Masashi. – Singapore: NUS Press in association with Kyoto University Press, c2009.

p. cm.
Includes index.
ISBN-13: 978-9971-69-463-0 (pbk.)

1. Asia – Civilization – 17th century. 2. Asia – Civilization – 18th century. 3. Asia – Civilization – European influences. 4. Intercultural communication – Asia – History. 5. Harbors – Asia – History – 17th century. 6. Harbors – Asia – History – 18th century. I. Haneda, Masashi.

DS33.7
950.3 – dc22 OCN301110102

Typeset by: Scientifik Graphics
Printed by: Markono Print Media Pte Ltd

Contents

List of Illustrations vii

Preface xv

Introduction: Framework and Methods of Comparative Studies on Asian Port Cities in the Seventeenth and Eighteenth Centuries 1

1. Canton, Nagasaki and the Port Cities of the Indian Ocean: A Comparison 13
Haneda Masashi

2. The Legal Position of Foreigners in Nagasaki during the Edo Period 24
Matsui Yoko

3. The Commercial Culture of the VOC in Canton in the Eighteenth Century 43
Liu Yong

4. Western and Chinese Influences on Japanese Paintings in the Eighteenth Century 63
Ito Shiori

5. Jingdezhen and *imari*: Communication and Competition between Chinese and Japanese Porcelains in the Seventeenth and Eighteenth Centuries 88
Liu Zhaohui

6. On the Waterfront: Life and Labour Around the Batavian Roadstead 119
Leonard Blussé

7. Dutch Interaction with Siamese Law and the City Rules of Ayutthaya in the Seventeenth and Eighteenth Centuries 139
Bhawan Ruangsilp

8. Cultural Interaction between the British Diaspora in Madras and the Host Community, 1650–1790 162
Søren Mentz

9. The Hindu Courtier and the French Governor: Pondicherry, 1744–60 175
Philippe Haudrère

10. The Factories and Facilities of the East India Companies in Surat: Locations, Building Characteristics and Ownership 192
Nagashima Hiromu

Contributors 229

Index 230

List of Illustrations

Chapter 4

Fig. 1 *喜多元規 Kita Genki,* 王心渠図 Oh Shinkyo zu (Portrait of Oh Shinkyo) 64

Fig. 2 *河村若芝 Kawamura Jakushi,* 布袋渡水図 *Hotei Tosui zu* (Deity Budai Crossing a River) 65

Fig. 3 *渡辺秀石 Watanabe Shūseki,* 寿老図 *Juroh zu* (God of Longevity and Cranes) 66

Fig. 4 *石崎元章 Ishizaki Genshō,* 倣沈銓花鳥図屏風 *Hou Shinsen Kachozu Byobu* (Birds and Flowers in the Style of Shen Nanpin, screen painting) 67

Fig. 5 *渡辺秀実 Watanabe Shūjitsu* (1778–1830) painted 覆瓶画箋 Fukuhei Gasen (Pot with a Lid album) 68

Fig. 6 *黒川亀玉 Kurokawa Kigyoku,* 海棠白頭翁図 Kaidō Hakutoō zu (Crab Apple and Chinese Bulbul) 69

Fig. 7 *諸葛監 Shokatsu Kan,* 芥子に鶏図 Keshi ni Niwatori zu (Poppy and Chicken) 69

Fig. 8 *宋紫石 Sō Shiseki,* 鯉図 Koi zu (Carps) 70

Fig. 9 *熊斐 Yū Hi,* 登龍門図 Toryūmon zu (Toryūmon Gate) 71

Fig. 10 *宋紫石 Sō Shiseki,* 獅子図 Shishi zu (Lion) 72

Fig. 11 *沈南蘋 Shen Nanpin,* 獅子戯児図 Shishi Giji zu (Lion with their babies) 73

Fig. 12 *小田野直武 Odano Naotake* 獅子図 Shishi zu (Lion) 73

Fig. 13 *小田野直武 Odano Naotake* 唐太宗・花鳥山水図 Toh Taisō Kachō Sansui zu (Chinese Emperor Taizong Birds and Flowers with Landscape) 74

Fig. 14 *司馬江漢 Shiba Kōkan*, 相州鎌倉七里ガ浜図 Sōshu Kamakura Shichirigahama zu (Landscape of Shichirigahama beach, Kamakura, Sōshu) 75

Fig. 15 *司馬江漢 Shiba Kōkan*, 犬のいる風景図 Inu no iru Fūkei zu (Landscape with a Dog) 76

Fig. 16 *司馬江漢 Shiba Kokan*, 異国工場図 Ikoku Kōjō zu (Factory in a Foreign Country) 76

Fig. 17 *西村重長 Nishimura Shigenaga*, 浮絵海士龍宮玉取之図 Uki-e Ama Ryūgū Tamatori no zu (A Woman Diver Determined to Recover Treasure Ball from Dragon's Palace) 77

Fig. 18 *歌川豊春 Utagawa Toyoharu*, 浮絵和国景跡風流和田酒盛之図 Uki-e Wakoku Keiseki Furyū Wada Sakamori no zu (Party of Wada from the series of Japanese noted places and scenes) 78

Fig. 19 *勝川春潮 Katsukawa Syunchō*, 筋違橋前 Sujitagaibashi-Mae (In front view of Sujitagaibashi Bridge) 79

Fig. 20 *葛飾北斎 Katsushika Hokusai*, くだんうしがふち Kudan Ushiga Fuchi (Landscape of Kudan Ushiga Fuchi) 79

Fig. 21 *葛飾北斎 Katsushika Hokusai*, 富嶽三十六景 隠田の水車 Fugaku Sanjurokkei Onden no Suisya (Watermill at Onden from the series Thirty-six Views of Mt. Fuji) 80

Fig. 22 *石崎融思 Ishizaki Yūshi*, 双鶏図 Sōkei zu (Hen and Cock) 81

Fig. 23 *若杉五十八 Wakasugi Isohachi*, オランダ海港図 Oranda Kaikō zu (Dutch Port) 82

Chapter 5

Fig. 1 Blue-and-white plate with human figure, imari, 1610–30s 92

Fig. 2 Blue-and-white bowl with human figure, Jingdezhen, 1573–1628 92

Fig. 3 Blue-and-white bowl with the decoration of Old Man Longevity, imari, 1660–70s 92

Fig. 4 Blue-and-white bowl with the decoration of Old Man Longevity, Jingdezhen, 1600–40s 92

Fig. 5 Blue-and-white plate with landscape design, imari, 1630–40s 93

Fig. 6 Ko-sometsuke square plate with landscape design, Jingdezhen, 1621–28 93

Fig. 7 Blue-and-white plate with landscape design, imari,1640–50s 93

Fig. 8 Blue-and-white plate with landscape design, Jingdezhen, 1628–44 93

Fig. 9 Blue-and-white plate with rabbit design, imari, 1620–30s 94

Fig. 10 Blue-and-white plate with rabbit design, Jingdezhen, 1610–20s 94

Fig. 11 Fragments of late-Ming Jingdezhen blue-and-white wares unearthed at Kaga-han Maeda-ke Edo-yashiki site 加贺藩前田家江户屋敷 94

Fig. 12 Plate with flower and lion design, imari, 1630–40s 95

Fig. 13 Jar with flower and lion design, Jingdezhen, 1573–1628 95

Fig. 14 Plate with the design of grapes, imari, 1610–30s 96

Fig. 15 Jar with the design of grapes, Jingdezhen, early 17th century 96

Fig. 16 Plate with the decoration of Sushi sightseeing at Chibi, imari, 1630–1940s 96

Fig. 17 Plate with the decoration of Sushi sightseeing at Chibi, Jingdezhen, 1610–30s 96

Fig. 18 Imari inscription of “Tai Ming Chenghua Nianzhi” 太明成化年制 97

Fig. 19 Jingdezhen inscription of “Da Ming Chenghua Nianzhi” 大明成化年制 97

Fig. 20 Imari inscription of “Fu” 福 98

Fig. 21 Jingdezhen inscription of "Fu" 福 98

Fig. 22 Shonzui bowl unearthed at Bunkyou-ku in Toukyou-to 100

Fig. 23 Shonzui plate, imari 1640s 100

Fig. 24 Shonzui fresh water jar, Jingdezhen, early 17th century 100

Fig. 25 Polychrome plate with the decoration of landscape, birds and flowers, imari, 1640s 101

Fig. 26 Polychrome plate with the decoration of landscape, birds and flowers, Jingdezhen, 1620–40s 101

Fig. 27 Bottom of the polychrome plate with the decoration of landscape, birds and flowers, imari, 1640s 101

Fig. 28 Bottom of the polychrome plate with the decoration of landscape, birds and flowers, Jingdezhen, 1620–40s 101

Fig. 29 Gourd shaped pilgrim flask with ribbon handles, imari, 17th century 102

Fig. 30 Gourd shaped pilgrim flask with ribbon handles, Jingdezhen Yongle 102

Fig. 31 Blue-and-white vase reflecting Tang poetry moods 103

Fig. 32 A part of the blue-and-white vase reflecting Tang poetry moods 104

Fig. 33 Illustration for *Zhu li Guan, Tangshi Huapu* 104

Fig. 34 *Zhu Li Guan* poem 104

Fig. 35 Blue-and-white plate with the design of human figures in a snowy landscape 105

Fig. 36 Illustration for "Lodging on Hibiscus Mountain after Encountering Snow" *Tangshi Huapu* 105

Fig. 37 Plate of a shepherd boy playing the flute with Chuimo method, imari, 1610–30s 106

Fig. 38 *Mushu* 牧竖 (shepherd boy) *Tangshi Wuyan Huapu* 106

Fig. 39 Plate with human figure and pavilion design imari, 1610–30s 107

Fig. 40 *Xiju* 溪居 (pavilion along the riverside) *Tangshi Wuyan Huapu* 107

Fig. 41 Plate with human figure and zigzag bridge design, imari, 1640–50s 108

Fig. 42 *Chunye* 春夜 (spring night), *Tangshi Wuyan Huapu* 108

Fig. 43 Patra decorated in underglaze blue and overglaze enamels with human figure in the boat design imari, 1640s 108

Fig. 44 Songren You Hunan 送人游湖南 (farewell to a friend setting off for Hunan), *Tangshi Wuyan Huapu* 108

Fig. 45 Polychrome plate with the decoration of human figure, imari, mid-17th century 109

Fig. 46 Jiachuan Dufan 葭川独泛 (boating alone at Jiachuan), *Tangshi Wuyan Huapu* 109

Fig. 47 Plate decorated with flowers and panels, imari, 1680–1710s 110

Fig. 48 Plate decorated with flowers and panels, Jingdezhen, 1573–1620 110

Fig. 49 Plate decorated with flowers and panels, imari, 1660–80 111

Fig. 50 Blue-and-white Kendi decorated with flowers and panels. Left: imari, Right: Jingdezhen 111

Fig. 51 Pitcher with the decoration of human figures and tulips. Left: imari, Right: Jingdezhen 112

Fig. 52 Blue-and-white bottle with a bulbous mouth. Left: imari, Right: Jingdezhen 112

Fig. 53 Blue-and-white rolwagen with human figures, imari, 1660–80 112

Fig. 54 Blue-and-white bottle with a bulbous mouth, Jingdezhen, 1628–44 112

Fig. 55 Kakiemon polychrome pot with a flower design 113

Fig. 56 Polychrome pot with a flower design, Jingdezhen, 1690–1700 113

Fig. 57 Polychrome chrysanthemum plate with petal rim, imari, 18th century 114

Fig. 58 Polychrome chrysanthemum plate with petal rim Jingdezhen, 18th century 114

Fig. 59 Polychrome plate with the Parasol design, Jingdezhen, 1730–40s 115

Fig. 60 Polychrome plate with the Parasol design, imari, 1730–40s 115

Fig. 61 Sample manuscript by the European purchasers, 1734 115

Chapter 6

Fig. 1 View on the Batavian Roadstead by Johannes Rach (1720–83) 119

Fig. 2 Map of Batavia, circa 1660 123

Fig. 3 View on Batavia's inner harbor 127

Fig. 4 View on the Bay of Batavia 131

Fig. 5 Maritime network of the VOC 132

Chapter 8

Fig. 1 "William Palmer and his family," by Johan Zoffany 163

Chapter 10

Fig. 1 Map of Surat in 1877 193

Fig. 2 Map of northwestern corner of Surat in the 1660s 197

Fig. 3 The 1817 Map of Surat: Remains of the factories 198

Fig. 4 Northwestern corner of the inner wall area of the 1817 map of Surat 199

Fig. 5 Southwestern corner of the inner wall area of the 1817 map of Surat 200

Fig. 6 The northwestern corner within the inner wall on the 1730 Map of Surat 201

Fig. 7a The western part of the inner wall area of the Fort of Surat on the 1730 map 204

Fig. 7b	The northwestern part of the inner wall area of the Fort of Surat on the 1730 map	205
Fig. 7c	The southwestern part of the inner wall area of the Fort of Surat on the 1730 map	206
Fig. 8	The 1758 French map of Surat	210
Fig. 9	Northern corner inside the outer wall of the 1817 Map of Surat	211
Fig. 10	The so-called "English Factory at Surat in 1638"	216
Fig. 11	The so-called Dutch factory at Surat	216
Fig. 12	The ground plan of the Dutch factory at Surat around 1699	217
Fig. 13	The mausoleum of Baron van Reede tot Drakesteijn (d. 1691)	219
Fig. 14	The mausoleum of George Oxenden (d. 1669)	219
Fig. 15	The Dutch cemetery at Pulicat	220

Preface

This volume proposes a new methodology in comparative studies of the history of Asian port cities. It is the product of a joint research programme entitled "Comparative studies on the cross-cultural contacts in Asian port cities in the seventeenth and eighteenth centuries" that my colleagues and I launched in April 2005, supported by a grant-in-aid from the Japanese Society for the Promotion of Sciences. More than twenty Japanese historians, including post-graduate students, took part in the programme. After several research meetings that were rich in discussion, we organized, in Tokyo in October 2007, an international workshop on the cross-cultural contacts in Asian port cities, to discuss the theme we were developing. We invited four participants from overseas, asking each of them to prepare a paper concerning the port city he or she was studying that would develop an argument based on at least one of six points for comparison that we were developing (see Introduction). The workshop was so animated and successful that all the participants wanted to publish a book putting their articles together. Six articles in this book (Bhawan, Blussé, Haudrère, Matsui, Mentz, Nagashima) are revised versions of papers presented at this workshop.

Even before the start of our joint research, Professor Leonard Blussé of Leiden University showed a strong interest in our programme, and he continued to encourage us as the project developed, suggesting to me that an international conference comparing Canton and Nagasaki be held with our Chinese colleagues in Guangzhou. I accepted his proposal, and an exploratory conference took place in Guangzhou and Macao in December 2007. Four articles in this book (Haneda, Ito, Liu Zhaohui, Liu Yong) have come from papers presented on this occasion. I am happy to add more East Asian views and flavour to the book.

The Introduction sets out a common framework for these ten articles and proposes a new methodology for comparative studies of Asian port cities. I am well aware that many points still need improvement, but I believe that the present volume shows at the very least the promising future of the methodology it proposes.

I would like to express my deep gratitude to the tenacious and enthusiastic efforts by my Chinese colleagues in Guangzhou and Macao, who made the "Canton and Nagasaki Compared" conference extremely interesting and fruitful.

Special acknowledgements go first to Drs. Zhou Xiang and Jiang Yinghe of Zhongshan University and to Ms. Marie Imelda MacLeod at the Macao Cultural Affairs Bureau. It was Mr. Evert Groenendijk of the Dutch Consulate General in Guangzhou who took charge, despite of his busy work schedule, of the very complicated communications with all the participants and made the conference successful. I am grateful to him for his patience, consideration and accuracy.

I have to specify that the above-mentioned two academic meetings were realized thanks to a grant-in-aid from the Japan Society for the Promotion of Science. I very much appreciate the appropriate support by the Society.

I would like to underline the strong backup by Professor Iwai Shigeki of Kyoto University, who took part in the conference at Guangzhou and Macao and kindly introduced our joint research programme to Kyoto University Press. Without his good offices, this book would never have been published.

I would like to express my sincere acknowledgement of my colleagues at the Institute of Oriental Culture at the University of Tokyo, who graciously accepted my request and decided to spend a substantial amount from the Institute's budget for the publication of this book. I am also grateful for the efficient work of the Institute's administrative staff.

It is impossible for me to close the list of acknowledgements without again mentioning the name of Professor Leonard Blussé of Leiden University. He has constantly supported me with his unparalleled scholarship, world-wide personal relationships, devoted friendship and cheerful sense of humour. It would not too much to describe him as the co-director of our research programme.

Haneda Masashi

INTRODUCTION

Framework and Methods of Comparative Studies on Asian Port Cities in the Seventeenth and Eighteenth Centuries

Haneda Masashi

World History and the Maritime Worlds of Asia

At the beginning of the twenty-first century, we most definitely need a new model of world history that is pertinent to, and corresponds with, the reality of our globalizing, transforming and interconnected world. How can we better understand the formation of the contemporary world, free from the powerful Eurocentric viewpoint? We have to seek out carefully another approach through which to view, analyze and describe world history. This is certainly an important issue worthy of the scrutiny of all historians. The model and meaning of the new world history has been discussed intensively since the 1990s and mainly among English-speaking scholars,[1] and these discussions have centred particularly on economic history-oriented and comparative approaches. The concept of "maritime world"[2] has received a significant amount of attention, and there can be no doubt that it constitutes a promising framework for structuring a new world history.

The present collective work on Asian port cities illustrates various aspects of cross-cultural contacts in Asian port cities on the basis of comparative studies, and draws a general plan, at least in part, of the various Asian maritime worlds in the seventeenth and eighteenth centuries. In doing so, it makes a modest contribution to efforts to describe world history from a new angle.

"Asian maritime worlds" denotes a vast geographical sphere that extends from the Japanese and Chinese coasts surrounding the East China Sea in the east to the East African coast in the west, and embraces Southeast Asia, the coast of the Indian subcontinent, and the coast of the land mass surrounding the Arabian Sea with its two extensions to the northwest, the Red Sea and the Gulf. The past of the Asian maritime worlds is a key element in the history of the world, and the authors in this volume examine and interpret events there in the context of a broader world history.

One problem with the Eurocentric historical view is that it presents world history as a dichotomy — Europe versus non-Europe — and then describes and interprets European history and Asian history separately. The concept of "Europe" and various positive values associated with it, such as liberty, equality, democracy, progress, science, technology and secularization gradually took shape in the course of the nineteenth century and it continues to evolve today with the construction of the political and economic entity of the European Union. Negative values associated with terms such as "Asia", "Orient" and the "Islamic World" have played a significant role in conceptualizing a positive "Europe".[3]

In this volume we do not view Asia as a single entity, nor do we regard it as something contrastive to Europe. We use "Asia" and "Europe" as geographical terms and employ them in discussion because we have no expressions to designate the continental mass that includes both regions. We divide "Asia" into several parts (such as East Asia, West Asia, Central Asia) to speak about specific regions, but this should not be taken to imply that the characteristics of all of these regions resemble one other or that they are necessarily different from those of Europe. The same thing can be said concerning the Asian maritime worlds, a point we try to emphasize by using the term in the plural.

We see people from Europe as one of the many groups of actors operating in the plural Asian maritime worlds of the seventeenth and eighteenth centuries, in conjunction with people from the various regions of Asia. Japanese people of the seventeenth century, for example, saw Europeans as foreigners, but no more so than Chinese or people from other parts of Asia. One goal of this book is to demonstrate that it does not make sense to distinguish between "European" and "Asian" in the Asian maritime worlds under investigation. There is no point reaffirming that the division between Europe and Asia was the result of self-consciousness by people who regarded themselves as Europeans. As Andre Gunder Frank, Kenneth Pomeranz and others have already stated powerfully, the Asian maritime world was situated at the centre of world economy in the seventeenth and eighteenth centuries.[4]

The term "maritime worlds" as used in this study implies a sphere with the sea at its centre. The common understanding of historical studies is that the sea is situated at the periphery of an area or country and that it separates two or more regions. Here, the sea is regarded as something that connects two or more regions, joining rather than dividing them. It should be noted, though, that this term never assumes a closed or a homogeneous area. Rather than cutting world-wide and linked commercial activities into several independent parts, we seek to grasp and understand them as an entity.

Ethnic, social, cultural and environmental layers do not always correspond with a political territory, and the concept of maritime worlds that we introduce here is, in contrast to the hard framework of the nation state, a loose geographical unit wide open to the outside. It is a kind of atelier for historians to examine, analyse and synthesize all kinds of cross-cultural contacts, and the influence of political power on diverse economic and cultural activities. We are able to presuppose several maritime worlds in Asian waters, each with specific features but all interconnected in complex ways, and linked with the Pacific, Mediterranean and Atlantic maritime worlds as well. We do not take as given a chronological history of a certain maritime world, since this would only produce another type of "nation state".

Viewing the past using the framework of the maritime world is an effective means of relativizing the powerful narrative of national history and, not being restricted to the confines of a particular nation, of shedding light on people's lives and activities. In the field of Asian history, important achievements have already been made using this new perspective.[5] However, some authors treat the Asian maritime world as a single geographical unit and oppose it to the Mediterranean maritime world, trying to analyze and explain what happened in the Asian maritime world only within its own context. In this sense, they maintain a dichotomous view in the world history.

Angela Schottenhammer proposes that the concept of maritime world should be understood "as one characterizing the dynamics of exchange in a geographical and geopolitical area whose neighbouring countries were linked and related with each other by sea routes".[6] Although our above-mentioned definition of "maritime worlds" is not far from hers, I would like to repeat that the term as we use it does not assume a closed geographical sphere. It is rather a framework for productive scientific discussion. Moreover, we always have to analyze what happened in a maritime world in connection with world history. The comparative approach is very useful at that juncture.

Significance of Comparative Studies of Port Cities

Port cities are a common and ordinary type of city found everywhere in the world. Before the age of train, car and airplane, they were often important political centres, hubs of regional economies and places where new arts, ideas and technologies were developed in the melting-pot of overseas and home cultures. A port city belongs to a country but, at the same time, it belongs to the maritime world that fronts it and connects it with the outside world. It represents the local culture of the country to which it belongs but it also appears alien to the people of that country owing to the presence of foreign peoples and cultures. Port cities are the site of cross-cultural exchanges of all kinds and are naturally of great interest to historians and to scholars of the other human and social sciences.

In the field of research on Asian port cities, important studies by Frank Broeze and his colleagues have been published in two substantial books discussing the past and the present of a number of port cities situated within Asian waters, ranging from Kobe and Niigata in Japan to Aden and Jidda in the Arabian Peninsula.[7] Since a multi-disciplinary approach is a feature of these two books, an article on Aden from the thirteenth to sixteenth centuries and an analysis of Bangkok in the nineteenth and twentieth centuries may appear side by side in the same volume, allowing different aspects and phases of the evolution of Asian port cities to be compared, although the choice of port cities, the periods examined and the topics discussed are rather too diverse and scattered for any meaningful comparison.

Murai Shosuke, Fukasawa Katsumi and I have recently edited three volumes of historical studies on port cities.[8] It was audacious to put more than thirty-five articles on various port cities from all over the world together and find a new perspective on world history. The period and the topics covered by the articles are vast: from a small port in northern Japan in the eleventh century through various port cities in East Asia, Southeast Asia and West Asia to London in the eighteenth century. As with the books edited by Broeze, the topics are disparate and not well-focused. We tried to arrange them according to a certain logic, but I have to confess that our work was really difficult and not always successful. Full discussion and consensus on the comparative viewpoint by the authors before starting the project was not sufficient.

In contrast to these earlier attempts, the approach we adopt in this book is simple and more consistent. We limit discussion and analysis to port cities where at least one European East India Company established a fort or factory,[9] and all the articles discuss cross-cultural contacts in port cities during the seventeenth and eighteenth centuries. The time span is limited, since it was only in those two centuries that the European East Asian Companies were active in Asian waters. Though the British East India Company survived exceptionally until the middle of the nineteenth century, its character changed considerably after 1800, and we have omitted port cities connected with the EIC in the nineteenth century.

Restricting the subject of research in this way allows us to examine, analyse and compare cross-cultural contact in each port city from almost the same angle. The main difficulty of a comparative approach in historical studies is the different characteristics of local sources. Over and above differences in language, they were often written in a specific context of local authorities and societies and consequently do not always offer parallel materials for comparison. Most of these problems disappear, however, when we examine port cities with forts or factories belonging to the European East India Companies. They shared the common feature of cross-cultural contacts, that is, cultural interactions between Europeans and local people. It is on this basis that we have tried to make comparisons between ports, though we never ignore relations among other groups.

Rich archives of the East India Companies exist for most of the port cities their ships visited and where their agents were stationed, and their records provide comparable content for each port city, notwithstanding slight differences of style, quality and quantity from one port city to another, as well as from one East India Company to another. Comparing specific points clearly brings out both common and different characteristics of Asian port cities. Moreover, by gaining a foothold in a port city, we may compare features of its hinterland at a specific period and thereby obtain a new image of the history of a certain country or a maritime world, suggesting ways of describing the new world history of our age.

East India Companies' Archives for the Comparative Studies of Asian Port Cities

I stressed above that we should not make a great distinction between what was European and what was Asian, at least in Asian waters in the seventeenth and eighteenth centuries. This does not mean however that differences did not exist. For example, we cannot ignore the different trading methods used by European and Asian people at the time. While Europeans created special trading organizations like the East India Company and maintained financial arrangements in connection with them (like the Bank of England and a stock market), Asians developed no comparable institutions. This difference may, however, be explained, at least partly, by geopolitics. Europe is situated very far from Asian waters and Europeans had to prepare a huge amount of capital in order to take part successfully in commercial activities on a large scale. A joint-stock company holding a monopoly over certain elements of Asian trade was certainly the best arrangement for them. This type of enterprise was quite exceptional in Europe at the time, although it offered a model for later industrial enterprise. Most of the overseas trade within European waters was conducted either on a personal or a familial basis until the early nineteenth century.[10]

One consequence of setting up joint-stock trading companies was that the Europeans recorded, whether they liked it or not, all their activities in their various documents. These papers contain information not only on aspects of maritime and commercial activities, but also on various interactions between Europeans and local people in almost every part of Asia. For our purpose, journals, letters, reports and account books, which were written in much the same manner whatever their provenance, along with minute books from the home country, are particularly significant. The Dutch East India Company archives are the most valuable and important in terms of comparative studies, since their forts and factories were dispersed across Asia. The English East India Company archives come next, followed by documents from the French, Swedish and Danish companies.

There are differences of size, structure, management, usage of ships, and so on among European trading companies, and researchers interested in the European East India Companies have hitherto paid attention to these matters, focusing mainly on the differences among European companies. Consequently, they have generally discussed a single company in the framework of either a national history, or the company's own history.[11] However, all European companies had features in common. The final goal of their various activities was the same: they sought maximum profits from their commerce in Asian waters. Company employees were expected to act always on the basis of this expectation, and company documents served to develop the company's activities and generate profits. It is at this point that we can look at the documents of all the East India Companies together for comparison, of course after subjecting them to strict textual analysis.

These archives, which remain intact in some cases even today, provide us with valuable material to study cross-cultural contacts in different port cities. They have not yet been fully explored for the kind of comparative research on Asian port cities that we intend to undertake.[12] The enormous number of pages (25 million just for VOC documents, for example), the difference of language, the framework of national history and a lack of interest in the topic among local historians have prevented scholars from organizing joint research on a large scale.

Of course, the archives of the East India Companies speak mainly about the cultural interactions between Europeans and the Asian people of various regions, and there are few remarks and descriptions concerning cross-cultural exchanges among local peoples in the Asian maritime worlds, such as the Japanese and Chinese, or Iranians and people from northern India. Although this is a weak point in those archives, the blanks can be filled to some extent by using local sources. For example, Japanese studies on the port city Nagasaki and Japanese foreign relations have the potential to change the situation.

Japanese Studies on Nagasaki and Japanese Foreign Relations

In contrast with the situation of many other Asian countries, where relations with European countries are not always a popular topic for historical studies, Japanese historians have been particularly interested in Japan's foreign relations during the Edo period (1601–1867) and have amassed a great many works on the subject. In this connection, they have also been interested in the urban history and topography of Nagasaki, which was the only official port city open to foreign merchants at that time.

Although most of the studies are bound by the framework of Japanese national history and the discussions are strongly influenced by the general interpretation of Japanese history, the historical evidence and facts they have elucidated, based on a strict criticism of historical sources, are for the most part reliable.[13] In Japan modern historical studies have been fully developed in the national language. It should therefore be sufficient for us to reanalyze and reinterpret this evidence in the context of world history.

After a careful reading of the important and interesting studies on Nagasaki and Japan's foreign relations already done by Japanese historians, it occurred to me that the comparative study of Asian port cities based on these works about Nagasaki was a promising line to pursue. In order to make an effective and meaningful comparison with other Asian port cities, I set up six points of cross-cultural contacts, which I will briefly explain before introducing the relationship between those points and the articles included in this book.

Six Points for Comparison

Many aspects of cross-cultural contacts at one Asian port city can be compared with those in another. The following six points seem to me to be particularly important because they reveal features of the political, economic and social conditions of the port city and the country to which it belongs. These six points raise interesting questions that have not been fully discussed before. All such information is indispensable to a new world history.

The principal analysis and discussion concerning cross-cultural contacts in most of the articles of this book focus on the relationship between Europeans and local people. Thanks to the archives of the East India companies, this situation is easier to study than to that of other overseas people within the Asian maritime world, but we have to take care to regard them not as an exception but simply as overseas people like those from other places.

The first point of comparison is the location, ownership and architectural features of the forts and factories of the East India Companies in the port cities. Was the company permitted to establish its factory anywhere in the city?

What was the significance of the location of the European factory for the Europeans themselves and for the local people? Was ethnic segregation involved in city planning? What kind of building materials, ornamentation and style did the factory's buildings have: European, local or a fusion of different styles? Could the company own the factory building and the land on which it stood? Could foreigners purchase real estate? All these questions concern the first point and have to be compared. In addition to sources from the East India Companies, local sources, maps and city plans can be helpful.

Articles by Leonard Blussé on Batavia and Nagashima Hiromu on Surat discuss this point. Neither in Batavia, where the Dutch were masters and were able to build the city and determine its plan, nor in Surat, where Europeans were only permitted to build their factory following the orders of the local authority, can we find any strict ethnic segregation. The situation was very different in Nagasaki, Guangzhou and Madras. In Nagasaki, the Dutch were confined to a small island called Deshima, just off the coast, and the Chinese were obliged to live in their special quarter called Tōjin-yashiki (Chinese residence), situated outside of the city. In Guangzhou, Europeans were only permitted to stay in their special quarter, situated in the western side of the city wall, during the trading season. Once that ended, they had to retreat to Macao. Madras, as described by Søren Menz, was composed of two different parts: the White town where the English population resided and the Black town for local people. How is this difference to be explained, and what is its significance?

The second point concerns communications between Europeans and the local people in a port city. Usually, an interpretation service bridged the divide between local people and those from overseas. Did Europeans employ local interpreters, or did they train their own language specialists? Did the local government have an office of interpreters? What was the situation for communications between people from various parts of Asia? What was the role of the interpreter? Was it the same as today's interpreter? Was there no common language between visitors and local people? These questions are related to the view and attitude of local people and their government towards people from overseas. Was there a clear distinction or boundary between people living inside of a country and people from elsewhere residing in Asian port cities?

Haneda Masashi's article discusses this topic and compares the interpreter's position in Nagasaki and Guangzhou and in Bandar Abbas in Persia. The article highlights the difference of attitude among local people towards overseas people in the East Asian maritime world and in the Arabian Sea maritime world. One could say that it is a question of a difference in self-consciousness. Philippe Haudrère explains the intimate but delicate relationship between French governors and a local broker in Pondicherry. Although the power balance between Europeans and local people was not the same, this relationship could be comparable with that of Europeans and the *hong* merchants in Guangzhou, and one might draw interesting conclusions.

The third point of comparison is how trade was conducted. Trading methods and the various formalities were not the same everywhere in Asian waters. How did merchants from overseas come into contact with local merchants? Was there any procedure *vis-à-vis* the local authority at the point of trade? What kind of duties did merchants pay? Were there any restrictions on the goods imported and exported as far as the local authority was concerned? Were there any special rules and arrangements for particular communities, or were merchants coming from abroad all treated in the same way? By examining such questions, we will be better able to know the practices in each port city. In fact, employees of European companies would have wanted to conduct trade in their accustomed way anywhere in Asia as they did in Europe with local people. However, the reality is that they had to trade in ways that differed from European practices except in those rare places where they had total political and military supremacy, such as Batavia. How trade was conducted in Asian port cities depended mostly on the customs and intentions of the local populace and the instructions of those in authority. Leonard Blussé's article on Batavia, Liu Yong's article on Dutch merchants in Guangzhou, as well as Bhawan Ruangsilp's article on merchants in Ayutthaya, explain and describe this aspect of cultural interaction.

There are many Japanese studies on Nagasaki.[14] Most are reliable but they are not known well among non-Japanese historians. Drawing on this work to compare Nagasaki with Batavia, Guangzhou and Ayutthaya, we may find a number of points in common as well as many differences in their respective trading systems. Unfortunately this kind of comparison remains a privilege of scholars who understand the Japanese language. Japanese historians have to make more effort to publish their works in foreign languages, particularly in English, so that scholars around the world interested in comparing Asian port cities can obtain relevant information.

The fourth point to be compared is the legal settlement of conflicts and incidents involving the factories of European companies representing European interests and the local people under their governor. Since there was no common international law at that time, they had to negotiate and compromise to reach some sort of agreement each time an incident occurred. Did local law have priority, or was the law of European countries respected? When a foreigner was judged guilty by the local authority, was he punished in exactly the same way as local people? How did the local governor judge crime against foreigners who were not under his jurisdiction? These questions are important, not only for what they reveal about the pre-modern legal system of each region but also in connection with the issues of modern European concepts of sovereignty, nationality, citizenship and extraterritoriality, all of which would be introduced willy-nilly to Asian countries in a later period. One of the topics discussed by Matsui Yoko is how conflicts and disputes were settled in Nagasaki.

The fifth point is relations between men and women, particularly between overseas men like Europeans and local women, and the social position of children of mixed parentage in a port city. Foreign visitors to port cities were predominantly male, and sexual relations with local women and the birth of children of mixed parentage were inevitable. Were there any consistent policies regarding this matter, whether developed by local authorities or by the East India Companies? Were there any restrictions on relationships from either side? It appears that the attitude towards this problem was subtly different even among the European East India companies themselves.

Matsui Yoko studies the situation in Nagasaki in her article and points out the reason for the change of policy concerning the nationality of a child of mixed parentage by the Tokugawa government. The question enables us to elucidate the mentality of local people *vis-à-vis* those from overseas, as well as the location of boundaries fixed by governments between people under their control and those outside their control. Søren Menz points out the different attitude towards mixed marriage between the Portuguese and the English in India and discusses the delicate identity of a British man married to a local woman. Leonard Blussé frankly confesses there have been no reliable studies on this issue in the case of Batavia, but Batavia is not exceptional in this regard.[15] Although the study of this topic is not easy, I believe it is worth doing in as many Asian port cities as possible so that the results can be compared.

The sixth point is less clearly focused, but since it is related to people's everyday life, we cannot neglect it. Cultural exchanges in Asian port cities, that is, the acceptance or rejection of foreign clothing, food, technologies, arts and ideas (including religious thought) should be compared. We must first elucidate the general features of the cultural exchanges in each port city and its hinterland. When was something originating abroad accepted in a port city and when was it rejected? How did something from abroad penetrate the society of the port city and its hinterland? What was the nature of cultural fusion? For example, we know that Christianity was rejected and strictly banned by East Asian countries like Japan and China, while it was permitted in India and Persia. What lies behind this difference? As we answer such questions, we will develop a better understanding of the society and culture of a port city.

Although they do not use the archives of the East India Companies in a systematic way, both Ito Shiori's article on the reception of Chinese paintings in Nagasaki and in Japan, and Liu Zhaohui's article on the relations between Jingdezhen and Imari porcelains deal with this point, and their contribution reveals certain aspects of cross-cultural contacts within Asia.

The European presence in Asian waters cannot be ignored, but we must bear in mind that there were also a great any intra-Asian cultural contacts in the period studied in this volume. Furthermore, various products, designs and ways of living originating in Asian regions, including textiles and porcelain, entered Europe at that time. The world was truly interconnected.

Notes

1. In the United States, the World History Association was established in 1982 and 19 volumes of the *Journal of World History* have already been published. Another important academic journal, the *Journal of Global History*, began publication through the London School of Economics and Political Science in 2006. Until quite recently, researchers interested in joining the movement for world history have been predominantly from North America or from other English-speaking countries like the UK and Australia. However, the movement has been gradually gaining ground in other parts of the world as well. The European Network in Global and Universal History was founded mainly by German scholars in 2002 and had its second congress in 2008. The Asian Association of World Historians (AAWH) was founded on May 4, 2008.
2. The origin of the concept is Fernand Braudel's famous work: *La Mediterranée et le monde mediterranéen à l'Epoque de Philippe II* (Paris, 1949). Its impact on later historians is important, and attempts to apply his theory to other periods and spheres have since been made. Principal works among them include: K.N. Chaudhuri, *Trade and Civilization in the Indian Ocean: An Economic History from the Rise of Islam to 1750* (Cambridge: Cambridge University Press, 1985), Anthony Reid, *Southeast Asia in the Age of Commerce 1450–1680*, 2 vols. (New Haven: Yale University Press, 1988, 1993), R.J. Barendse, *The Arabian Seas 1640–1700* (Leiden: Research School CNWS, 1998), Yajima Hikoichi, *Kaiiki kara mita rekishi (History from a viewpoint of the maritime world)*, Nagoya daigaku shuppankai (Nagoya: University Press of Nagoya University, 2006). A German group led by Angela Schottenhammer started a research project entitled "'The East Asian Mediterranean', c. 1500–1800: A New Quality in the Development of its Neighbouring Countries" in 2002 and it has already published three volumes of collective work under the series title "East Asian Maritime History".
3. Edward Said, *Orientalism* (Vintage Books, 1978). Concerning the notion of the Islamic World, Haneda Masashi, "Modern Europe and the Creation of the Islamic World", *International Journal of Asian Studies* 4, 2 (Summer 2007): 201–20.
4. Andre Gunder Frank, *Reorient. Global Economy in the Asian Age* (Berkeley and Los Angeles: University of California Press, 1998), Kenneth Pomeranz, *The Great Divergence: China, Europe and the Making of the Modern World Economy* (Princeton NJ: Princeton University Press, 2001).
5. Chaudhuri, *Trade and Civilization in the Indian Ocean*; Yajima, *Kaiiki kara mita rekishi.*

6. Angela Schottenhammer, "The East Asian maritime world, 1400–1800: Its fabrics of powers and dynamics of exchanges — China and her neighbours", Angela Schottenhammer (ed.), *The East Asian Maritime World 1400–1800: Its Fabrics of Power and Dynamics of Exchanges* (Wiesbaden: Harrassowitz Verlag, 2007), p. 5.
7. Frank Broeze (ed.), *Brides of the Sea, Port Cities of Asia from the 16th to 20th centuries* (Honolulu: University of Hawaii Press, 1989), Frank Broeze (ed.), *Gateways of Asia. Port Cities of Asia in the 13th–20th Centuries* (London and New York: Kegan Paul International, 1997).
8. *Minatomachi no sekaishi (Port cities in world history)* (Tokyo: Aoki shoten). Vol. 1, *Ports and Maritime Worlds*, ed. Murai Shosuke (2005); Vol. 2, *The Topography of Port Cities*, ed. Fukasawa Katsumi (2006), Vol. 3, *Living in Port Cities*, ed. Haneda Masashi (2006). All articles are written in Japanese.
9. Leonard Blussé has already done a similar attempt in a little bit small scale with three Asian port cities, that is, Batavia, Canton and Nagasaki. See his *Visible Cities* (Cambridge, Mass: Harvard University Press, 2008).
10. Fukasawa Katsumi, *Shonin to sarasa (Merchants and chintz)*, Tokyo daigaku shuppankai (Tokyo: University of Tokyo Press, 2007), p. 43.
11. Some general comparative studies on Dutch, English and French companies mark the exception. See J.R. Bruijn, F.S. Gaastra and I. Schoffer (eds.), *Dutch-Asiatic Shipping in the 17th and 18th Centuries*, vol. 1, The Hague, 1987; Philippe Haudrère, *Les Compagnies des Indes orientales* (Paris : Editions Desjonqueres, 2006); Gérard Le Bouëdec and Philippe Haudrère, *Les Compagnies des Indes*, (Rennes : Editions Ouest-France, 1999).
12. A series of admirable initiatives by Dutch scholars to promote historical studies on Asia and Africa by using Dutch archives and to train young Asian and African students who can use both Dutch and local sources are a rare and distinguished exception. See the website of following two research-education programmes: TANAP (Towards A New Age of Partnership) programme (<http://www.tanap.net/>) and ENCOMPASS (Encountering a Common Past in Asia) programme (<http://www.hum.leiden.edu/history/encompass.jsp>). One of the contributors to this book, Leonard Blussé, is the leader of these programmes.
13. A list of principal works on Nagasaki and Japanese foreign relations in connection with the six points of comparison explained later is on the following website (in Japanese): <http://www.ioc.u-tokyo.ac.jp/haneda/data-base-nagasaki.htm>.
14. See the above-mentioned list of Nagasaki studies on the web. Shimada Ryuto gives a brief sketch concerning Japanese historical studies on the Japan trade of the VOC in his recently published book. See Shimada Ryuto, *The Intra-Asian Trade in Japanese Copper by the Dutch East India Company during the Eighteenth Century* (Leiden and Boston: Brill, 2006), pp. 150–54.
15. Leonard Blussé himself published an interesting monograph on the life of a Dutch-Japanese woman married to a high-ranking VOC employee in Batavia. See his *Bitter Bonds: A Colonial Divorce Drama of the Seventeenth Century* (Princeton, NJ: Markus Wiener Publishers, 2002).

Chapter 1

Canton, Nagasaki and the Port Cities of the Indian Ocean: A Comparison

Haneda Masashi

If we choose the appropriate elements and objects carefully, comparison is a good way of improving our understanding of the characteristics of a certain society or area, enabling us to discover important and interesting aspects that may otherwise be neglected. The main purpose of the first international conference "Canton and Nagasaki Compared" was to compare the history of Canton and Nagasaki during a specific period. In addition to doing this, however, I will also attempt, in this article, to make a broader comparison; that is, between the East Asian maritime world (including both Canton and Nagasaki) and the Indian Ocean maritime world.

I will first discuss the role and parameters of the interpreters, who were indispensable during the communication between Europeans and the local people, and compare the case of Nagasaki with that of Canton. I will also look briefly at the status of children of mixed parentage, born of European men and local women. I will then demonstrate the differences in the situation of Nagasaki and Canton on the one hand, and Bandar Abbas in Persia on the other. The attitude of the state towards foreign trade will be the focal point of the discussion. The results will demonstrate the similarity, in the broader sense of the word, between Nagasaki and Canton, so far as the state control of foreign trade is concerned, and prove the efficiency of tackling the historical development of Japanese and Chinese societies together.

Interpreters in Nagasaki

There are several works written in Japanese on interpreters (*tsūji*) in Nagasaki acting as intermediaries between the Japanese authorities and the VOC (the Dutch

East India Company), the only European company that had the right to engage in commerce there. Among others, Matsui Yoko's recent article[1] discusses all of the important work done so far on the Oranda-tsūji (interpreters of Dutch), and demonstrates the characteristics and role of interpreters in Nagasaki, as well as the evolution of the interpreter system, which had become firmly established around the turn of the eighteenth century. The following are the major points that should be noted when attempting to compare questions related to interpreters in Nagasaki under the direct control of the Tokugawa government with those in other Asian port cities.

(1) Foreigners' circumstances: Foreigners were, in principle, forbidden to learn the Japanese language. They were prohibited from living on Japanese soil. As a result, the Dutch traders were confined to a small artificial island called Deshima, located just outside the Nagasaki city area.

(2) Interpreters' situation: It was only the Japanese side which provided interpreters to communicate with the Dutch. The Nagasaki Bugyō, the officer responsible for law, order, and trade with foreigners in Nagasaki, employed the interpreters. They were all local Japanese. Theoretically, they were the local staff of the Bugyōsho; that is, the Nagasaki local government. Their social position was civilian (*chōnin*) rather than samurai (warrior).

(3) Interpreters' income: Interpreters obtained their income from their salary as well as from commission at the point of trade. In addition, they had priority when purchasing some portions of imported goods at cost before the start of official negotiations.

(4) Interpreters' post and their hierarchy: By around the turn of the seventeenth and eighteenth centuries, hierarchical grades of interpreters had been formed. At the top of the hierarchy, there were two *tsūji metsuke* (superintendents) and four *daitsūji* (senior interpreters); below them were four *shōtsūji* (junior interpreters) and eleven *keiko tsūji* (trainees). The formal interpreter's community consisted of these twenty-one people. There was another category of interpreter called *naitsūji* (lower interpreters), who dealt with the incidental communications necessitated by the daily life in Deshima between the Dutch and the Japanese. There was a gap between the two communities of interpreter. The *naitsūji* could not, in principle, be promoted to *keiko tsūji*, the lowest level of the upper category. The post of interpreter was often hereditary. Therefore, interpreters had no right to change their job. Sons succeeded to their fathers' positions. If the son had no linguistic talent, a man who was proficient in Dutch was adopted into the family as a son-in-law and succeeded to his adoptive father's position.

(5) Number of interpreters: The number of interpreters grew over time, although the Dutch-Japanese trade itself gradually declined. In 1750, there

were forty-four interpreters, and fifty-five belonging to the upper category by 1822.

(6) The duties of the upper level interpreters consisted of:
   (a) Interpreting for audiences and visitors.
   (b) Translating various kinds of document, such as orders from the Bugyō, lawsuits by the Dutch, and the demands and reports of the Dutch to the authorities.
   (c) Producing various kinds of document concerning the Dutch trade and aspects of life on Deshima; for example, attestations that a newly-arrived ship was really Dutch, crew lists and lists of goods loaded onto Dutch ships, lists of goods stored at Deshima, etc.
   (d) Mediating during negotiations between the Dutch and the various levels of Japanese authorities. Their role was not simply translating words; they themselves discussed problems concerning the mediation and often proposed compromises.
   (e) Watching the Dutch in Deshima so that they did not do anything that was prohibited.
   (f) Transmitting all kinds of information to the Dutch.
   (g) Taking care of the Dutch when they went to Edo for the Shogunal audience.

The *tsūji* differed from modern interpreters in several ways. Interpretation and translation were certainly among their most important tasks, but, in addition, they produced every kind of document relating to the Dutch trade and were involved in all aspects of the sojourn of the Dutch in Japan. They often worked as negotiators. Dutch sources call them "tolk" and, in English, they were called "linguists". I use the term "interpreter" in this paper to avoid confusion, but we should understand that the meaning is not equivalent to that of a modern interpreter.

To reiterate, the interpreters were all Japanese and were employed not by the VOC, but by the Japanese government. The VOC had no right to employ interpreters. By making use of interpreters, the Japanese government intended to control all aspects of the foreign trade and activities of foreigners in Nagasaki. The interpreters were expected to keep an attentive watch over the Dutch and to report any unusual activity to the Bugyōsho.

The other foreign ethnic group in Nagasaki, the Chinese, was also confined to an area reserved specifically for them in the west end of the city that was controlled through interpreters specializing in Chinese (*tōtsūji*). The government seems to have been determined to take the initiative in their foreign relations. Such an action *vis-à-vis* foreigners would have been impossible had the Japanese and their government not had a sense of distinction between themselves (the Japanese people living inside) and foreigners (people coming from outside). They perceived the Dutch and Chinese as foreigners, different from themselves. This is a very important point that will be compared with the situation in other port cities.

Interpreters in Canton

I would like to sum up the parameters of interpreters in Canton during the period when the Canton system functioned, from 1757 to 1842, mainly making use of Paul Van Dyke's recently published work.[2] Unlike Nagasaki, the ships of several nationalities came to Canton, including English, Dutch, French, Swedish, Danish and, later, American, which naturally complicated the situation regarding the use of interpreters. The common Western language in Canton until around 1730 was Portuguese, but, after that, pidgin English (broken English and an amalgam of many languages) prevailed. In addition to this, local languages, Cantonese and Mandarin were also indispensable. The following points are important when we analyse the characteristics of the interpreter in Canton.

(1) Foreigners' circumstances: It was forbidden for foreigners to learn Chinese. The Chinese were not permitted to learn foreign languages systematically (there was no foreign language school in Canton). Europeans were permitted to go to Canton and live within an area specifically allotted to them outside the walled city. They could stay there only during the period of trading and were compelled to return to Macao once the transactions had been completed.

(2) Interpreters' situation: The interpreter was not a government official, but needed a license from the Qing government. The interpreter was Chinese and could not quit his job or change profession without the consent of the Hoppo (*hubu*, customs superintendents). It is true that he was not a state official, but neither was he free from government control. Unlike Nagasaki, it was not impossible for European companies to have their own interpreters, but the Chinese local authorities did not apparently welcome this. The interpreters were not expected to have the ability to translate anything accurately, because they spoke only pidgin English, an unsophisticated language. This fact demonstrates that the Chinese administrators wanted only as much contact with, and understanding of, foreigners as was necessary in order to conduct their commerce.

(3) Interpreters' income: They obtained their income from the engagement fee for every ship served, the commissions on the imports and exports of merchandise, and gratuities.

(4) Number of interpreters: The number of interpreters varied from two to five. Compared with Nagasaki, to which only a couple of Dutch ships

sailed every year, the number of interpreters in Canton appears to be very small. This may be partly due to differences in the government's attitude towards foreigners, but, as I will now discuss, a more important reason is that the working style of the interpreters in Canton was slightly different from that of those in Nagasaki.

(5) Interpreters' duties: Compared with interpreters in Nagasaki, who were government staff under the authority of the Nagasaki Bugyō, interpreters in Canton seem to have been more independent and formed a kind of guild in order to conduct their work more efficiently. An interpreter had a couple of assistants and five or six pursers. Their corporation could undertake all of the necessary services to accommodate the trade of their client: obtaining chops (official seals or stamps) for going up the Pearl River to Whampoa (Huangpu, the harbour for Western ships at the lower part of the river off the city of Canton), hiring sampans and labourers to bring goods from Whampoa to Canton, preparing documents for customs, paying customs in place of foreigners, and hiring labourers in Canton and giving them wages, tips, and various fees on behalf of their client. Without the assistance of the interpreters' corporation, the European companies would not have been able to engage in trade. Since the number of such corporations was very limited, an interpreter sometimes provided services for more than ten ships at a time. European companies had practically no choice of interpreter.

As is shown above, there are differences between the situation of interpreters in Nagasaki and that of their counterparts in Canton. Interpreters in Canton were not governmental staff, while, in Nagasaki, the local government employed them. The organization of interpreters in Nagasaki seems to have been more systematic and the political influence and pressure of the government on the interpreters was apparently stronger. The language skill of the Japanese interpreters was sometimes excellent. It was one of the interpreters in Nagasaki who invented the word *sakoku* (closing the country) when he was translating Engelbert Kaempfer's famous description of Japan. Such a thing never happened in Canton.

We must, however, pay attention to the common aspects of the circumstances surrounding interpreters in the two port cities. First, in both cases, the interpreters were local people. Second, they were professional interpreters and not merchants. Third, they were governmental employees or worked under government license and had no special relations with the European companies. Chinese control over foreigners in Canton seems to have been less extensive than in Japan. Still, it is clear that the Chinese authorities distinguished foreigners, especially Westerners, from local people and attempted to control their activities. We can understand better what these common features signified when we examine the interpreters working in Bandar Abbas in the Persian Gulf region, but, first, let us examine the situation of children of mixed parentage in Nagasaki and Canton.

Children of Mixed Parentage in Nagasaki and Canton

The Tokugawa government strictly prohibited the Dutch and the Chinese from having relations with Japanese women in Nagasaki after it forced foreigners to live in the settlements reserved especially for them. The Dutch and the Chinese were able to enjoy intimate relations only with professional women (*yūjo*) from the special entertainment districts of Maruyama-machi and Yoriai-machi, who were exceptionally permitted to enter the foreigners' settlements. As a result, children of mixed parentage were born, for the most part, to these women. According to Matsui Yoko, it was because the *yūjo* was outside the Japanese *ie* (household) system that she was allowed to enter the foreigners' settlements and have relations with the Dutch and the Chinese. I should emphasize, however, that many *yūjo* maintained their ties with their parents and often returned to their parental homes once their contracts ended.

In 1715, the Nagasaki Bugyō issued an instruction which ordered *yūjo* and their relatives to report the birth of a child of mixed parentage to the authorities, without exception. People may have kept the birth of a child secret until then. The instruction emphasized that it was relatively normal for *yūjo* to have children with Dutch and Chinese men and permitted them to live together as a family while the fathers remained in Nagasaki. What is important for us is that the instruction forbade fathers to take their children with them when they returned home. The government had a clear intention of placing the children of mixed parentage under its control. They were certainly regarded as Japanese and people of the "inside" by the government. So far as the relevant studies have clarified, after 1715 foreigners could not take their children born in Nagasaki abroad. (In fact, this is an important change in Tokugawa policy towards children of mixed parentage. In the first half of the seventeenth century, it deported children born of European men and Japanese women to Macao and Batavia due to the threat of Christianity.)

We can thus confirm that there existed the sense of a clear distinction between Japanese and foreigners, at least at the government level, at the beginning of our period (1730), and there was seemingly no change until the end of the Edo period.

In the case of Canton, I have not found any precise or reliable references to this issue. Paul Van Dyke indicates the existence of "flower boats" stationed along the Zhu Jiang, especially for the service of foreigners. He doesn't discuss in detail, however, the question of children of mixed parentage. Information regarding how they were treated by the Qing government and their status in Canton society would prove extremely useful. Nevertheless, since the Qing authorities drew a clear distinction between Westerners and local people, we can safely assume that there might have been some kind of distinction between Eurasians and local people.

Interpreters and Children of Mixed Parentage in Bandar Abbas

I have already referred to a couple of articles, in Japanese and Western languages, on interpreters in Bandar Abbas, the most important Persian port city in the seventeenth and eighteenth centuries.[3] The following are the main points related to the questions under discussion at present.

(1) Foreigners' circumstances: There was no restriction on foreigners learning Persian or any other local language in Persia. The EIC encouraged some of its staff to learn Persian. Neither the Safavid government (until its collapse in 1722) nor the Afghan government, its successor, maintained interpreters systematically. In principle, the foreign visitors provided interpreters to facilitate smooth communication with the government. Therefore, the European companies required interpreters when they needed to negotiate about various political and commercial issues with the Persian government. Foreigners could live wherever the king permitted and there are a couple of pieces of evidence to suggest that Europeans purchased houses in the city of Isfahan.

(2) Interpreters' situation: Most interpreters for both the EIC and the VOC were Armenian Christians. They were the subjects of the Persian government, although they were employed by the European companies. The Europeans attempted to obtain some privileges for their Armenian interpreters in order to increase their willingness to work with them. For example, the EIC asked the Safavid government to exempt its interpreter from the *jizya* (poll tax), which they theoretically had to pay as infidels living in a Muslim state.

(3) Number of interpreters: Both the EIC and the VOC had only one interpreter, although there were several interpreters of the lower class as well.

(4) Interpreters' duties: Interpreters were not simply translators, but, like interpreters in Nagasaki and Canton, also negotiators. They were also called "linguists". Indian brokers also played an active part in communications at every stage of the commercial activities, in addition to interpreters of the lower class. The Armenian interpreters of the upper class took charge of more political and diplomatic issues. I have highlighted the important

role assumed by the interpreter of the EIC as a mediator, when the chief of the Dutch factory at Bandar Abbas was arrested by the local Afghan government official, and an armed conflict resulted between the Afghans and the Dutch in 1728–29. The interpreter of the Dutch factory, who was not in Bandar Abbas when the Afghans captured the Dutch chief, hid himself inside the Dutch factory when he returned there and narrowly escaped from a search by the Afghans. In fact, the origin of the conflict between the Afghans and the Dutch was the negotiation of surrender with people on the island of Hormuz, several miles off Bandar Abbas, which the Dutch interpreter had undertaken without the consent of the Afghan government.

(5) Interpreters' income: At present, it is uncertain whether or not they received a fixed salary from the European companies. However, even if they received a salary, it would not have constituted their main income. They offered some services to the European companies as interpreters and mediators between them and the local government. This collaboration brought them certain privileges, such as exemption from *jizya*, priority in acquiring some imported goods, and the use of the holds of European ships. It was not the salary, but such privileges and the profit they made as a result of their private commerce through their use of the networks of the European companies that the interpreters expected. In fact, the Armenian interpreters were themselves merchants. They engaged in trade on their own account. They formed their own caravans, sent their agents to important cities in the Iranian Plateau and the Persian Gulf region and obtained useful trading information by themselves. They often communicated such information to the Europeans. They seemed to be rich, and, at the beginning of the eighteenth century, the Dutch interpreter had a large residence next to the Dutch factory.

In terms of the children of mixed parentage, it is certain that many European men had sexual relations with local women, like in Nagasaki and Canton, and we can expect that children would have been born. There might have been some kind of discrimination, but we have no clear evidence of this from the narrative sources. In fact, it is impossible to distinguish insiders from outsiders in Bandar Abbas society. We have considerable evidence of people living at the fringe of different ethnicities and cultures; for example, there was a French captain commanding a local ship, a converted Muslim commander of the castle who was originally Banyan (Hindu merchant from North-western India), a French military leader and Dutch deserters under the command of a pseudo-Safavid prince, converted Portuguese serving the Safavid court, etc.

Members of a number of ethnic groups resided in Bandar Abbas: Turks, Afghans, Georgians, Armenians, Jews, Arabs and Iranians lived together in the city. The religious groups were also quite complex: Sunni and Shiite Muslims, Jews, Armenian and Georgian Orthodox, Catholic and Protestant Christians, Hindus, etc. In such a multi-layered society, a child of mixed parentage would not cause a serious problem.

Two Features of East Asian Port Cities

After discussing the questions related to interpreters and children of mixed parentage in Bandar Abbas, I wish to point out two interesting features of the two East Asian port cities, Nagasaki and Canton, which are in sharp contrast with those of Bandar Abbas.

(1) Foreigners' activities, especially those of Westerners, were strictly controlled in the two East Asian port cities, because of the clear distinction between insider and outsider. It was clearer in Nagasaki, and less clear in Canton, but the distinction still existed there. Interpreters stood between the insider and the outsider and worked to mediate between the two parties. In Bandar Abbas, however, there was no clear distinction between the local people and foreigners. For example, Armenian interpreters were local in the sense that they fell under the jurisdiction of the Safavid government, but they were employed by Europeans and possessed a network which linked them to their colleagues and relatives overseas in India, South-East Asia and Europe. In this sense, they could be called outsiders. Some Indian merchants also worked for themselves and as brokers for the European companies in Bandar Abbas. Although they were from North-western India, they had lived in Bandar Abbas for a certain period and were incorporated within the economic activities there. We cannot define them either as insiders or foreigners. Thus, neither ethnicity nor religion can be indices of the distinction between insider and outsider here.

(2) In the two East Asian port cities, the government strictly controlled foreign trade, but it did not trade on its own behalf, nor did it profit directly from trade. The reason it controlled the foreign trade seems to be related to security, social stability and the prosperity of the state (*kokka*, *goujia*). This attitude on the part of the government is relatively similar to that of the modern sovereign state. In Bandar Abbas, by contrast, the Safavid government had little intention of controlling foreign trade as a whole. The levy of duties at Bandar Abbas was often farmed out to courtiers and the government was content to receive a fixed sum from customs. The royal family itself sometimes traded in competition with other lords and merchants. We cannot find here any existence of a kind of "sovereign state" like East Asia during the same period. This was not because the Safavid

> Empire was weak and had no power, since it was one of the most powerful states in the world at that time. It was simply a question of a difference in governmental attitude towards maritime trade. Safavid and other political powers in the Indian Ocean maritime world adopted a *laissez-faire* policy, while countries in the East Asian maritime world attempted strictly to control the commercial activities of the maritime trade.

It is noteworthy that these two particular features had not been present for long. A completely different situation prevailed in the Japanese port cities of the sixteenth and the early seventeenth centuries. Let us consider the situation at this time through the studies of Arano Yasunori.[4] He refers to Hirado, a port city situated in the far west of Kyūshū, as *shominzoku zakkyo* (a city where multi-ethnic people live together), and points out that Chinese, Korean, Spanish, Portuguese and English people lived side by side along with the local Japanese. Chinese, Korean, Spanish, Scots and Japanese interpreters worked in the EIC factory that operated in Hirado between 1613 and 1623, and Malay, Portuguese, Spanish and Japanese were employed as the common languages by those living there. Moreover, Chinese documents were still being employed. Arano underlines the multi-ethnicity of the interpreters and mentions that they were merchants and sometimes traded for themselves. It can be concluded, therefore, that a drastic political and social change occurred in the Japanese archipelago during the first half of the seventeenth century. Although we know what happened, we do not know the reason why.[5] The severe governmental control of maritime trade seems to be quite natural within the context of East Asian history. A *haijin* policy already existed in the Ming dynasty and a similar policy was enacted by the Qing dynasty in the middle of the seventeenth century. Once we understand that a very different attitude towards maritime trade existed in South and West Asia (there is no room to outline the policy of the other political powers in the Indian Ocean maritime world, but the Persian case was not exceptional), we have to admit that intervention in, and the control of, maritime trade by the state is a feature of East Asia. Although we use the same word, "state", to indicate the political power in various regions of Asia, its character may not be the same.

Notes

1. Matsui Yoko, "Edo-jidai Deshima niokeru Nichiran-kankei-no Ninaitetachi" (Those in Charge of the Japanese-Dutch Relations at Deshima in the Edo Period), in *Yūrashia-niokeru Bunka-no Kōryu-to Tenpen* (Cultural Interaction and Translation in Eurasia), ed. Haneda Masashi (Tokyo: Institute of Oriental Culture, University of Tokyo, 2007) (Proceedings of the second French-Japanese colloquium between the University of Tokyo and École Pratique des Hautes Études).

2. Paul A. Van Dyke, *The Canton Trade: Life and Enterprise on the China Coast, 1700–1845* (Hong Kong: Hong Kong University Press, 2005), pp. 77–93.
3. Bandar Abbas and Nagasaki, "An Analysis of the Reaction of the Safavid Government to Europeans from a Comparative Perspective", *Annals of the Japan Association for Middle East Studies* 20–2 (March, 2005): 119–30; "Les compagnies des Indes orientales et les interprètes à Bandar 'Abbas", *Eurasian Studies* 5, no. 1–2 (2006): 175–94; "Europeans at Bandar Abbas and the 'state' of Persia in the Seventeenth and Eighteenth Centuries", Birgitt Hoffmann, Ralph Kauz and Markus Ritter, eds., *Iran und iranisch geprägte Kulturen: Studien zu Ehren von Bert G. Fragner; überreicht an seinem 65. Geburtstag* (Beiträge zur Iranistik) (Wiesbaden: Reichert, 2008), pp. 97–104.
4. Arano Yasunori, "Tsūyaku-ron. Josetsu" (Introductory Remarks on Interpreters) in *Ajia-no naka-no Nihonshi*, vol. 5 (Japanese History from the Asian Perspective), ed. Arano Yasunori, Ishii Masatoshi and Murai Shosuke (Tokyo, 1993), pp. 243–63; *Kinsei-Nihon-to Higashiajia* (Early Modern Japan and East Asia) (Tokyo, 1988).
5. The idea that such a change took place is accepted by most specialists. See, for example, Momoki Shiro and Hasuda Takashi, "A Review of the Periodization of Southeast Asian Medieval/Early Modern History, in Comparison with that of Northeast Asia", *Osaka University, the 21st Century COE Program, Interface Humanities Research Activities 2004–2006* 4: 77–78.

CHAPTER 2

The Legal Position of Foreigners in Nagasaki during the Edo Period

Matsui Yoko, Translated by Reinier H. Hesselink

1. Introduction

This paper discusses the ways of settling conflicts and disputes concerning legal questions, issues relating to men and women, and the social recognition of children of mixed parentage in Nagasaki in relation to six themes of this comparative study project.

Nagasaki, at the beginning of the seventeenth century, was a city where a variety of people resided who had come from overseas; that is, it was a town of mixed nationalities. Trade flourished there between the Japanese and foreigners, as well as among the foreigners themselves. These foreigners could freely move about the city, choosing where they wanted to live, and intercourse between Japanese women and foreign men was common.

The 1630s changed this situation. The laws issued by the Bakufu during this decade were to become the standard for the relations between Japanese and foreigners for the rest of the Edo period. These laws were aimed at forbidding the Japanese to travel overseas, tightening the prohibitions on Christianity, and bringing trade under Bakufu's control.

In this paper, I will first review these laws paying particular attention to the way in which foreigners were perceived and how they were supposed to have been treated in Japan. Next, I will trace how, thereafter, foreigners were actually treated in Nagasaki, limiting myself to two topics: (1) crime and punishment; and (2) children sired by foreigners.

2. Japanese and Foreigners

(1) The provisions contained in the laws of the 1630s

The attached table provides a list of the various laws issued during the 1630s relating to Japan's foreign relations. Please refer to the appendix for the relevant passages of each law.[1]

A, B, D, and E are orders that were issued, between 1633 and 1636, by the Senior Councillors to the Governors of Nagasaki upon their departure from Edo for their tour of duty. Their articles are virtually identical in content. The first article of each contains a general prohibition on foreign travel for Japanese vessels, while article 2 prohibits the Japanese from going overseas. While, in 1633 and 1634, these articles contained exceptions for Japanese vessels carrying a letter of authorization (*hōsho*) from the Senior Councillors themselves, in 1635, the overseas traffic was completely halted. On 23 June 1634 (Kan'ei 11, 5th month, 28th day), these prohibitions were announced to Nagasaki's inhabitants via wooden placards (C), article 3 of which adds to the prohibition on overseas travel the provision that foreigners domiciled in Japan will be treated like Japanese.

Article 3 of the orders issued by the Senior Councillors prohibits the return to Japan of Japanese who have gone abroad. The texts of 1633 (A) and 1634 (B) contain the proviso that "those who have resided abroad for unavoidable reasons and return to Japan within five years will be allowed to stay, but those who wish to leave again will be executed", but the order of 1635 omits this. Because there are no longer any Japanese who are going abroad, article 3 now deals only with those Japanese who have already left Japan and have spent time or resided abroad.[2]

On the other hand, the order of 1636 (E) adds two new articles dealing with those who are not Japanese, that are referred to as *nanbanjin* or Southern Barbarians. Article 9 contains a prohibition on leaving behind Southern Barbarian progeny, and article 10 orders that any children born of Southern Barbarians in Nagasaki, their birth mothers, as well as their adoptive parents, should leave Japan together with the Southern Barbarians.

Moreover, the orders issued in 1639 to the Governors of Nagasaki after the Amakusa-Shimabara Rebellion (F) forbid the Dutch, in article 3, to have children in Japan, and orders that such children and their mothers must leave the country, together with their Dutch fathers.

Article 9 deals with Chinese residents of Nagasaki, informing them that those who wish to return home will not be allowed to reside in Japan should they return there subsequently, but they are allowed to return home accompanied by their wives and children if they wish to do so. Article 10 contains the same regulation for the Dutchmen residing in Nagasaki.

Finally, the order prohibiting Portuguese ships from coming to Japan (G), dated 4 August 1639 (Kan'ei 16, 7th month, 5th day), by which the Portuguese lost their permission to trade in Japan, is well-known.

(2) Criteria for distinction: domicile

According to the depth of their relationship with Japanese society, Arano Yasunori has divided the foreigners who came to Japan before the 1630s into three groups: (1) those who stayed for a short period of time; (2) those who stayed for a long period of time; and (3) those who were assimilated into Japanese society. He concluded that the policy of the period now removed the second, "marginal" group, from Japanese society. Also, he pointed out that the second criterion for deciding who in the third group could become Japanese citizens was: (1) not being Christian and (2) having adopted Japanese manners and customs. According to Arano, race was not an issue, and it was these two issues that decided who was to be included among the Japanese people during the early modern period.[3]

Where the expulsion of those who had been in Japan for a long period of time is concerned, I agree with Arano, but I think that, in order to distinguish foreigners from Japanese, the criterion of domicile (*jūtaku*) is a more concrete keyword that appears in the various laws dealing with this issue. Domicile in these ordinances means more than just a physical dwelling place, and is often used as a verb meaning "to take up residence" or "to make a home". In C, it is translated into Chinese as "to nationalize" (*kika* or *tōka*),[4] an expression which can be clarified as "possessing residence and family, and living permanently in Japan". Japanese who had traveled overseas and lived in foreign countries did not fall under the jurisdiction of the Japanese authorities. On the other hand, those who make their domicile (*jūtaku suru*) in Japan, that is: "have both residence and family" there and thus are governed as a "household" (*ie*) by the Japanese authorities, will be treated, regardless of their bloodline, in the same manner as Japanese. This seems to be the basic thinking underlying the ordinances quoted.

In ordinance F, dating from 1639, the Chinese and Dutch who made their domicile (*jūtaku*), that is: "lived" in Nagasaki, are urged to choose whether to "return home" (*kikoku*) or not. As we can see from the wording of the text, to "return home" means: not to belong to a "household" (*ie*) in Japan; that is: not to live permanently in Japan and not to have a wife or children there. Such people, when they come to Japan, will only be allowed to stay for a short period of time, and belong to the category of "foreigners" (*ikokujin*). As far as I am aware, there is no example of a Dutchman who chose, at this time, not to "return home", but it is well-known that, among the Chinese of Nagasaki, there were, beginning with the families that had received official appointments as interpreters, a considerable number who chose this option. Thereafter, these people were known as "resident Chinese" (*jūtaku tōjin*), who had wives and children in Japan, had established a hereditary household (*ie*), were included in the temple registers (*shūmon ninbetsu aratame-chō*) and so were fully-fledged members of Japanese society.[5]

I should point out that these ideas occurred within the context of the continuing effort to control everyone residing in Japanese territory (that is: the Japanese) in terms of the "household" (*ie*). In order to tighten its prohibition against Christianity, the Bakufu enforced the custom that everyone was registered as a parishioner of a temple somewhere and underwent an examination of their religious beliefs (*shūmon ninbetsu aratame*). The registers resulting from this examination, or *shūmon ninbetsu aratame-chō*, were prepared and filed throughout Japan annually from the 1660s onward, but they were started in the 1630s and maintained more rigorously after the Amakusa-Shimabara rebellion.[6]

On 5 May 1639 (Kan'ei 16, 4th month, 3rd day), during his stay in Edo, Chief Factor François Caron wrote in his diary that he had heard from Nagamura Sumimasa, a senior retainer of Hirado-han, that his lord and all other daimyo of Western Japan had had an audience with Shōgun Iemitsu on that day and "had again been ordered to conduct another severe search for Christians throughout Japan".[7] What Caron heard about the methods to be employed in this search was, first, that the existing organization of the five-household units (*gonin-gumi*), bearing responsibility as a group and responsible for watching over each other, would be tightened, and second, that everyone would have to prove that they were not Christian and that they belonged to some Japanese sect before two witnesses. They would also have to document to which temple's parish they belonged. Of Hirado machi (which had been among the first streets of Nagasaki since its foundation) we have, beginning with the *ninbetsu chō* of 1634, which is said to be the oldest such surviving register in Japan, several other registers dating from the Kan'ei period, and so we know that this policy was already being implemented by 1639. Among these Hirado machi registers, the most detailed is that of 1642, and, looking at its entries, we see that several Chinese, Koreans, and others who came from outside Japan are included in it. These people had obviously either declined to or could not "return home" and had a household (*ie*) in Japan, so they were registered in the *ninbetsu chō* in the same manner as "Japanese".

(3) The children of foreigners and their mothers

The principle governing this distinction between Japanese and foreigners becomes even clearer when we analyze the policy pursued at the time of the banishment of children sired by foreigners and their mothers. Why, for example, were the children of Dutchmen and their wives sent into exile, while the Dutch themselves continued to trade in Japan? This cannot be explained simply by referring to a fear of Christians or a dislike of a European bloodline.

It is believed that, in 1634, the year when the construction started of what would become the artificial island of Deshima, it had been decided to limit the sojourn of the Portuguese to the duration of their embassy and to separate them from the city. On 22 June 1636 (Kan'ei 13, 5th month, 19th day), the offspring of the Southern Barbarians were ordered to be expelled from Japan, which order was implemented the same year. On 20 October 1636, we read in the diary of the chief factor of the Dutch trading house in Hirado that 287 people had been sent to Macao on four galliots: "among them were not only the children of the Portuguese, but also Japanese women who had lived with Portuguese men for a few years, but later had married Japanese men and borne them five, six or even more children, and now had to separate from their children and husbands. Among them were also Japanese who were exiled because they had adopted and brought up children of mixed blood". This shows that the orders had been carried out to the letter. The number 287 is confirmed by the records of Ōmura-han, which was charged with policing the city at this time.[8]

This order exiling the "offspring of the Southern Barbarians" not only concerned their children, but also the women who had previously had sexual relationships with Portuguese men, or even Japanese who had brought up the children born of such relationships, which seems to show an excessive zeal to get rid of all of those who had had anything to do with the children of the Southern Barbarians, who were closely associated with Christianity. However, the deportation of the wives and children of the Dutch was implemented under a different policy.

In the fall of 1638, the Nagasaki representative of the Hirado factory, Willem Versteegen, petitioned the Governors of Nagasaki for permission to leave for Batavia, accompanied by his wife and child, as well as his parents-in-law, who were Melchior van Santvoort, and his Japanese wife. Van Santvoort was the last survivor of *De Liefde*, which had been stranded off Kyūshū in 1600, and who had, since then, been in Japan.[9]

Vincent Romeijn, a Dutch free trader in Nagasaki, submitted a similar petition. Versteegen had applied for permission from Edo in this matter as well and, on 2 February 1639, a messenger came from Edo with the news that "the many Chinese who were living in Nagasaki, had married there, and had sired a number of children" had also asked "to leave this country for China", but that the decision concerning all of those cases had been postponed.

On 6 May 1639, this permission finally arrived in Nagasaki. Immediately afterwards, on 9 May, an investigation was held into the names of the Japanese women and the children they had borne to Dutch fathers, and, on 16 June, all of the Japanese women, together with the children whom they had borne to Dutchmen and Englishmen, were ordered to sail for Batavia on the ships leaving that year. At the same time, intercourse between Dutchmen and

Japanese women was strictly forbidden in Hirado as well as in Nagasaki. All of this was based on articles 3 and 9–11 of the orders (F) issued to the Governors of Nagasaki on 25 March 1639 (Kan'ei 16, 2nd month 21st day), mentioned above. When the Governors reached Nagasaki at the beginning of May, these policies are thought to have been put into effect immediately. The Dutch heard that the same order that had been issued to their women and children had also been applied to the Chinese, who were subject to the same severe penalties.[10]

On 31 October 1639, twenty-five people set off for Batavia on the ship *Breda*. Stopping off at Taiwan on the way, it is said that four couples were formally married.[11]

The measures taken towards the exile of the women and children of the Dutch can be summarized as follows: (1) these measures applied to both the Dutch and the Chinese; (2) it had been decided to allow their Japanese women to leave as an exception to the general prohibition on foreign travel; and (3) from now on, all intercourse between foreigners (*ikokujin*) and Japanese women was to be proscribed.

In this way, the households (ie) of foreigners disappeared from Japan, while those foreigners who continued to come to Japan all belonged to the category of those who stayed for only a short period of time.

(4) The extent of Japan's authority

How and where was the reasoning behind this distinction between Japanese and foreigners actually applied? Since the Dutch ships had been coming to Japan, the Dutch had usually been labeled as *pirates* by both the Southern European missionaries and the Chinese.[12] In 1621, the Bakufu issued orders prohibiting the export of slaves bought in Japan as well as all military equipment, and it forbade foreigners to engage in piracy at sea.[13] The Chief Factor at that time, Jacques Specx, was aware that, in this connection, he needed to have clear directions regarding how far Japan's territorial waters extended, for inside these territorial waters it would be dangerous for the Dutch to make prizes of enemy ships.[14] This, however, did not stop the Dutch from taking enemy ships, as the Portuguese and Chinese complained to the Bakufu every year. According to an entry in the diary for 27 August 1637, the Chinese on a junk that had arrived in Nagasaki had lodged a complaint with the Governors of Nagasaki that, on their way from Cochin China, they had been diverted to Taiwan by a Dutch ship, where their cargo had been stolen. They were now asking the Governors to order the Dutch to pay them an indemnity. Chief Factor Coeckebacker said that he had heard from members of the crew that it was true that the junk had been brought to Taiwan, but that no theft had taken place, and he petitioned for the complaint to be dismissed. The Dutch were no longer concerned about this matter, for the Governors stated that the actions of the Dutch while at sea were no concern of theirs, but they warned that to be called a pirate was the worst type of blemish on one's name possible in Japan, and that, if they expected the shogun's favour, the Dutch should be careful about this.[15]

The Dutch, however, were not the only ones who attracted complaints. On 30 July 1639, it was reported by a ship arriving from Taiwan, among the news of all the Dutch activities in the area, that a junk dispatched from Tonkin to the Pescadores in January in the preceding year "had been pursued by Chinese living in Japan (*Japansche Chinesen*), seized, and 19 people had been killed".[16] Chief Factor Caron noted on 31 August in Nagasaki that, "the captain, the owner of the junk, and the other interested parties were all residents of Nagasaki, where they owned houses and had wives and children" and "that we would have liked to identify all of these people so that we might hold them responsible before justice and the law". Thus complained the Dutch to the Bakufu about the behaviour of the Chinese living in Japan; that is, the Chinese who fell under the jurisdiction of the Japanese authorities. However, according to the Governors of Nagasaki, it was forbidden for the Chinese of Nagasaki who fell under the jurisdiction of the Japanese authorities to go overseas. Therefore, the perpetrators of this affair were not people who lived in Japan, and so they consequently did not have women and children in Japan. They declined to consider the complaint, stating that the Dutch should appeal to the authorities of the place where the criminals lived.

Obviously, the Bakufu feared there was a real danger that it might become involved in the disputes between the different powers sailing the China Sea, either through its own red-seal ships and the activities of the Japanese living abroad or through the advent in Japan of Europeans and Asians living along the coasts. If faced with complaints, how was the Bakufu to handle or solve disputes occurring either within the area under its jurisdiction or those that concerned the people living there? In any case, whether it was an internal or an international matter, the Bakufu needed to devise solutions that would hurt neither its power nor its honour. It was important for that purpose to define how far Japan's jurisdiction extended. Geographically, some research indicates that the desire to fix the borders of Japan dates back to Hidetada's time.[17] During the 1630s, the Bakufu also decided who was going to be considered Japanese; that is, the people who lived in this area under its jurisdiction. As it had experienced several international disputes and ruptures during the 1620s,[18] we may say that the Bakufu chose to avoid potential problems by limiting the extent of its power in so far as it was sure to be able to dominate.

3. The Treatment of Foreigners

(1) Crime and punishment

Let us now review some actual cases to see how foreigners were treated.

(a) The execution of Hans Andriesz

In January 1640, an employee of the Dutch Factory in Hirado, the assistant Hans Andriesz, and a Japanese woman were executed by an official of Hirado-han "because he had slept with the wife of a Japanese man and (according to Japanese law) had been condemned in court to be executed". The domain officials reported to the chief factor that they had wanted to save him somehow in order to maintain their friendship with the Dutch, but, because "this affair had received too much publicity and would otherwise have had grave repercussions", they had been unable to let the Dutchman go free, for "in Japan, cases of adultery are handled with great severity". They explained that the shogun had, moreover, issued orders forbidding all intercourse between foreigners and Japanese women, so that this really was a case of a double crime.

(b) A Dutch sailors' brawl and the principle of *kenka ryōseibai*

On 15 October 1646, a brawl occurred among Dutch sailors who had come ashore and got drunk. One of them incurred a grave injury, being stabbed in the chest. His attacker, sure that he had killed his man, then turned the same knife on himself and committed suicide.[19] When the chief factor reported this incident to the Governors of Nagasaki, they let it be known at first that "according to Japanese law, it did not matter whether a wound was self-inflicted or not, so that the wounded man should be executed as well", suggesting that the principle of "punishing both parties to a quarrel" (*kenka ryōseibai*) applied here.[20] When the chief factor stressed that no Japanese had been involved in this affair, and that, after a careful investigation, justice would be done according to Dutch law, he was permitted, for the moment, to investigate the circumstances of the affair. Next, on 20 October, the chief factor petitioned for permission to send the wounded man under arrest off on the ship that was currently preparing to sail, and to be allowed the right to apply Dutch law to Dutchmen. The next day, the Governors gave their permission for this. However, they made it known that, because this was the first time that this had happened, they would allow the wounded man to be sent off at the request of the Dutch, and would refrain from executing him, but if, hereafter, a similar affair occurred, after which one man was left dead, the other would be executed, regardless of the rights and wrongs of their quarrel and without any special treatment for anyone on the basis of his rank.

(c) The expulsion of Andreas Cleyer

Fujita Kayoko has published a detailed study of the affair of the chief factor who was found to have been involved in smuggling and was expelled from Japan in 1686. The eight Dutchmen who had actually been engaged in the smuggling were led before the Governors' office by the interpreters, where the Governor investigated the affair, after which they were all sent back to Deshima in shackles. Finally, the Governor ordered the old and the new chief factors that: "19 Japanese will be executed, and these eight men should be tried in their homeland according to the laws applying there", and they announced that, because the incident had occurred due to lack of supervision, Chief Factor Cleyer "was expelled from Japan and forbidden to return on pain of death".[21] Later, after a hearing before the Batavia Council of Justice, all of the men involved were cleared of wrong-doing.

Similarly, in the smuggling case of 1691, the Dutch accomplice was simply handed over to the chief factor and ordered to be expelled from Japan. In the cases of Chinese smugglers also, it was only the Japanese accomplices who were severely punished, while their Chinese counterparts got off with being expelled and did not lose their lives.[22]

In case (a), the idea of the husband's right to punish (that is: take revenge on) his wife and her accomplice in adultery was generally accepted at the time as an inalienable male right. Moreover, it may be surmised that concern for the shogun's prohibitions on the part of Hirado-han made it exercise its right to investigate the affair, try those involved, and punish them. In case (b), the Governors showed that they thought that, again, the generally accepted principle of "punishing both parties to a quarrel" should be applied here, but they accepted the chief factor's argument that this was a case in which no Japanese were involved and admitted that the Dutch had the right to conduct their own investigation, hold their own trial, and mete out their own punishment. Both sides agreed, therefore, that Dutch law would ensure a proper trial and punishment. Case (c) was a large-scale smuggling affair implicating both Japanese and Dutchmen, and the investigation was conducted by the Japanese side. The only punishment for the Dutchmen was to be expelled from Japan. However, this certainly did not mean that they had been sufficiently tried and punished according to the Japanese side but simply shows the Japanese expectation that they would now be properly tried according to Dutch law.

These punishments of foreigners for smuggling, as well as the criminal liability of foreigners in general, have been regarded as too lenient, or "soft" on foreigners.[23] It certainly cannot be denied that depending on the time and the officials responsible, there may have been a tendency to overlook certain matters through a fear of a deterioration in relations and other problems. However, the principle governing the treatment of foreigners was that the right to punish non-Japanese should be exercised by the appropriate authority with power over those foreigners. This is likely to be the main reason why the response to the crimes of foreigners was to expel them from Japan.

(2) Children sired by foreigners

When, in 1639, the children sired by the Dutch and their mothers were ordered to leave the country, the Dutch were at the same time also forbidden to have intercourse with Japanese women. An exception to this prohibition was intercourse with prostitutes (*yūjo*).[24] Why would only these women have been allowed to have intercourse with foreigners? This is because they led an existence apart from that of normal households (*ie*). Women in Japanese society of the Edo period were conceptualized in terms of some sort of relationship to a specific male head of household: as his wife, or as his concubine with the position of servant, or as his daughter, either genuine or adopted. To have a relationship with a male without a household (*ie*), that is a foreigner, was only possible for prostitutes who did not belong to any specific man, or who belonged, one might say, to the provisional household (*ie*), that was her brothel.

It can be easily imagined that the Dutch established such relationships with prostitutes soon after their move to Deshima,[25] for, already, by 1649; these had become so frequent that the chief factor asked the Japanese side to provide some regulations.[26]

It is certain that the relationships between the port town prostitutes and the foreigners who stayed for only a short period of time were originally designed to be of a transitory nature, without assuming that children might be born of such unions. However, in reality, some relations became intimate and children were born. The ordinance addressed to Maruyama machi, Yoriai machi, and the compound of the Chinese (*tōjin yashiki*) issued by the Governors of Nagasaki in 1715 (Shō toku 5) clearly recognizes this reality.[27] Its contents are: (1) pregnancies with children sired by foreigners, their births, and deaths should not be kept hidden but reported; (2) while their fathers are in Japan, they may be brought up by them; (3) after their fathers have returned home, they should be reared in the brothel, but when their fathers returned to Japan, the fathers would be consulted about their children; (4) the Chinese should be consulted about their upbringing; (5) it is prohibited for foreigners to take these children home.

From this time onwards, we find the news of such pregnancies and births scattered among the sources of Nagasaki's Yoriai machi, although it is uncertain whether all cases were reported in this manner. Also, there are almost no records of what became of these children. However, I would like to present one example, dating from the middle of the eighteenth century, which proves that this order may have been well observed.

On 28 March 1757 (Hōreki 7, 2nd month, 9th day), a daughter was born to the factory assistant, Abraham Verspijk, and Wakaura, a prostitute held in bondage by the brothel owner Aburaya Risanta. This pregnancy as well as the birth had been reported by Aburaya,[28] but on 20 December of the same year,

Chief Factor Vermeulen petitioned Governor Masaki Shima-no-kami to allow the child to accompany her father back to Batavia.[29] In reply, they were notified in the name of the mayor-on-duty for that year (*nenban machidoshiyori*) that children related by blood to the Dutch as well as the Chinese were not permitted to leave the country since the Bakufu's order of 1714.[30] The chief factor stated that there was no record of that order in the factory, and he appealed once more to the Governor, claiming that, "at the time, such cases may not have occurred, but now, because there are, apart from this case, two other children like this, would the Governor be so kind as to ask Edo if, from now on, the Dutch might be permitted to return to Batavia with these children?"[31] There is no record showing whether or not the Governor indeed enquired about this matter in Edo, but it seems that the person in question had been asked if she had any inclination to hand over her child, for we have a record dated 7 January 1758, in which the mother of the child, Wakaura, and her parents replied that, if they were ordered to do so by "the authorities" (*kōgi-sama*), it could not be helped, but that, otherwise, they definitely did not want to part with the child.[32]

The final decision of the Governor is not found in either the Japanese or the Dutch sources. However, the Dutchmen were not allowed to take their children back to Batavia, and Wakaura's daughter was living in the Aburaya until she was reported missing in 1786.[33] What we often see with the Nagasaki prostitutes, and also in Wakaura's case, is that she gave birth in the house of her parents. The baby may have been brought up by her grandparents or in the brothel. In some cases, such children may have been put up for adoption by another household.

The offspring of foreigners may have been expelled from Japan in 1639, but, after that date, it was forbidden for foreigners to take their children home with them. This seems either contradictory or evidence of a change in policy. However, the principle that foreigners did not have a household (*ie*) in Japan remained unchanged. Moreover, the ordinance of 1715 shows clearly that those who were actually born in the territory governed by the Japanese authorities were treated as Japanese. Consequently, those children were considered to belong to some household in Japan.

Among Japanese males, too, there were those who could not have their own household,[34] but, for males who had foreign fathers, it was particularly difficult to become heads of their own independent households. Ishii Renpei, son of the Chinese Zhou Ai-t'ing, is an exception, who managed to have his own household as a local official in Nagasaki. Calling himself the natural son of a Japanese man, he possessed the right to inherit the headship of a household of a local official.[35] Michitomi Jōkichi, son of Chief Factor Hendrik Doeff, was another special case who managed to establish a new household as a local official through the merit and persistent petitioning of his father.[36] Both cases were made possible by the intimate relationship of the fathers with the high and mighty of Nagasaki as well as the change of hands of a considerable amount of money. However, when all is said and done, that it was possible at all was, of course, due to the recognition that, although both children had foreign fathers, they were considered to be Japanese.

Conclusion

As we have seen, the position of foreigners in Nagasaki during the Edo period was characterized by their being short-term residents who did not have a household and, as such, were not considered to fall under the jurisdiction of the Japanese authorities. It was thought that their crimes should be punished in the place where they were domiciled. Moreover, the children born to Japanese prostitutes and these foreigners were considered Japanese and were forbidden to accompany their fathers on their return home.

This way of conceiving foreigners is the reverse of how the Japanese were defined and administered by the authorities, and reflects the structure of Japanese society at this time. Viewed from the perspective of the comparative history of port towns, we should not only examine parallel cases of port towns in Asia, but should also analyze the special characteristics of the countries and regions of the world where port towns have thrived, and then contrast them to other towns and regions that do not belong to that category.

Notes

1. Since the systemization by Iwao Seiichi, A, B, D, E and G have been commonly accepted as the so-called five-step "Sakoku Legislation" in Kan'ei, which implemented, step by step, the Closed-Country system (Iwao, 1963, 1966a). During the 1970s, a complete reversal occurred in the Japanese approach to the concept of "sakoku" (closed country). According to research by Yamamoto Hirofumi, who analyzed the form and transmission route of each of the documents involved, A, B, D and E were, unlike G, internal orders of the Bakufu addressed to the Governors of Nagasaki upon the occasion of their departure for Nagasaki to provide them with guidelines for their tour of duty. The contents of these orders were not necessarily made public in every detail and the Governors of Nagasaki were advised to inform the interested daimyō, the citizens of Nagasaki, and the Dutch of only those parts that directly concerned each of these groups. Moreover, each of these guidelines addressed particular problems relating to the time at which they were issued and they do not show a gradual implementation of the so-called Closed Country policy foreseen from the start (Yamamoto, 1995). In this chapter,

I analyze these orders that deal with Japanese and foreigners, not confining myself to the so-called "Sakoku Legislation". (For a review of the concept of "Sakoku", see, inter alia: Arano, 1987; Blussé, 1979; Kato, 1989; Tsuruta, 1997; *Acta Asiatica* 67, 1995.)

2. Actually, there were quite a number of people who made their base in foreign places (Iwao, 1966b, 1987).
3. Arano, 1987, 2004.
4. Hizen no kuni Nagasaki kō kinrei (*Tsūkō Ichiran* vol. 170).
5. As for the Chinese, we can find some examples of permission to be considered "Domiciled Chinese" (*Jūtaku Tōjin*) even in the late seventeenth century, e.g., in 1672 (Kanbun 12), Wei Jiu-guan, well known as the interpreter of Tonkin (*Tonkin Tsūji*), his two sons born in Tonkin and his servant as well as seven other Chinese were allowed to reside in Nagasaki (*Nagasaki jūtaku*) (Nakamura, 1973, p. 208).
6. Hayami, 1979, pp. 52–60.
7. *Daghregister*, 5 May 1639.
8. Gonoi, 1986, p. 13.
9. *Daghregister*, 26 and 29 Nov. 1638; 2 Feb. 1639; 9–10 and 18 May 1639.
10. *Daghregister*, 24 Oct. 1639.
11. Iwao, 1987, pp. 17–22, 294, and its appended sources 6 and 7.
12. Nagazumi, 1981, pp. 18–21; Kato, 1993, pp. 29–32, 97–9.
13. *Dainippon Shiryō* 12–38, Genna 7, 7th month, 27th day, pp. 183–207.
14. Valentijn 1724, vol. 5 part 2, pp. 30–2. (*Dainippon Shiryō* 12-43, Genna 7 zassai, pp. 209–18.)
15. *Daghregister*, 30 Oct. 1637.
16. This ship, shipwrecked by a storm, was attacked by fishermen in Fu Zhou and brought to Ji Long. The silk goods in her cargo were sold to the Spaniards there. After that, she reached Cambodia, and Chief Factor Van der Haghen managed to reclaim the ship and a part of her cargo after persistent lawsuits (*Daghregister*, 30 July 1639). Amidst such troubles, both sides usually appealed to the local authorities that had some kind of jurisdiction related to the problem to see if it were possible to obtain an indemnity. In some cases, the Dutch were ordered to pay compensation.
17. Takeda, 2005, p. 157.
18. In 1624, Japan broke-off its relations with the Spanish. From 1628 to 1630, trade with the Portuguese was interrupted in the wake of their attack on a *shuin-sen.* Dutch trade was also halted from 1628 to 1633 due to the Nuyts affair.
19. *Daghregister*, 15–16 and 20–21 Oct. 1646.
20. For *kenka ryōseibai*, see *Hō shakai shi*, 2001, pp. 215–7, 292–4.
21. Fujita, 1998.
22. Matsuo Shin'ichi insists that, beginning with *Shotoku shinrei*, the Bakufu changed its policy, deciding to regard the Chinese and their junks as acting illegally as pirates, and to use hard-line measures like gunfire (Matsuo, 2004). But in individual

cases, the Chinese smugglers were neither sentenced to death nor executed. Even though the policy concerning the punishment of Japanese smugglers underwent several changes (Nishimura, 1973; Shimizu, 1979), the treatment of foreigners in Nagasaki does not seem to have been affected very much.

23. Harafuji, 1953; 1956. H. Can Erkin pointed out a similar tendency in the laws of the sixteenth century and explained it with reference to *sengoku daimyō* awareness of other domains as foreign countries (Erkin, 2000).
24. Maruyama machi and Yoriai machi formed the licensed red-light district in Nagasaki. For the intercourse between Maruyama prostitutes and foreigners, see Koga (1969). Compared to other red-light districts, such as the Yoshiwara (in Edo) or Shimabara (in Kyoto), Maruyama prostitutes enjoyed greater rights: they were allowed to go outside of their compound and to keep any children they had by their clients (Miyamoto, 1984).
25. Two months after their removal to Nagasaki, a wooden placard was erected in front of Deshima. According to the *Daghregister*, its contents included the following prohibition: Prostitutes may enter Deshima, but other women may not (*Daghregister*, 19 Aug. 1641), while Chief Factor Elserack lamented in the instruction to his successor that many sailors came ashore to get drunk and visit prostitutes. (Instructie van Jan van Elserack voor Pieter Anthonissen Overtwater, Nangasacquy, 20 Nov. 1644. VOC 1148.)
26. *Daghregister*, 13 Aug. 1649.
27. Shōtoku go nen itsubi no toshi roku gatsu, Tōjin yashiki hattogaki jōjō (*Tsūkō Ichiran* vol. 204); Shōtoku go itsubi no toshi shichi gatsu Maruyama machi Yoriai machi e jōjō (*Tsūkō Ichiran* vol. 244); Koga, 1969, pp. 108–11. The order for the Dutch cannot be found, but I presume that the same sort of order should have been issued to them; see note 30.
28. *Yoriaimachi shoji kakiage chō* (Part II), pp. 115–6.
29. Brief van H. Vermeulen aan Masaki Shima-no-kami, Nagasaki, 20 Dec. 1757 and 30 Jan. 1758. "Allerlei stukken van en betreffende Japan, 1734–1778" (NFJ495).
30. As mentioned above, the order to prohibit foreigners from removing their children from Japan was issued in 1715. It is unclear whether 1714 is simply an error, or whether the Dutch had received this order a year earlier.
31. Letter of Vermeulen dated 30 Jan. 1758; see note 29.
32. *Yoriaimachi shoji kakiage chō*, p. 123; Koga, 1969, pp. 111–3.
33. *Yoriaimachi shoji kakiage chō* (Part II), pp. 223–4.
34. Except for the successor to the headship of a family, other sons of the household, who did not have enough of the family business and property to divide between them, should belong in their brother's household as collateral family or in an employer's household as apprentices, in case they were not able to inherit other households as adoptees.
35. When it became known that Renpei was a son of a Chinese national, he lost his household and official position; see Koga, vol. 2, pp. 142–4.
36. About Jōkichi, see Koga, vol. 2, pp. 401–55, *Daghregister* 1817.

Appendices

Table Orders related to the treatment for *Japanese* and *Foreigners*

	Japanese calendar (A.D.)	*from*	*to*	*number of items / our subject*
A	Kan'ei 10, 2nd month, 28th day (16330406)	Senior Councilors of the Bakufu	Governors of Nagasaki	17 items / (2)(3)
B	Kan'ei 11, 5th month, 28th day (16340623)	Senior Councilors of the Bakufu	Governors of Nagasaki	17 items / (2)(3)
C	Kan'ei 11, 5th month, 28th day (16340623)	Governors of Nagasaki	Wooden placards addressed the people of Nagasaki	3 items / (3)
D	Kan'ei 12, 5th month, 28th day (16350612)	Senior Councilors of the Bakufu	Governors of Nagasaki	17 items / (2)(3)
E	Kan'ei 13, 5th month, 19th day (16360622)	Senior Councilors of the Bakufu	Governors of Nagasaki	19 items / (2)(3)(9)(10)
F	Kan'ei 16, 2nd month, 21st day (16390325)	Senior Councilors of the Bakufu	Governors of Nagasaki	15 items / (3)(9)(10)
G	Kan'ei 16, 7th month, 5th day (16390804)	Senior Councilors of the Bakufu	All daimyō, Portuguese, Chinese, Dutch	3 items

Sources

A 覚 Memorandum (*Buke genseiroku* 武家厳制録) (B, D, E almost the same)

(1) Sending vessels overseas is strictly prohibited <u>except *hōshosen*</u> (vessels carrying a letter of authorization from the Senior Councilors). (D&E lack <u>except *hōshosen*</u> and give *Japanese vessels* for *vessels*.)

異国え奉書船之外 (D･E 下線部を日本之とする) 舟遣候儀、堅停止之事

(2) Other than *hōshosen* no vessel can send Japanese people overseas. If someone travels illegally, this person should be executed, and the vessel and its captain should be arrested. The Governor of Nagasaki should report it to the Bakufu. (D&E lack Other than *hōshosen*.)
奉書舟之外 (D･E 下線部を欠く) 日本人異国へ遣し申間敷候、若忍ひ候て乗参候者於有之ハ其者ハ死罪、其舟并船主ともに留置、言上可仕事

(3) If someone who has gone abroad and taken up residence there returns to Japan, he/she will be executed. (D&E end here.)
However, in case he/she stayed there by some force of circumstance and returns within five years with the intention to stay in Japan, he/she will be acquitted after investigation. But if he/she intends to go back, they will be executed.
異国え渡り、住宅仕有之日本人来候は、死罪可申付候、(D･E 以下を欠く) 但不及是非に仕合有之て、異国ニ逗留いたし、五年より内に罷帰候者ハ、遂穿鑿、日本にとまり可申に付てハ御免、併異国え亦可立帰におゐては、死罪に可申付事

C 禁制 Prohibition (*Buke genseiroku* 武家厳制録)

(3) (It is prohibited for) Japanese people to travel overseas other than on *hōshosen*.
Supplement: Same as above for foreigners domiciled in Japan.
奉書船之外、日本人異国江渡海事　附　日本住宅之異国人同前事

E 定 Decree (*Kenkyō ruiten* 憲教類典)

(9) The Governor should strictly prohibit the Southern barbarians to leave their children in Japan. Anyone who violates this order will be executed, and all the members of the clan will be punished depending on the gravity of their crime.
南蛮人子孫不残置詳ニ堅可申付事、若令違背残置族有之におゐては、其者は死罪一類之者科之軽重により可申付事

(10) Although the children born of Southern barbarians' in Nagasaki as well as their adoptive parents should be executed, they are acquitted and given away to the Southern barbarians. If some of them return or correspond

with Japan, such persons will be executed, and all the members of the clan will be punished in accordance with the gravity of their crime.

南蛮人長崎にて持候子并右之子共之内養子に仕族之父母等悉雖為死罪、身命を助ケ南蛮人江被遣候間、自然彼者共之内重而日本江来る歟又者書通於有之は、本人は勿論死罪親類以下迄随科之軽重ニ可申付事

F 覚 Memorandum (*Nagasaki oyakusho dome* 長崎御役所留)

(3) Dutchmen should stop having children in Japan. Children already born and their mothers will be sent abroad with the fathers.

おらんた人於日本子を持候儀可為停止、此跡持候子は其父につけ母ともに異国え可遣の事

(9) If Chinese people who have taken up residence in Nagasaki ask to return to their home country, they will be permitted to go and take their wives and children, as they wish, on condition that they will never come to live in Japan again.

長崎住宅の唐人致帰国度と申者の儀、以来商売に付渡り候とも居住不仕様ニ申付、望次第妻子ともに可遣の事

(10) Same as above for Dutchmen who have taken up residence in Nagasaki.

長崎に令住宅おらんた人右同前の事

BIBLIOGRAPHY

Manuscript

Dagregisters van de factorij te Hirado en te Deshima, 1633–1833 NFJ53-249. (Partly published by Historiographical Institute University of Tokyo. *Nihon kankei kaigai shiryō Oranda shōkanchō nikki*. Tokyo: Tokyo daigaku shuppankai, 1974–.)

Nagasaki oyakusho dome at Naikaku Bunko.

Nederlandse Factorij Japan (Deshima Archive: NFJ) at Nationaal Archief (NA), the Hague.

Vereenigde Oost-Indische Compagnie (Dutch East India Company Archieve: VOC) at NA. *Overgecomen Brieven en Papieren uit Indië* (OB).

Printed

Buke gensei roku. Kinsei hōsei shiryō sōsho vol. 3. Tokyo: Sōbunsha, 1959.

Hayashi Akira *et al.*, eds. *Tsūkō Ichiran*. Osaka: Seibundō, 1967.

Kenkyō ruiten. Naikaku Bunko shozō shiryō sōkan 37–43. Tokyo: Kyūko shoin, 1984–.

Kuroita Katsumi, ed. *Tokugawa jikki*. Tokyo: Yoshikawa kōbunkan, 1964–66.

Kyūshū shiryō kankōkai, ed. *Nagasaki Hirado-machi ninbetsu chō*. Fukuoka: Kyūshū shiryō kankōkai, 1965.

Tōkyō daigaku shiryō hensanjo, ed. *Dainippon Shiryō*. Tokyo: Tokyo daigaku shuppankai, 1901–.

Valentijn, François*: Oud en Nieuw Oost Indiën*, 6 vols. Amsterdam: Gerard Onder de Linden, 1724.

Yoriaimachi shoji kakiage hikae chō. Nihon toshi seikatsu shiryō shūsei 6–7. Tokyo: Gakushū kenkyū sha, 1975–76.

Books and Articles

Arano Yasunori, "Nihongata ka'i chitsujo no keisei". In Asao Naohiro, Amino Yoshihiko, Yamaguchi Keiji and Yoshida Takashi, eds. *Rettō naigai no kōtsū to kokka*. Vol. 1 of *Nihon no shakaishi*. Tokyo: Iwanami shoten, 1987, pp. 184–226.

________, "Kinsei Nihon no kokka ryōiki to kyōkai: Nagasaki yūjo to konketsuji kara kangaeru-". In Shigakukai, ed. *Rekishigaku no saizensen*. Tokyo: Tokyo daigaku shuppankai, 2004, pp. 199–231.

Erkin, H., Can "16 seiki Nihon ni okeru 'gaikokujin' no hō teki ichi", *Rekishigaku kenkyu* 740 (2000): 1–15.

Fujita Kayoko, "Jōdaka-sei to Nagasaki shōkanchō Kuraiyā (Cleyer) tsuihō jiken". In Ōsaka daigaku bungakubu nihonshi kenkyūshitsu, ed. *Kinsei kindai no chiiki to kenryoku*. Osaka: Seibundō shuppan, 1998, pp. 299–323.

Gonoi Takashi, "Kinseika ni okeru Ōmura-han to kirishitan senkyōshi-Ōmura-han no gun'yaku wo chūshin to shite-", *Nagasaki dansō* 71 (1986): 1–38.

Harafuji Hiroshi, "Kinsei Nagasaki ni okeru ikokujin no keiji jō no ichi". In Miyamoto Mataji, ed. *Kyūshū keizaishi kenkyū*. Kyoto: Sanwa shobō, 1953, pp. 249–67.

———, "Nukeni' zai zakkō", *Hōseishi kenkyū* 6 (1955): 177–223. (*Both in Harafuji Hiroshi, Bakuhan taisei kokka no hō to kenryoku IV Keiji hō to minji hō. Tokyo: Sōbun sha, 1983.*)

Hayami Akira, "Kokō". In *Nihon komonjogaku kōza* vol. 7 *Kinsei hen* II. Tokyo: Yūzankaku shuppan, 1979, pp. 52–60.

Iwao Seiichi, "Sakoku". In *Iwanami kōza Nihon rekishi* vol. 10 *Kinsei* 2. Tokyo: Iwanami shoten, 1963.

———, *Sakoku*. Vol. 14 of *Nihon no Rekishi*. Tokyo: Chūō kōron sha, 1966.

———, *Nanyō Nihonmachi no kenkyū*. Tokyo: Iwanami shoten, 1966.

———, *Zoku Nanyō Nihonmachi no kenkyū*. Tokyo: Iwanami shoten, 1987.

Kanai Madoka and Katō Eiichi, eds. *Foreign Relations of Tokugawa Japan: Sakoku reconsidered. Acta Asiatica* 67. The tōhō gakkai, 1994.

Katō Eiichi, "Sakokuron no Gendankai", *Rekishi Hyōron* 475 (1989): 2–25.

———, *Bakuhansei kokka no keisei to gaikoku bōeki*. Tokyo: Azekura shobō, 1993.

Koga Jūjirō, *Shintei Maruyama yūjo to tō-kōmō jin*. Nagasaki: Nagasaki bunkensha, 1995, first published in 1969.

Leonard Blussé, "Japanese historiography and European sources". In *Reappraisals in Overseas History*. The Hague: Leiden University Press, 1979.

Matsuo Shin'ichi, "Bakuhansei kokka ni okeru 'tōjin' 'tōsen' mondai no suii: 'Yūwa' seisaku kara 'Kyōkō' seisaku e no tenkan katei to sono ronri", *Higashi Ajia to Nihon-Kōryū to henyō* 1 (2004): 17–32.

Miyamoto Yukiko "Maruyama yūjo no seikatsu –'Nagasaki bugyōsho hanketsu kiroku *Hanka chō* wo chūshin to shite–", *Komazawa Shigaku* 31 (1984): 19–46.

Mizubayashi Tadashi, Ōtsu Tōru, Nitta Ichirō, and Ōtō Osamu, eds. *Hō shakai shi*. Tokyo: Yamakawa shuppansha, 2001.

Nagazumi Yōko."Hirado Oranda shōkan nikki". In *Hirado Oranda shōkan Igirisu shōkan nikki*. Tokyo: Soshiete, 1981, pp. 11–241.

Nakamura Tadashi, "Kinsei no Nihon kakyō-Sakoku to kakyō shakai no henyō-". In Fukuoka Yunesuko (Unesco) kyōkai, ed. *Gairai bunka to Kyūshū*. Vol. 2 of Kyūshū bunka ronshū. Tokyo: Heibon sha, 1973.

Nishimura Keiko, "Edo bakufu no nukeni torishimari rei wo meguru hō ishiki no hensen", *Nihon joshi daigaku bungakubu kiyō* 23 (1973): 11–36.

Shimizu Hirokazu, "Nukeni kō-Kyōho ki no nukeni taisaku wo chūshin to shite", *Chūō daigaku bungakubu kiyō: shigakuka* 24 (1979): 1–38.

Takeda Mariko, *Sakoku to kokkyō no seiritsu*. Tokyo: Dōseisha, 2005.

Tsuruta Kei, "Sore wa *sakoku* dattanoka?" *Rekishi chiri kyōiku* 568 (1997): 24–31.

Yamamoto Hirofumi, *Sakoku to kaikin no jidai*. Tokyo: Azekura shobō, 1995.

CHAPTER 3

The Commercial Culture of the VOC in Canton in the Eighteenth Century

Liu Yong

Right from the moment the European East India companies began to trade in the port of Canton at the beginning of the eighteenth century, the trade representatives of these companies were obliged to take up their station and live together on a small strip of land outside the city walls of Canton, where they were expected to reside and conduct their business. Under the strict regulations promulgated by the Chinese authorities, they were not allowed to enter China proper, not even the city of Canton itself.

Half a century later, when the Canton System (1760–1842) was officially introduced in 1760, the regulations designed to govern the business affairs and the daily lives of the Europeans were considerably tightened. The European trade was meticulously organized and followed an invariable pattern. Each step was strictly controlled by Chinese officialdom. This system was the brainchild of the highest-ranking mandarins in Canton; namely, the *Tsongtou* (Governor-General of the Provinces of Guangdong and Guangxi),[1] the *Fooyuern* (Governor of Guangdong Province),[2] and the *Hoppo* (Superintendent of Maritime Customs).[3] Although they had devised it, such high officials remained aloof from its actual workings; all the relations between the European traders and Chinese officialdom were mediated by the Hong merchants and interpreters (*linguists*), since the Confucian administrative elite of China held their compatriot merchant class in great disdain. This condescension became even more apparent when they had to deal with foreign merchants. In fact, the *Hoppo* was the only relatively high-ranking official with whom foreign traders were able to make contact on a regular basis, as he was directly in charge of the customs administration and of supervising the Canton trade.

Obliged by the inexorable constraints of this strictly regulated trade system, each foreign company were compelled to engage several Hong merchants as security to guarantee the payment of their customs duties. Far from being merely financial guarantors, the security merchants were also responsible for the behaviour of the foreigners. Despite the many frustrations this entailed, invariably locked in fierce competition with the delegates of other companies, the European trade representatives had no choice but to negotiate with their Chinese partners (security merchants) in order to expedite the sale and purchase of goods.

Conducting business in an alien country required and still requires more than simply financial acumen. The core functions of the European business management in Canton, which included marketing, negotiation and procurement, also required that they should take into account the cultural differences and cross-cultural relations in the business context in such an exceptional local commercial environment. The values influencing Chinese business behaviour and style of communication, including *Guanxi* (or Chinese "networking"), the concept of "face", and, above all, Chinese commercial culture, could never be overlooked for an instant whenever the European trade representatives were conducting their business in the Canton market. They had constantly to be aware of the correct manner in which to initiate contact, what to expect during meetings, and how to behave during negotiations and communications, if they were to achieve their goal: business profits. Accordingly, the foreign traders in Canton developed a distinct commercial culture.

The finer details of this commercial culture were exhibited in various aspects. For instance, for the European trade representatives, who needed to present and maintain a positive, unblemished commercial profile to their trading partners, comprehend Chinese expectations of business relationships, master Chinese business etiquette and protocol, maintain consistent contact with the key person, and appreciate the mandarins' role in trade, it was imperative to understand Chinese bargaining and negotiating tactics if they were to obtain a win-win contract conclusion. This all required familiarity with Chinese etiquette and manners, as well as an awareness of taboos and preferences. The correct management of meetings and participation in Chinese banquets were likewise essential.

An examination of the commercial culture of the Dutch East India Company (VOC) and the way in which this developed within the course of its trade representatives' business negotiations and daily life in Canton presents itself as an attractive research topic. Such patterns of behaviour incontrovertibly reveal the organization and management of the VOC personnel, providing invaluable clues to the VOC trade representatives' co-operation and negotiations with their Chinese trading partners, their dealings and communications with the

Chinese authorities and their competition and collaboration with other foreign traders, not to mention their contact with and co-ordination of the VOC local employees.

Organization and Management of VOC Personnel

As a professionally organized eighteenth century trading company, the VOC had made elaborate projections of its successful China trade. As those responsible for operating the trade in China, the VOC trade representatives followed the prescribed Company orders to the letter and behaved carefully, both within the organization of the VOC personnel and in conducting their business. Simultaneously, they wisely never lost sight of the crucial policy imposed by the Chinese authorities on the Europeans in Canton.

The VOC personnel in the Canton factory consisted of supercargoes, assistants, bookkeepers, stewards, cooks, valets, ushers, medical orderlies, night-watchmen, drummers and others. They maintained a distinct hierarchy among themselves. This was reflected in the way in which they sat down to dine, since the seating plan was fixed according to rank, from the top downwards: the "first table", "second table" and "third table". There was a huge difference in the sumptuousness and copiousness of the meals at the various tables. Outward appearance was, as it still so often is, an indication of one's social status, and a person's ranking was easily intimated to outsiders by his clothing and behaviour.

The Dutch trade representatives set up the 'Rules and Regulations for the Servants of the Trade' to maintain correct relations between themselves and to ensure that their conduct towards one another remained proper in every way. The details of this ordinance laid down that there would be: no smoking in the warehouses; no lewd or offensive words on the doors and windows of rooms; no rowdiness in the factory; much less drumming and letting off firecrackers; the keeping of good company and an avoidance of becoming overly familiar with subordinates; moderation in drinking; neatness in attire; and a curfew of returning home by ten o'clock in the evening.[4] All these rules and regulations were unconditionally obeyed by everyone.

A great deal of time and energy was devoted to maintaining the security of the factory. Twice daily, at eight o'clock every morning and evening, the watch was drawn up and checked. Strict instructions were issued to the corporal that the men should come on duty properly dressed and groomed. To ensure this, they were issued with the requisite items of clothing and soap. The corporal was forbidden to strike or abuse his men in the presence of the Chinese, to avoid damaging the image of the Europeans as a group.[5] Thanks to the effective security maintained by the garrison and sentries, there were no large-scale thefts of the goods in store.

The deliberative organ of the trade representatives in Canton, the Trade Council, was called into session during the trading season to draw up the resolutions germane to the Company's business.[6] The Trade Council consisted of several supercargoes and their assistants. Each supercargo had one conclusive vote, while the assistants had an advisory vote. Should one or more of the supercargoes be absent from the meeting of the Council for some reason, the assistant next in rank might be selected to cast a conclusive vote.[7]

All the business concerning the sale and purchase of goods at Canton was subject to the control of this Council. Contracts were made or approved in the presence of all its voting members, unless some were unable to attend due to illness or some other, unavoidable reason. The Trade Council was ordered to take charge of all sale and purchase contracts and the proper reception of the goods. Whenever the Council members took a particular decision, the reason also had to be clearly stated. Not all of the trade representatives in Canton could attend the Trade Council, but, according to the instructions of the China Committee, they were detailed definite assignments by the Council.[8]

The Trade Council took decisions about the disbursement of funds and the delivery of goods after the process of the sale and purchase, each time taking due care to explain why such a decision had been made. If a unanimous agreement was not obtained, a decision could be made based on the majority vote. In that case, the reasons for taking this decision had to be noted, including the particular objections voiced by the dissenting members in support of their own sentiments. In the event of the votes of the two opposing sides being equally divided, the Dutch chief (the first supercargo), who presided over the Council, always had the right to cast a double, deciding vote to ensure that a definitive conclusion was reached. This gave the Dutch chief a special position in the Trade Council: in the deliberations and management of all other business, he was authorized to take the lead and nothing could be undertaken unless he had previously been informed.

In order to safeguard the Company's commercial interests, all the members of the Trade Council present swore a solemn oath that they would discuss the Company's business only with those who had an indisputable acquaintance with it. The Council members should disclose the state of affairs fully and report directly or indirectly, before deliberating on or resolving to proceed with the sale and purchase of goods, the disbursements, the making of contracts with Chinese merchants, and so on.

During the sojourn of the Company's servants in Canton, at the factory each chest containing the ready money required for trade was furnished with four different locks and keys, and the Dutch chief and three other subordinate supercargoes in descending order of rank retained a different key under his personal control respectively, so that any money had to be taken out in the presence of the said supercargoes. The supercargoes and the assistants kept a note of the commerce as well as of the housekeeping in a daily record. In minute detail, and with great accuracy, the daily record noted the arrival of any foreign ships, their names, who the supercargoes and captains were, from where they had sailed, in what business they were engaging, and what merchandise they took for the return voyage. All this information could be useful for the instructions that the Company would issue pertaining to the sale of foreign goods which had been brought to Canton.[9]

The general trade books, which include the ledgers, journals, and cash-books, were also kept in Canton by one individual who was ordered to append his signature after the balancing of these books. All the information contained in these books would be helpful to the successive trade representatives who were to fulfil the same function in later years. It would aid them to understand how their predecessors had fared, what the conditions at the lodge were, and, if some debt had to be paid back on the Company's account, where and in whose hands the contracts had been signed, and so on.

Every year, upon finishing their business, the supercargoes drew up a copious memorandum replete with the necessary instructions to provide detailed information for those who would leave for China the following year. This memorandum contained a description of the state of the factory together with an inventory of the furniture and other chattels. Above all, they had to note meticulously the principal events which had befallen them, with which merchants they had transacted business, what goods they had sold and purchased there and at what price, and what they thought about the state of business in Canton and other such commercial matters. The memorandum was also useful in assisting their successors to pursue their business profitably.[10]

By the time that the commercial dealings had been completed, some of the Company servants were invariably plunged into debt, having sold or purchased some goods privately, or having engaged in buying and selling with local dealers, shopkeepers, and smugglers, who, it transpired, were impecunious/short of cash on receipt or delivery of the goods, which meant that dues were not paid on time. All of the Company's servants were ordered to be wary of becoming embroiled in such difficulties. Notices were posted, warning Chinese and other European merchants that the Dutch Company would not be responsible for the credit or debts of its servants. Extremely conscious of financial etiquette, the trade representatives attempted to pay off all the tolls and other duties exacted on the exports and imports punctiliously in an effort to protect the good name and interests of the Company.[11]

To preserve trade secrecy, orders were issued that all the official VOC reports and correspondence should be sent only via company ships. However, should some private letters be sent home by the Company servants in China via the ships of other nations, in these letters the senders were not supposed to mention anything pertaining to the VOC's business in China which might prove detrimental to the Company; as an additional guarantee of the delivery of the letters, the sender was to inform the VOC administration in the Dutch Republic, under a separate cover, on which ship the letters had been sent.

In Co-operation and Negotiation with Chinese Trading Partners

For the sake of the long-term development of the VOC's business in China and its perennial interests, the VOC trade representatives preferred and always tried to select reliable, creditworthy Hong merchants as their stable trading partners. Having taken so much trouble, likewise, they did not dismiss them casually. They never lost sight of the fact that maintaining consistent contact with the right key person equalled attaining twice the achievement by putting only half of the effort into the business. Apparently, choosing such a satisfactory partner was not an easy job for any foreign trader, for the chosen merchants should be prominent enough in trade to be acceptable to them and, conversely, had to have found favour with the Chinese officials, particularly the *Hoppo*. Any oversight or misjudgement could harm the interests of the Company, particularly when the merchants went bankrupt because, for example, they had fallen out with the officials and lost their support or when the latter subjected them to extortion.

At different stages in the eighteenth century, the VOC trade representatives cautiously selected eligible trading partners. In the early decades of the China trade, the Dutch trade representatives appointed Tan Honqua as guarantor and trading partner because he was trustworthy and credible. In the 1750s, Swetja, the son of the prominent Cantonese merchant, Texia, in the 1740s, became the security merchant of the VOC,[12] and was succeeded in 1763 by his brother Inksja, whom the Dutch considered a man with a reputation for courage and resolution,[13] and to whom all the European companies with which he worked accorded great credit in the 1760s and 1770s.[14] Another two security merchants of the VOC in the 1760s were Tsja Hunqua and Tan Chetqua. The former was the leader of the three security merchants for the VOC,[15] and, in the eyes of the Dutch, was: "The most upright of all the Chinese who have ever passed through this world" and "... has never misled us [the Dutch]".[16] The latter was Tan Chetqua, who had the unenviable reputation, as the Dutch recorded, of being known as an indecisive person who would take exception to even the most trifling matter.[17] In the 1780s–90s, sooner or later, the VOC trade representatives chose as their regular trading partners, Tan Tsjoqua, Tsjobqua, Tayqua, Consciens Giqua, Kousia, Pinqua, Kiouqua, and Monqua, according to the afore-mentioned stringent standard laid down for selecting a Hong merchant.

In the 1760s, Poan Keequa was appointed the head of the Co-hong and held that position until it was dissolved in 1771. Despite the fact that all the other Co-hong members revolted against Poan Keequa in the 1760s, he made himself master of the European trade until his death in 1788.[18] In the opinion of the Dutch, he was a "sly fox", always brimming with intrigues, and attempting to bring the whole European trade under his control.[19] The Dutch by no means applauded his "grandiose way of life, giving banquets for the mandarins, building splendid houses and paying the expenses of his sons, who are mandarins".[20] Therefore, when selecting their trading partner, an important criterion for the Dutch trade representatives was that he never poked his nose directly or indirectly into their affairs, although he was the most powerful and famous Hong merchant of his day.

The business negotiations were the most strenuous task for both the Dutch supercargoes and their trading partners. These ordinarily began after the departure of the VOC ships in the first quarter of each year, sometimes in February or early March. On paper, it seemed simple. During the process of negotiation, the trading partners presented the goods samples with their asking price, and then the Dutch supercargoes put in their bidding price after checking the samples. Finally, both parties came to an agreement and fixed a price. In practice, it was an extremely protracted process and there was a great deal of ostensibly polite to-ing and fro-ing between the two parties, which was a true mirror of Chinese and Dutch commercial astuteness and shrewd trading.

Once the negotiations were under way, the trading partners usually urged the Dutch side not to dally and to accept their offer at the earliest possible opportunity. They hinted that, the earlier the Dutch accepted their offer, the better the quality of the goods they could obtain at a lower price and the sooner they could pack them up. The Dutch took a slightly different view of the matter, reasoning that, the earlier they did so, the less opportunity they would have to put pressure on the sellers and the higher the price they would actually have to pay. That was the reason why, after the VOC ships departed, the Dutch representatives frequently attempted to leave Canton as late as possible.

When the supercargoes engaged in negotiations with their trading partners at Canton, they were often urged by the Chinese to accept gifts. All of the trade representatives had strict instructions not to accept gifts from the Chinese merchants. They should refuse such prohibited articles, albeit they were allowed to give gifts to the Chinese, according to the Company regulations. Should it really prove impossible to refuse such gifts without prejudicing the Company's business, the members might accept them and would then be obliged to explain the reasons for their action. Such gifts should be dispatched with the Company's goods, to be placed at the disposal of the VOC administration when they reached the Netherlands. Come hell or high water, every servant should be assiduous in his solicitude regarding the interests of the Company.[21]

In practice, the VOC trade representatives and the Hong merchants regularly exchanged some business gifts, for example, when the VOC trade representatives returned to Canton at the beginning of the trading season and visited their trading partners. Gift-giving was a good way for the Dutch supercargoes to strike up and improve their friendships with their trading partners. The gifts might consist of cloth, wine, mirrors, clocks, watches and other items. Most of them were just playthings to indulge a Chinese hobby, while others were extremely practical, like a fire-engine (water pump) which could be used with its appliances to protect the goods stored in the warehouse from fire.[22] In return, the Hong merchants normally gave fine tea, excellent quality silk, porcelain, and other examples of Chinese art.

As a rule, it was impossible for the Chinese merchants ensconced in their residences in the city and the European trade representatives confined to their factories outside the city walls to hold business banquets at which they might entertain each other. In order to build up good business relationships with the European traders, the Chinese merchants occasionally used to invite the supercargoes of European companies to their residences and country houses on a narrow strip of land along the river opposite Canton for a party, a meal, or even fireworks, on the pretext of some celebration, such as the Emperor's (or the merchants' own) birthday, the Chinese New Year, some well-known national festivals, weddings and other special events. On these occasions, food was served in abundance and some well-chosen entertainment was usually presented. The host formally expressed his good wishes and hoped that the celebration would bring joy, and the guests paid elaborate compliments in return. The solitary Dutch, and indeed the other European, supercargoes looked forward to attending such occasions, regardless of being somewhat apprehensive about the performance of "Chinese comedies", which were usually fairly protracted and made it impossible for the guests to leave early without displeasing their host.[23]

In Dealings and Communication with the Chinese Authorities

Throughout the eighteenth century, because of the influence exerted on Chinese commercial culture by the fact that the Confucian administrative elite (and even the common people) showed great disdain for the merchants and the merchant class, by attributing to them a comparatively inferior social status, plus the Chinese world view that all foreigners (except those of a few tributary countries) were uncivilized "barbarians", the Chinese authorities had never placed the slightest value on communicating and dealing with the foreign traders on an equal footing. The Chinese government considered that permitting European trade in Canton was a beneficent indulgence towards European countries, and it did not place any particular value on the European trade. The European traders had constantly to bear in mind that they should never have any confrontation with the authorities of this vast Empire if they wished to conduct their business successfully in China.

Given these circumstances, it was difficult for the European traders to have personal contact with the mandarins in Canton, either regarding matters of business or more personal relationships. Audiences with the *Tsongtou* and the *Fooyuern* were granted only under very special conditions, such as being informed of the Chinese authorities' solutions to the European traders' grievances and negotiating the settlement of failed Hong merchants' debts.[24] During such audiences, it was customary for the Europeans not even to be invited to sit down but to be ordered to remain standing before the mandarins.

Other close encounters with high officials might happen occasionally. Such sporadic events occurred when the Dutch and other foreign trade representatives were invited by the mandarins to gatherings when officials from Peking occasionally visited Canton; when the Canton mandarins took up or left their posts; or when officials from neighbouring provinces passed through on their way to a new appointment. On these occasions, naturally, the foreign supercargoes could not have any communication about matters of business with the Chinese officials, and only formal greetings were exchanged.

Because of the power inherent in his position as head of the customs administration and supervisor of Canton trade, the *Hoppo* was, as mentioned earlier, the only relatively high-ranking official with whom the European trade representatives were able to make contact on a regular basis.

In the first half of the eighteenth century, the Dutch, as well as other European, supercargoes could request a personal audience with the *Hoppo* at his residence in Canton. By the late 1730s, once the Canton trade had settled down into a relatively well-balanced track, the granting of such audiences was becoming less frequent. Meetings with the European trade representatives at the *Hoppo*'s residence in the city were granted more selectively, since he was bored by listening to the oft-repeated, long-standing complaints of the Europeans. From the late 1750s onwards, the European trade representatives were ordered to send their security merchants and interpreters to act as proxies in submitting their petitions or complaints in an audience with the *Hoppo* at his residence in the city.[25]

Should the matter be urgent, a petition might be delivered personally to the sentry at the city gate near the factories on the south-western corner of the new city wall. The sentry would deliver the petition to the *Hoppo*'s residence. The drawback to this arrangement was that the petitioners had to wait at the gate for several hours while the document was received by the *Hoppo*, read and explained to him, and finally a reply was sent back, informing them that their request was under consideration.[26] Any visit by the *Hoppo* and his mandarins to the factory was a very rare event indeed.

Besides all these, there was one other good opportunity for the VOC trade representatives to speak directly to the *Hoppo* in order to convey their problems or requests: when he went down to Whampoa to measure the ships. This ceremonial event took place a day or two after the ships' arrival, and the intercourse between the Dutch traders and the *Hoppo* is described around 1760 as follows: "… as soon as the train or procession of the *Hoppo* appears, it is the custom to greet him with a salute from the cannon, send an officer with a interpreter to meet him and pay him the usual compliments … the interpreter states the name of the ship from which the officer comes, pays him a compliment and, having greeted the Chinese, returns to his ship again. As soon as the *Hoppo* nears the ship, the supercargoes receive him on the manrope or, should he so wish, even in his own galley; having come on board and a second salute having been fired, he sets to work on the measuring and, having completed it, he is invited to enter the cabin, where a table of sweetmeats has been prepared; when he has partaken of these, he is always served fine liqueurs; then he goes back on board his galley again and is saluted by the cannon for the third time".[27]

During the measuring ceremonies, both the *Hoppo* and foreign trade representatives had their men play music to create a lively atmosphere. The *Hoppo* made a speech of welcome and the foreign traders made the reciprocal speech expected of them, conveying their formal greetings. All Chinese and foreign officers and merchants dressed formally in order to stress the dignity of their business.[28] The *Hoppo* might receive small gifts from the Dutch supercargoes during his measuring, but the private gift (or the present charge) offered to him by each ship was officially fixed at 1,950 taels (roughly 7,020 guilders), cast in the form of what was known as the measurage fee, which, after the other port charges had been added to it, placed a heavy burden on the foreign trade representatives.

Any positive result of the communication with the *Hoppo* on the occasion of the measuring of the ships would be very rare indeed. The *Hoppo* might measure several ships on the same day, and, after such exhausting work and so much eating of sweetmeats as well as drinking of wine, he might easily be forgiven for forgetting the supercargoes' requests or complaints. In a later period, the *Hoppo* did not even appear personally at the measuring ceremonies but delegated the task to his deputies,[29] who very rarely reacted to the Dutch trade representatives' requests.

Although it was extremely remote, in every sense of the word, something can be said about the VOC trade representatives' communication with the Qing court in Peking. Even as the Canton trade developed, by the latter decades of the eighteenth century, the European traders had realized that their export trade to China could not yet be expanded as widely as they had hoped. The major problem was financial uncertainty. The prices on the Canton market frequently fluctuated and the taxes and levies imposed by the customs officials increased sharply. It was a problem which forced the European companies to seek a solution. Direct contact with the Qing court was considered as a good strategy, although it presented a virtually insurmountable difficulty. Setting his sights on establishing trade and diplomatic intercourse with the Empire of Qing China on the basis of equality, the British King George III sent George Macartney to the Qing court as his envoy for the years 1792–93. The Macartney mission failed, partly because of the cultural clash between the Chinese and the English attitudes towards Chinese court etiquette, which required all visitors to show homage to the Qianlong Emperor.

Not to be outdone, the Dutch immediately followed in the English footsteps and sent their embassy to Peking in 1794–95 to congratulate the Emperor on the sixtieth anniversary of his reign, with the ulterior motive of obtaining better trading conditions, and also of discussing the increasing extortion at Canton. At the court, the Dutch performed, without a murmur, the three genuflections and nine prostrations, and complied with all the demands of Chinese court etiquette. They worked on the pragmatic assumption that they merely represented a trading company and could not be regarded as representatives of a foreign monarch, so, if they appeared at a foreign court, they had to comply with its etiquette. Such had been their conduct with numerous Oriental potentates and they made no distinction in the case of the Chinese.[30] The Emperor was deeply satisfied with the Dutch behaviour at court and bestowed his benevolence on them, from which the VOC benefited in subsequent years.

In Competition and Collaboration with other Foreign Traders

Throughout the course of its direct China trade (1729–94), the VOC conducted its business at the port of Canton. Outside the city walls, during the trading season, the VOC trade representatives, as well as their fellow merchants from other companies, were restricted to their factories located on a small plot of land. Such enforced close proximity meant that, in terms of business, they not only competed but also collaborated with each other, depending on the situation.

Besides the VOC trade representatives, there was also a host of trade representatives from other nations vying in the Canton market, representing such organizations as the English East India Company (EIC), the Danish Asiatic Company (DAC), the Swedish East India Company (SOIC), the French East India Company (CFI), and, later, the United States. Among them, the EIC (and, from 1784, the Americans as well) was the biggest competitor to the VOC, and traces of its influence could even be found in the business contracts between the Dutch supercargoes and their trading partners, in the drawing up of which an EIC business contract with Chinese merchants was often used for comparison.[31] Apart from these foreign rivals, Chinese junk people, sailing for South-East Asia, were also important competitors in both the export and import of goods, because they could always easily obtain a lower price for Chinese goods from their compatriots and never hesitated to sell their imported East Indies goods at a lower price in the ruthlessly competitive market of Canton.

It was by no means out of the question that some of the trading partners of the VOC might also do business, particularly in tea, with other foreign traders. Being thoroughly aware of this, the Dutch trade representatives attempted to ensure that they did not have close contact with those who were the principal partners of their competitors, such as the EIC. For a long time, the name of the most powerful Hong merchant, Poan Keequa, who undertook a great deal of business with the EIC after 1760 and on whom the English always showered praise, had the dubious honour of taking pride of place on the blacklist of the Dutch supercargoes. Strikingly, in the European trade in Canton, he used to be the most powerful opponent of Tsja Hunqua, the leader of the security merchants of the VOC in the 1760s.[32]

During the negotiations with their trading partners, the Dutch supercargoes were skilled in making use of the market intelligence they obtained in a number of different ways in order to persuade the Chinese merchants to accept their proposal so that the contract could be concluded. The Dutch trade representatives foraged for such information principally by putting out feelers among their security merchants and interpreters. These people could either pass on information about other foreign traders' states of business by word of mouth, or hand in more detailed written information copied from the *Hoppo*'s book regarding such pertinent matters as the invoices of either other companies' ships or Chinese junks, including the quantity, assortment, and price of exported and imported goods, the name of the captains and *nachoda*s, and even the port from which the junks from South-East Asia had set sail.[33]

Shrewdly, the Chinese trade partners also knew how to take advantage of their negotiations with other foreign traders, above all the EIC, to urge the apparently hesitant Dutch to take the plunge. The fear that their competitors would steal a march on them was the real reason why the Dutch trade representatives sometimes hastened to conclude the negotiations, less because they were truly satisfied with the Chinese offer, but more because they were acutely aware that other competitors also had their eye on the same goods or had already put in a higher bid. In such a situation, he who hesitates is lost!

Facing fierce competition from other foreign traders in purchasing tea, the VOC trade representatives dallied, trying to leave Canton as late as possible after the trading season had been concluded. On occasion, they tarried so long that they were even actually forced to withdraw because of the threats issued by the Chinese officials. Their tardy departure meant that they were able to buy the 'old teas' that remained unsold on the market. They obtained the "old teas", of which the Bohea provided the bulk, at a far lower price, although the quality of the tea was, accordingly, highly inferior. This kind of tea elicited a host of complaints from the tea-buyers in the Dutch Republic. After the middle of the eighteenth century, they frequently complained to the VOC about the dusty nature of the tea bought, in spite of the fact that, since 1760, this matter had already attracted the undivided attention of the Gentlemen Seventeen.[34]

Although this played a very large role, unquestionably, the business relationship between the Dutch and other foreign trade representatives in Canton was not purely one of fierce competition. To a certain extent, they also assisted and collaborated with each other, and these rapprochements could sometimes have an important bearing on their own affairs in China, of which perhaps the best example was their stand against the Co-hong. The Co-hong, which was privileged to decide the prices of import and export goods, was founded in 1760 by the Hong merchants on the instructions of the Chinese authorities. Its task was to regulate the Canton trade of their respective members and to consolidate their monopoly over the European trade.[35] In co-operation with the English and Swedish, the Dutch supercargoes courageously led a protest against the establishment of "such a pernicious association", because it would definitely be deleterious to the business of them all in China.[36] Unfortunately, they finally gave up after learning of the Chinese officials' official confirmation in support of its foundation.

In 1777, "having for many years past been subject to great impositions resulting from the rapaciousness of the Chinese at the different custom houses", the English supercargoes persuaded the Dutch, as well as the French, Danish, and Swedish supercargoes, to join with them in making a representation on this subject to the *Fooyuern* and the *Hoppo*. On the occasion when the *Hoppo* measured the first ship, a supercargo from each nation came on board to deliver a petition seeking redress in this instance.[37]

They also co-operated when physical danger menaced. Fires posed a frequent danger in Canton and posed a universal threat. When a fire broke out in the vicinity of the foreign factories, all of the foreign trade representatives, including the Dutch of course, would rush to the scene to offer assistance, bringing with them their pumps and able-bodied men.[38] This proved a prime opportunity for desertion for the servants, seamen in particular, of all foreign companies during their sojourn in China. The Dutch trade representatives made an agreement with the English that deserters should be sent back.[39]

On their arrival in Canton from Macao at the beginning of each trading season, the Dutch supercargoes paid official courtesy visits to the various other factories, which were reciprocated. In time of war, for example, during the Fourth Anglo-Dutch War (1780–84), mutual relations were inevitably strained, but, because Canton was a free port, the situation never developed into a full-scale, open conflict. All foreign trade representatives endeavoured to avoid any face-to-face confrontations, but some skirmishes could and did occur sporadically, although these were usually no more than quarrels, brawls, or fights between their lower-ranking servants, seamen in particular. The Dutch supercargoes were accustomed to solving these problems by means of a written communication with other foreign top-ranking supercargoes, by visiting them in person, or, as a last ditch attempt to restore order, by asking the Chinese authorities to intervene directly.[40] The number of such incidents rose considerably in the second half of the eighteenth century, fuelled by the entry of the private free traders who arrived to claim their share of the profitable China trade. The group known as the English Country traders obtained their licences from the EIC to trade in their own vessels between India and Canton, but it soon transpired that they refused to surrender to the authority of the EIC trade representatives in Canton because of their strong position within Sino-British trade. This obstreperous behaviour foreshadowed the English supercargoes' dilemma in seeking to maintain a peaceful co-existence with other foreign traders.

In Contact with and Co-ordination of the Local Employees

Working alongside the Dutch trade representatives themselves were also Chinese people who were temporarily or permanently employed in Canton by the VOC, including interpreters, *compradors* — both factory and ship *compradors* — and other employees hired by these *compradors*, such as coolies, cooks and their mates, barbers, carpenters, bricklayers, painters, and water carriers in the factories. In earlier times, the Dutch factory was shut at ten o'clock in the evening and all of the Chinese present had to leave. This changed in 1772, when the (factory) *compradors* and permanent Chinese personnel were given living-quarters to the rear of the premises, near the gate.

The art of creating a close, smooth co-ordination with the local Chinese employees was an essential skill which the Dutch trade representatives had to acquire if they were to succeed in business. It was an art principally manifested in their direct relationship with the interpreters and *compradors*. Their contact with the more menial servants was more distant. Should any problem arise, the Dutch were under strict orders not to strike them but to complain directly to the *compradors*.

The interpreters were the appointed mediators between the Dutch trade representatives and the Chinese officials. They were responsible for the communication between the two parties. Therefore, in addition to their word-of-mouth reports, they were required to hand in the translated petitions of the supercargoes to the mandarins and carry back the latter's reply, and it was their responsibility to teach the supercargoes the correct protocol to be observed during an audience with the mandarins. The interpreters performed their duties for the VOC by scheduling the *Hoppo*'s measuring date for the ships, taking care of the export and import duties and customs fees for each ship, applying the *Hoppo*'s permit for the sampans to be used as lighters, and collecting wages, tips and so forth. Besides their regular work, the interpreters were sometimes asked by the Dutch to assist in such emergencies as fires and shipwrecks, and attend events such as non-business gatherings with the Chinese officials.

In all the matters set out above, the Dutch trade representatives, of course, expected the interpreters to behave properly, prioritising the Company's interests at all times. Their devoted service could mean huge savings for the Dutch trade representatives in making their business contracts with the Chinese merchants, not to mention enhancing their relationship with the Chinese officials, which might prove helpful if they were in need or difficulty.

As mentioned above, one of the methods, by which the Dutch trade representatives gathered pertinent information, was to ask their interpreters to report any useful market intelligence that they might come across in Canton. Generally speaking, information about other foreign traders was not difficult to obtain from the customs house, as the customs officials were happy to spread this around among all other foreign traders to keep the competition between them simmering nicely, thereby compelling them to conclude their business quickly. Since the *Hoppo*'s trade book provided a very open database for all foreign traders, the only measure that the Dutch could take to preserve their very intimate business information was to demand that the interpreters, and the trading partners, should say as little as possible.

In the early decades of the eighteenth century, the interpreters came from Macao and communicated with the foreign traders in Portuguese. Probably, by the early 1730s, the interpreters began to make use of the so-called Pidgin English as the medium of communication with the foreigners. Pidgin English was a hotchpotch of English and Portuguese, interspersed with many words and expressions from Chinese and Malay. Speaking such language, the interpreters could be understood more or less passably by various foreign traders, although, as might have been expected, the clarity and accuracy of what they had to say could not be absolutely guaranteed.

As all the other foreign traders, the Dutch trade representatives were never one hundred per cent satisfied with the interpreters' work. In part, this dissatisfaction could be attributed to their somewhat unsatisfactory language skills, but it also arose from their reluctance to accommodate the Dutch trade representatives' petitions. The Dutch sometimes demanded that the interpreters deliver a petition in which the requests or complaints registered sounded uncivilized or beyond the bounds of reason to Chinese ears, and the interpreters did not dare to present a detailed, explicit translation. A knowledge of this shortcoming even prompted the Dutch to try to circumvent the interpreters and take more extreme measures to realize their intentions on occasions when the two parties disagreed with each other about the contents of a petition.[41]

Aggravated by these two factors, the Dutch trade representatives apparently had once even tried to train their own interpreters in order to reduce their dependence on the Chinese interpreters. Early in 1756, and again late in 1758, they paid for a Chinese teacher to teach them the Chinese language, but abandoned this endeavour in 1760, shortly after the *Flint* incident occurred in 1759 between the EIC and the Chinese authorities in 1759.[42] During this unfortunate incident, the Chinese teacher of Mr Flint, an English gentleman, was beheaded for teaching Mr Flint Chinese, because, under Chinese law, teaching foreigners Chinese was a crime punishable by death. The Dutch and the other foreign trade representatives had no option but to revert to the use of Chinese interpreters once again.

Factory *compradors* supplied all the provisions and hired the Chinese personnel for the factory. They were responsible for obtaining the *Hoppo*'s permit for the trade representatives to return to Canton from Macao after the off-season. They were also responsible for requesting a Macao pilot to guide the ships after they had arrived at Whampoa. The duties of the ship *compradors* were less taxing, as they did not have to negotiate with the authorities but simply supply all the provisions and labour for the VOC ships.

In the course of their contact over the years, the Dutch trade representatives and their *comprador*s, especially the factory *compradors*, became close and trusted friends, which certainly contributed to the stability and success of the VOC business in China. In the factory records, we can read an amazing story of the *comprador* Atack's life-long service of the Dutch trade representatives. Atack began as a *comprador* at the Dutch factory in 1737, at the age of fifteen. He, together with his brothers and other *comprador*s, took care of the Dutch household and supplied provisions for the VOC ships.

In the 1760s, Atack served the Dutch in partnership with two other factory *compradors*, Amie and Apo. They supplied all the provisions needed for both the Dutch factory and the VOC ships. They also ran the household and commissioned four ship *compradors* to supply the VOC ships with goods. Around 1774, when Atack was in his fifties, he started to remain in Canton throughout the year, taking care of the factory in the off-season, and then looking after the Dutch household when the trade representatives returned from Macao in August or September. The Dutch often sent Atack letters from Macao asking for business information or requesting him to visit some Hong merchants. He was even still employed to watch over the factory in his old age. In 1797, he fought off a big flood which threatened the premises. The elderly Atack died of an illness on 16 January 1798, at the age of 75. The Dutch trade representatives, who held Atack in great respect, sincerely mourned his death. He had been serving the VOC for so long that the Dutch trade representatives could not even remember for how many years he had worked for them.[43]

Concluding Remarks

In the course of their business transactions in Canton, the Dutch trade representatives in the eighteenth century created a very particular commercial culture, because they had no option but to take careful note of the extraordinary local commercial conditions existing in Canton in order to adapt themselves actively and flexibly to such an environment. The formation of the commercial culture of the VOC in Canton was a course whereby the VOC trade representatives both adhered to their basic commercial principles and also simultaneously tried to "do in China as the Chinese (merchant) does", adjusting each measure to suit the local conditions. The commercial culture of the VOC in Canton, therefore, had its idiosyncrasies born of adaptability and applicability when it came to the local social business relations in Canton.

In this great southern Chinese port, the Dutch trade representatives were well organized and disciplined to do business, strictly in compliance with the Company's instructions. The rules and regulations governing their business behaviour in China were clear and explicit. Simultaneously, the trade representatives also carefully complied with the local commercial rules and civil laws. In the patterns of behaviour revealed in the organization and management of the VOC personnel in Canton, we may see the embryo of the good functioning and running of a modern trading company.

The Dutch trade representatives carefully chose reliable, credible and regular trading partners to assist them in their business in Canton. They were well aware of the need to preserve agreeable contacts with these Chinese merchants, and did their best to negotiate and co-operate with their trading partners in order to achieve fair dealings. They tried to conclude win-win contracts with their trading partners, in order to establish a solid basis for their long-term stable business in China.

Both directly and indirectly, the Chinese officialdom controlled the European trade in Canton. This situation allowed the Dutch trade representatives to do their best to remain on good terms with the mandarins and create a favourable impression on the latter by presenting themselves as "honest men".[44] They pursued their business conscientiously, paying full respect to the Chinese authorities, as they were painfully aware of the dominant role of the latter in the European trade in Canton.

In such a fiercely competitive port as Canton, the Dutch trade representatives inevitably encountered various other rivals. They, therefore, adopted a business strategy in which they were naturally in competition with all the other foreign traders but were also happy to assist and collaborate with them should the need arise. Of course, their competition with their rivals, which involved long-range planning, went far beyond merely co-operating with them, a tactic which was effective only at a given moment. Nonetheless, the Dutch trade representatives still endeavoured to interact compatibly with their rivals in daily life in Canton and avoid engaging in direct open conflict with them, although some skirmishes might have been unavoidable on occasion.

The contribution of the local Chinese employees, particularly the interpreters and *compradors*, was also truly indispensable to the VOC business in China. The Dutch trade representatives relied utterly on the interpreters' work in both their business and daily life, but could not trust them completely, mainly because of their occasional reluctance to convey their employer's petitions. The Dutch trade representatives endeavoured to establish close, trusting friendships with their *compradors*, whose meticulous care of the logistics of the Dutch settlement in China ineluctably lightened the daily grind of the VOC trade representatives.

Notes

1. The highest civil official with authority over the Provinces of Guangdong and Gaungxi.
2. The subordinate colleague of the Governor-General or Viceroy in matters relating to Guangdong Province.
3. The Imperial Commissioner of the Guangdong Customs House, with headquarters in Canton.
4. *Nationaal Archief* (NA), The Hague, *Archieven van de Verenigde Oostindische Compagnie* (VOC) 4442, "Rules and regulations for the servants of the trade", included under the Judicial Papers of 1789–90, no date.
5. C.J.A. Jörg, *Porcelain and the Dutch China Trade* (The Hague: Martinus Nijhoff, 1982), p. 62.
6. NA VOC 4543, Particular instruction of the China Committee to the supercargoes and assistants, Article 3, 10 October 1759.
7. Ibid., Articles 2–4, 10 October 1759.
8. NA *Nederlandse Factorij te Canton* (NFC) 36, Resolution of the Trade Council, 25 August 1773.
9. NA VOC 4543, Particular instruction of the China Committee to the supercargoes and assistants, Articles 9–15, 10 October 1759.
10. Ibid., Article 18, 10 October 1759.
11. Ibid., Articles 19–21, 1757 and 1758.
12. Paul A. Van Dyke, *The Canton Trade: Life and Enterprise on the China Coast, 1700–1845* (Hong Kong: Hong Kong University Press, 2006), Chapter Five; and his "The Yan Family: Merchants of Canton, 1734–1780s", *Review of Culture* (International Edition 9) (Macao, 2004), pp. 30–85.

13. NA NFC 73, Daily record of the supercargoes, 24 June 1764.
14. NA NFC 38, Resolution of the Trade Council, 6 January 1774.
15. NA NFC 33, Resolution of the Trade Council, 2 August 1770.
16. NA NFC 73, Daily record of the supercargoes, 10 August 1764.
17. Ibid., 24 June 1764.
18. Ch'en Kuo-tung, 'Pan Youdu, a Successful Businessman for a Foreign Firm', in Liu Ping *et al.* (ed.), *Guangzhou shisanhang cangsang* (The Transformation of the Thirteen Hongs of Canton) (Guangzhou: Guangdongsheng ditu chubanshe, 2001), pp. 150–93; Dilip Kumar Basu, *Asian Merchants and Western Trade: A Comparative Study of Calcutta and Canton 1800-1840* (PhD dissertation, Berkeley: University of California, 1975), p. 355; Cheong, *Hong Merchants*, pp. 40–1 and p. 71 (note 79); Huang Qichen and Pang Xinping, *Mingqing guangdong shangren* (Guangdong Merchants in Ming and Qing Period) (Guangzhou: Guangdong jingji chubanshe, 2001), pp. 259–69; Liang Jiabin, *Guangdong shisanhang kao* (The Thirteen Hongs of Canton) (Guangzhou: Guangdong renmin chubanshe, 1999), p. 259; NA NFC 73, Daily record of the supercargoes, 18 April 1764.
19. NA NFC 73, Daily record of the supercargoes, 31 May and 23 June 1764.
20. NA VOC 4417, General report of the Trade Council, 24 January 1779.
21. NA VOC 4543, Particular instruction of the China Committee to the supercargoes and assistants, Articles 4–8, 10 October 1759.
22. In 1764, the Dutch provided their trading partner, Tsja Hunqua, with a fire-engine carrying all its appliances, which he installed in his warehouse. It attracted great attention in Canton. See Jörg, *Porcelain*, p. 71.
23. Jörg, *Porcelain*, p. 65.
24. British Library (BL) India Office Records (IOR)-R/10/4, Diaries and consultations, 6 December 1759 and 22 October 1779.
25. BL IOR-R/10/4, Diary and consultation, 18 January 1762.
26. Van Dyke, *The Canton Trade*, p. 21.
27. Refer to the copy in C.H. Gietermakers' manuscript *'t Vergulde Licht der Zeevaart ofte Const der Stuerlieden*, preserved in the Prince Hendrik Maritime Museum, Rotterdam, to which notes are added, entitled 'Regarding that which the supercargoes must observe in connection with the ceremonies which must be honoured on arrival at, during the stay in and on the departure from Canton' (anonymous). See also Jörg, *Porcelain*, p. 50.
28. Jan Parmentier, *Tea Time and Flanders: The Maritime Trade between the Southern Netherlands and China in the Eighteenth Century* (Ghent: Lundion Press, 1996), p. 95; Van Dyke, *The Canton Trade*, p. 24.
29. Parmentier, *Tea Time and Flanders*, p. 95; Van Dyke, *The Canton Trade*, p. 25.
30. J.J.L. Duyvendak, "The last Dutch embassy to the Chinese Court (1784–1795)", in *T'oung pao*, XXXIV (Leiden: Sinology Institute, 1939), p. 1.
31. NA NFC 26, Resolution of the Trade Council, 25 May 1763.
32. NA NFC 73, Daily records of the supercargoes, 31 May and 23 June 1764; Liu Yong, *The Dutch East India Company's Tea Trade with China, 1757–1781* (Leiden: Brill, 2007), p. 166 (note 49).

33. Liu Yong, *The Dutch East India Company's Tea Trade*, p. 82.
34. NA NFC 73, Daily Record of the supercargoes, 3 November 1764.
35. Liang Tingnan (ed.), *Yue haiguan zhi* (The Chronicle of the Guangdong Customs House) (Taipei: Chengwen chubanshe, 1968), vol. 25, p. 1797; Ch'en Kuo-tung, *The Insolvency of the Chinese Hong Merchants, 1760–1834* (Taipei: Institute of Economics, Academia Sinica, 1990), p. 8.
36. For a more detailed description of the European protest against the establishment of the Co-hong, see Liu Yong, *The Dutch East India Company's Tea Trade*, pp. 92–101.
37. BL IOR-R/10/4, Diary and consultation, 25 September 1777.
38. Van Dyke, *The Canton Trade*, p. 88.
39. Neither party, however, ever strictly complied with the agreement. This was because their ships were sometimes heavily undermanned and deserters were seen to be available as cheap labour for a small payment. See Jorg, *Porcelain*, p. 50.
40. Like the case of recapture of the ship the *Goede Hoop* in 1781, described in detail in Liu Yong's *The Dutch East India Company's Tea Trade*, pp. 111–7.
41. In 1747, the Dutch trade representatives threatened to keep their 'old linguist Ja-qua' under house arrest until he wrote a complaint against one of the Chinese merchants on their behalf. See NA NFC 8; Van Dyke, *The Canton Trade*, p. 78.
42. See Morse, *The Chronicles of the East India Company Trading to China 1635–1834* (London: Routledge, 2000), vol. V, pp. 68–107.
43. In the Canton factory records, even the Dutch supercargoes themselves were confused about the number of years for which Atack had served the Company. See NA NFC 97; Jörg, *Porcelain*, p. 334 (note 8); Van Dyke, *The Canton Trade*, p. 55.
44. BL IOR-R/10/4, Diary and consultation, 17 August 1760; NA VOC 4384, Order of the *Hoppo* to the English and Dutch, 16 August 1760.

Chapter 4

Western and Chinese Influences on Japanese Paintings in the Eighteenth Century

Ito Shiori

Introduction

In the period of national isolation during the Edo Period, Chinese and Dutch paintings (and also other Western paintings) were brought to Japan via Nagasaki and had various influences on the Japanese paintings of that time.[1] In particular, the influence of both Chinese and Western paintings became prominent in the mid-Edo Period or around the eighteenth century. I would like to provide an overview of and discuss the Western and Chinese influences on the Japanese paintings of this period.

Nagasaki was a port town, where the Dutch East India Company had a trading post. In the Edo Period, the town was not only a channel for Japan to import various Western cultures and technologies that were brought to the town by Dutch ships, but also a point of contact with China. Japanese culture has been greatly influenced by Chinese culture since ancient times; therefore, it is difficult to draw a clear line between the influence of Chinese culture up to that time and the influence of contemporary Chinese culture. Furthermore, in modern Japan since the Meiji Period, it has been considered more valuable to study the beginning of the Western influence, rather than to track the influence of Chinese culture.[2] In this context, Nagasaki has also been valued for its role and function as a channel for Western culture. We cannot ignore, however, the fact that Nagasaki was also a door to China. (The number of Chinese ships that arrived at Nagasaki port and the trade volume with China were greater than those of Holland.) In fact, some Western cultures and technologies came to

Japan via China in the form of Chinese-translated books. Furthermore, both Chinese and Western influences co-exist in Japanese paintings, and it is sometimes difficult to determine the boundary between the two.

In this chapter, we will examine how the Western and Chinese influences overlapped each other in eighteenth century Japanese paintings. First, I will present an overview of the domestic situation at that time by tracking how the phenomena of perspective and realistic representation gained popularity. Along with the painters in Nagasaki, we will also consider painters in Kyōto and Edo and how they came to accept the new painting styles. Furthermore, as the Chinese and Western influences sometimes co-exist in Japanese paintings, I will discuss how this situation came about.

Western and Chinese Influences on Japanese Paintings in the Eighteenth Century

In the mid-Edo Period, there were many painters with different styles. Today, we can see various styles of paintings in this period.[3] This new trend was stimulated by various influences of Western and Chinese cultures.

Firstly, Ōbaku-style paintings came to Japan with Ōbaku culture.[4] Ingen Ryūki came to Nagasaki by invitation in 1654 and established the Manpuku-ji Temple of Ōbaku Zen sect of the Rinzai School in Uji, Kyōto. Ōbaku culture spread across the country from this temple and supported the acceptance of Chinese culture in the eighteenth century. Painters such as Kita Genki (–1709) painted realistic shadows called *kumadori*, now known as a make-up technique of *kabuki* (Fig. 1). The *Kumadori* technique formalizes forms and also expresses realistic volume at the same time. This technique first appeared in the works of Zeng Jing (1568–1650), a portrait painter who was active at the end of the Ming Dynasty. Interestingly enough, Zeng Jing is

Fig. 1 *喜多元規 Kita Genki*, 王心渠図 Oh Shinkyo zu (Portrait of Oh Shinkyo). 1679. Kobe City Museum.

Fig. 2 河村若芝 *Kawamura Jakushi*, 布袋渡水図 *Hotei Tosui zu* (Deity Budai Crossing a River). Nagasaki Museum of History and Culture.

believed to have been influenced by the use of shadow with an implied light source found in Western paintings. Ōbaku portraits were actually influenced by the Western paintings brought to Japan via China.[5] Both portrait paintings by professional artists and *kara-e* paintings, influenced by the new Chinese style, also originated in Ōbaku culture.[6] Itsunen Shōyū was the monk of Ōbaku sect, and he was the main figure among those who invited Ingen. He also painted *kara-e* paintings. Itsunen's painting style was then succeeded by Kawamura Jyakushi (1638–1707) and Watanabe Shūseki (1639–1709) in Nagasaki (Fig. 2) (Fig. 3). Shūseki was appointed as the official painter and an authorized connoisseur of *kara-e* paintings. The establishment of polychrome *ukiyo-e* prints (*nishiki-e*) was enhanced by the introduction of colored fancy paper from China by Ōbaku culture. In this new genre of *nishiki-e*, *uki-e* gained popularity. *Uki-e* is a painting style characterized by a three-dimensional appearance and a sense of distance realized by using the technique of linear perspective.

Tokugawa Yoshimune (1684–1751), the eighth shogun of the Edo Shogunate, relaxed the restrictions on foreign books around 1720 and allowed the importation of books except those that taught Christianity. This marked the beginning of Dutch studies. In 1722, Shogun Yoshimune ordered the Nagasaki magistrate to import *kara-e* (Chinese paintings) and *oranda-e* (Dutch paintings) and, as a result, five oil paintings were brought to Japan in 1726 by a Dutch ship.[7] As for *kara-e*, the shogun issued an order in 1725 to import copies of masterpieces from the Ming Dynasty or earlier. However, a Chinese painter, Shen Nanpin (1683– (1760)–unknown) arrived in Nagasaki in 1731 instead, so it may have been too difficult to make copies of masterpieces in China.[8]

Fig. 3 渡辺秀石 *Watanabe Shūseki*, 寿老図 *Juroh zu* (God of Longevity and Cranes). Nagasaki Museum of History and Culture.

Hu Mei, the master of Shen Nanpin, is said to have excelled at painting birds and flowers that resembled the style of Lu Chi, an academic painter of the Ming Dynasty. Nanpin was also familiar with the gorgeous coloring of the classical paintings and minute representations.[9] Around the same time, in the Beijing court, Lang Shining (Giuseppe Castiglione, 1688–1766), who was thoroughly conversant with Western painting techniques, painted subjects such as portraits, birds, flowers, and horses using Chinese painting materials, under the strict restrictions on oil paintings by the emperors.[10]

In December 1731, Nanpin came to Japan with his disciples, including Gao Diao and Gao Qian, and stayed in a Chinese settlement in Nagasaki for eighteen months before returning to China in September 1733. Yū Hi (1712–72) often visited the house and studied directly under Shen Nanpin. He was able to visit the house so often because he was an adopted son of Kumashiro Hisaemon, who was one of the Chinese interpreters. In fact, it is also said that Yū Hi was actually willingly adopted by the family on 24 December 1732 in order to be able to study under Nanpin.[11] Before he was taught by Nanpin, he studied painting under the Watanabe family, a family of *kara-e* connoisseurs. Nanpin's realistic painting style was spread across the country by Yū Hi, who

Fig. 4 *石崎元章 Ishizaki Genshō*, 倣沈銓花鳥図屏風 *Hou Shinsen Kachozu Byobu* (Birds and Flowers in the Style of Shen Nanpin, screen painting). Nagasaki Museum of History and Culture.

completed works such as *Kachōzu Byōbu* (Birds and Flowers, screen painting, Tokugawa Art Museum), which was commissioned by Tokugawa Munekatsu, the lord of Owari.[12] Yū Hi never left Nagasaki; however Nanpin's style was more accepted in Kamigata (Kyoto and Osaka) and became more popular in Edo. Ishizaki Genshō (1731–78) painted a work called *Hou Shinsen Kachōzu Byōbu* (Birds and Flowers in the Style of Shen Nanpin, screen painting, Nagasaki Museum of History and Culture), which was a reproduction of a work by Shen Nanpin (Fig. 4). Watanabe Shūjitsu (1778–1830) painted *Fukuheigasen* (Pot with a Lid album, 1830, Nagasaki Museum of History and Culture) to hand down his painting techniques to his son, Shūkan (Fig. 5). We can see the clear Nanpin style in parts of this work. In Nagasaki, the Nanpin style was probably handed down as a part of the repertoire of *kara-e* connoisseur painters.

The Nanpin style was brought to Kamigata by Kakutei (1722–85), who studied under Yū Hi. He was also an Ōbaku Zen priest. Around 1746 or 1747,

Fig. 5 *渡辺秀実 Watanabe Shūjitsu* (1778–1830) painted 覆瓶画箋 Fukuhei Gasen (Pot with a Lid album). 1830. Nagasaki Museum of History and Culture).

Kakutei moved to Kyōto. We can also see the strong influence of the Ōbaku *kara-e* style in his paintings. It appears that the Nanpin style did not become the mainstream in the Kamigata area; instead, Maruyama Ōkyo (1733–95) and Itō Jyakuchū (1716–1800), who were influenced by the Nanpin style, became active in Kyoto.

Kurokawa Kigyoku (1732–56) emerged as the first Nanpin style painter in Edo City. He painted *Kaidō Hakutō zu* (Crab Apple and Chinese Bulbul, Chiba City Museum of Art) in 1755 (Fig. 6). Shokatsu Kan (1717–90) appeared next and painted *Keshi ni Niwatori zu* (Rooster and Poppy, 1758, Itabashi Art Museum) (Fig. 7). There is no record to suggest that these two painters ever visited Nagasaki. The direct Nanpin style was brought from Nagasaki to Edo by Sō Shiseki (1715–1816), who had studied under Yū Hi in Nagasaki. He also studied under Chinese painter Sō Shigan (who came to Nagasaki in 1758) and changed his name to Sō Shiseki, after his master. In his book, *Kokongasō go Hasshu* (Eight Patterns of Classic and Modern Painting), published in 1771, he wrote, "I visited Nagasaki and learnt the essence of Chinese painting in the Shen Nanpin school". He also wrote, in a hanging scroll in 1759, *Koi zu* (Carps, Tokuhon-ji Temple) (Fig. 8), that he had learnt the painting techniques of Sō Shigan. No painting of carp by Shen Nanpin is known today; however,

Fig. 6 *黒川亀玉 Kurokawa Kigyoku*, 海棠白頭翁図 Kaidō Hakutoō zu (Crab Apple and Chinese Bulbul). 1755. Chiba City Museum of Art.

Fig. 7 諸葛監 *Shokatsu Kan*, 芥子に鶏図 Keshi ni Niwatori zu (Poppy and Chicken). 1758. Itabashi Art Museum.

Fig. 8 *宋紫石 Sō Shiseki*, 鯉図 Koi zu (Carps). 1759. Tokuhon-ji temple.

Yū Hi has *Tōryūmon zu* (Tōryūmon Gate, Nagasaki Museum of History and Culture) (Fig. 9), and the carp motif was also included in the main repertoire of Nanpin followers. Nanpin style painters expressed the carp's body volume by depicting the scales in minute detail. The works by Sō Shiseki are characterized by a simple layout of motifs and a clear and light composition, compared to the works by Yū Hi and his other followers. In Edo, the sophisticated style of Nanpin paintings by Shiseki proved more popular. The feudal lords, such as Sakai Tadazane and Yanagisawa Korenobu, also painted some works in the Nanpin style.

Sō Shiseki illustrated *Butsurui Hinshitsu* by Hiraga Gen'nai, published in 1763. Among these illustrations, there is a work produced in the Western style that expressed the curves of flower petals by minutely placed lines, as if the artist were copying copperplate engravings, and a work produced in the Nanpin style also expressed the three-dimensional appearance of tree branches and trunks through brushstrokes and dots. This book indicates that Sō Shiseki had a connection with people in Dutch studies group, too. Of course, there

Fig. 9 熊斐 *Yū Hi*, 登龍門図 Tōryūmon zu (Tōryūmon Gate). Nagasaki Museum of History and Culture.

were also many illustrations that cannot be clearly described as following either the Western or Nanpin style. An illustration of saffron in the book was done in a style that resembles copperplate engravings. There is a note to this illustration, "This illustration is from a Dutch natural history book". There were, however, other illustrations produced in both the Western and Chinese styles, respectively, contained within the same book. A painting of a plum tree entitled "*Kanshu Dankōbai*" (Chinese Spicebush) uses both the Nanpin style expression of tree branches and also a three-dimensional representation by lines that resembles Western copperplate engravings. Sō Shiseki painted *Shishi zu* (Lion, the Museum Yamatobunkakan) (Fig. 10) in 1768 and left a note, "This painting of lions is from the illustrations in the *Banjū-fu* book in the collection of Mr. Hiraga. It is unlike those drawn by common painters. This is but a reproduction of Western illustrations". This indicates that he had seen *Historiae naturalis*, written by Johnston, in the collection of Hiraga Gen'nai.[13] The three-dimensional expression of the lion's face is clearly Western. However, if we compare this work with the works by Shen Nanpin, such as *Shishi Giji zu*

Fig. 10 *宋紫石 Sō Shiseki*, 獅子図 Shishi zu (Lion). 1768. The Museum Yamatobunkakan.

(Lion with their babies, Kōbe City Museum) (Fig. 11), Shiseki's expression of fur and body volume may be relatively dissimilar to the Western style.[14] Odano Naotake, a practitioner of the Akita *ranga* style, which will be discussed later, also painted a work entitled *Shishi zu* (Lion) (Fig. 12), which was also inspired by the illustrations of lions in the book by Johnston. While this work is partly done in the Western style, that resembles oil painting, Sō Shiseki only used Western expressions in a more limited way.[15]

Akita *ranga* (ranga means Dutch painting) painting appeared during the An'ei Era (1772–81). This was before Shiba Kōkan (1747–1818) started

Fig. 11 *沈南蘋 Shen Nanpin,* 獅子戯児図 Shishi Giji zu (Lion with their babies). Kōbe City Museum.

Fig. 12 *小田野直武 Odano Naotake* 獅子図 Shishi zu (Lion). Private Collection.

producing Western-style paintings.[16] The group of painters is so-called because the Akita domain lord and his followers were the key figures of the group. Despite its name, they were mainly active in Edo. Akita *ranga* painters used shadow with an implied light source and perspective that required a relatively higher level of understanding of the technique. Their expression of birds and flowers were closer to the Nanpin style. Among the Akita *ranga* painters, the only one who had an almost full understanding of linear perspective and

Fig. 13 *小田野直武 Odano Naotake* 唐太宗・花鳥山水図 Tōh Taisō Kachō Sansui zu (Chinese Emperor Taizong Birds and Flowers with Landscape). The Akita Museum of Modern Art.

aerial perspective was probably Odano Naotake (1749–80).[17] The Akita *ranga* style is characterized by its composition of arranging landscapes that resemble copperplate engravings in close-up in bird and flower paintings.[18] In order to place such landscapes in their paintings, the Akita *ranga* painters other than Odano Naotake probably re-used illustrations by Naotake or copied copperplate engravings. On the other hand, in *Tōh Taisō zu* (Chinese Emperor Taizong, hanging scroll) which is a part of *Tōh Taisō Kachō Sansui zu* (Chinese Emperor Taizong, Birds and Flowers with Landscape, important cultural asset, the Akita Museum of Modern Art) by Odano Naotake (Fig. 13), we can see that the painter attempted to use the one vanishing point perspective in the representation of the floor in a grid by placing the vanishing point outside the picture's plane. However, even Naotake almost always avoided the strict use of aerial and linear perspective by placing water surfaces in the middle distance in his landscape paintings. Shiba Kōkan probably studied under Naotake at one point.

Fig. 14 *司馬江漢Shiba Kōkan*, 相州鎌倉七里ガ浜図 Sōshū Kamakura Shichirigahama zu (Landscape of Shichirigahama beach, Kamakura, Sōshū). Kōbe City Museum.

Shiba Kōkan studied Dutch books with the help of Ōtsuki Gentaku, who knew Dutch, and completed a copperplate etching entitled *Mimegurinokei zu* (Landscape of Mimeguri, *megane-e*, peep-show pictures) in 1783.[19] This was the first copperplate etching produced in Japan. Subsequently, he took up oil painting (Kōkan called oil painting Western wax painting or *ranga* painting). He dedicated his framed works to temples and shrines in order to promote oil paintings. An early example of such paintings is *Soshu Kamakura Shichirigahama zu* (Landscape of Shichirigahama beach, Kamakura, Sōshū, Kobe City Museum), produced in 1796 (Fig. 14).[20] His name, Kōkan, is inspired by Chinese language and culture.[21] Before he started using this name, he was painting *ukiyo-e* in the style of Suzuki Harunobu, using the name Suzuki Harushige, and, after that, he studied the Nanpin style under Sō Shiseki. When he was calling himself Harushige during the Meiwa Era (1764–71), he became familiar with the exaggerated linear perspective that came to Japan via China and applied the *uki-e*-like perspective to his paintings of beauties produced in a style similar to his master, Harunobu.[22] When we examine Kōkan's works, we note the following two points: firstly, he shifted from the Nanpin style, to copperplate engraving, and then to oil painting in chronological order; however, these phases overlapped with each other at some point. For example, even after he started working on copperplate engraving, he was also painting commissioned works in the Nanpin style. Secondly, he visited Nagasaki from 1788 until the following year; however, he had already completed copperplate etchings before that time and taken up oil painting. It is obvious that his visit

Fig. 15 *司馬江漢 Shiba Kōkan*, 犬のいる風景図 Inu no iru Fūkei zu (Landscape with a Dog). Chiba City Museum of Art.

to Nagasaki, at least, was not the key turning point for him to absorb and learn the Western styles. Kōkan became familiar with the linear perspective from *uki-e* and *megane-e*, tried the Nanpin style, and then took up oil painting. So, how did his style change? In terms of his perspective technique, Kōkan probably had some knowledge of aerial perspective, as he used lighter colours for distant mountains in his *Inu no iru Fūkei zu* (*Landscape with a Dog*, Chiba City Museum of Art) (Fig. 15). However, aerial perspective is rarely used in Kōkan's work. One of the reasons for this is that his oil painting materials were unsuitable for expressing the tones that were needed for aerial perspective. As for linear perspective, Kokan had almost completely resolved the sense of incongruity that existed in the Akita *ranga* paintings by the time he painted *Ikoku Kōjō zu* (Factory in a Foreign Country, Kobe City Museum) (Fig. 16). The oil paint used by Kōkan was not ideal for expressing shadows with an implied light

Fig. 16 *司馬江漢 Shiba Kōkan*, 異国工場図 Ikoku Kōjō zu (Factory in a Foreign Country). Kōbe City Museum.

Fig. 17 *西村重長 Nishimura Shigenaga*, 浮絵海士龍宮玉取之図 Uki-e Ama Ryūgū Tamatori no zu (A Woman Diver Determined to Recover Treasure Ball from Dragon's Palace). Chiba City Museum of Art.

source. However, in this work, which is not an oil painting, we can see shadow work with an implied light source, although some inconsistencies persist in the relationship between the position of the light source and the shadows. The technique for using shadows had already appeared in the works of Hanabusa Icchō (1652–1724), who belonged to traditional Kanō-school. Therefore, the use of shadow is not necessarily Western. However, the use of shadow with an implied light source probably had a connection with the Western style, since it was used in the works of the Akita *ranga* painters and also in the landscape prints of Katsushika Hokusai that were clearly and intentionally produced in the Western style.[23]

Let us now consider how the use of perspective shifted from *uki-e* to landscape prints. An early example of *uki-e* is an *uki-e* painting called *Ichimuraza Jyōnai no zu (Inside of Ichimuraza Theater)*, produced around 1739. Also, in 1744, the works by Torii Kiyotada were published.[24] The early *uki-e* works were probably influenced by Chinese paintings and prints that used perspective.[25] As in the early *uki-e* works of *Uki-e Ama Ryūgū Tamatori no zu (A Woman Diver determined to Recover Treasure Ball from the Dragon's Palace*, Chiba City Museum of Art) (Fig. 17) by Nishimura Shigenaga or some by Okumura

Fig. 18 *歌川豊春 Utagawa Toyoharu*, 浮絵和国景跡風流和田酒盛之図 Uki-e Wakoku Keiseki Furyū Wada Sakamori no zu (Party of Wada from the series of Japanese noted places and scenes). Chiba City Museum of Art.

Masanobu (1686–1764), linear perspective is used to express only indoor structure and no perspective is used for outdoor scenery. Utagawa Toyoharu (1735–1814) began to produce *uki-e* paintings around 1767. As we can see in his *Uki-e Wakoku Keiseki Furyū Wada Sakamori no zu* (*Party of Wada from a Series of Japanese Noted Places and Scenes*, Chiba City Museum of Art) (Fig. 18), he used linear perspective throughout the work, although there are some inconsistencies. This means that the painter used the linear perspective (or a technique that is very close to it) not only for indoor structures, but also for outdoor scenery. The use of perspective by Kōkan (or Harushige) is close to that of Toyoharu. After that, there appeared landscape paintings that casually used linear perspective in paintings of beauties, which were not necessarily *uki-e* paintings, as in *Sujitagaibashi-Mae (A View of the Front of Sujitagaibashi Bridge*, Chiba City Museum of Art) (Fig. 19), a triptych by Katsukawa Syunchō (1786–88). In early 1800, after Shiba Kōkan succeeded in copperplate engraving, Katsushika Hokusai started to work on Western-style landscape prints, such as *Kudan Ushigafuchi* (Fig. 20), in which the artist intentionally emphasized the Western style by using the shadow technique that resembles copperplate engravings. The following masterpieces of landscape prints by Hokusai and Utagawa Hiroshige,

Fig. 19 *勝川春潮 Katsukawa Syunchō*, 筋違橋前 Sujitagaibashi-Mae (In front view of Sujitagaibashi Bridge), c. 1786–88. Chiba City Museum of Art.

Fig. 20 *葛飾北斎 Katsushika Hokusai*, くだんうしがふち Kudan Ushiga Fuchi (Landscape of Kudan Ushiga Fuchi). Nakau Ei Collection.

Fig. 21 *葛飾北斎 Katsushika Hokusai*, 富嶽三十六景 隠田の水車 Fugaku Sanjurokkei Onden no Suisya (Watermill at Onden from the series Thirty-six Views of Mt. Fuji). c. 1831–1833. Chiba City Museum of Art.

such as the *Fugaku Sanjuroku kei* (36 Views of Mt. Fuji) and *Meisho Edo Hyakkei* (100 Famous Views of Edo) series, are also mainly based on the logical spatial representation realized by the use of linear perspective (Fig. 21).

In the period of transition from early *uki-e* style to logical *uki-e* style during the Hōreki Era (1751–64), young Maruyama Ōkyo was painting *megane-e* (peep-show pictures) that use an exaggerated linear perspective. *Megane-e* is a series of pictures viewed through a hole with a lens. One enjoys the three-dimensional appearance of pictures that are drawn with perspective, which is further exaggerated by the lens. It is closely linked with the beginning of *uki-e*, and *uki-e* was also used in *megane-e*. (This does not mean that every *uki-e* was a *megane-e*.[26]) It is said that Ōkyo reproduced *megane-e* works that were originally produced in China under the influence of Western culture. Ōkyo painted landscapes based on his three-dimensional understanding of space. There, we can see the influence of linear perspective. In the following years, Western peep-show viewers and the accompanying copperplate peep-show pictures came to Japan via Dutch Ships. Shiba Kōkan produced an imitation of these peep-show viewers and also created *megane-e* that could be enjoyed using the viewer. In 1783, Kōkan completed the first copperplate etching *megane-e* works in Japan. Returning now to the situation in Nagasaki at that time. Shiba Kōkan was there

Fig. 22 *石崎融思 Ishizaki Yūshi*, 双鶏図 Sōkei zu (Hen and Cock). 1841 Nagasaki Museum of History and Culture.

from 1788 to the following year and met Araki Gen'yū (1728–94).[27] Gen'yū was an official painter and the leader of the *kara-e* connoisseurs. He studied painting techniques under his master, Ishizaki Gentoku, and learnt Western painting techniques from a Western painter. Gentoku is the foster father of Ishizaki Genshō, mentioned above. He was the painter who reproduced Shen Nanpin's work and used it for his folding screen work. Gentoku is said to have learnt Western painting techniques from a Dutch painter; however, no Western-style work by him is known today. His *Tōbōsaku zu* (Dong Fang Shuo, Nagasaki Museum of History and Culture) is a painting of a Chinese motif, produced in a style that is far from Western. Ishizaki Yūshi (1768–1846), the son of Araki Gen'yū, also became a *kara-e* connoisseur at the age of 14 and later became the leader of the connoisseurs. The works of Yūshi demonstrate that he was familiar with a broad range of painting styles. His *Tohrankan zu emaki* (Chinese and Dutch Houses, Nagasaki Museum of History and Culture) in 1801 reflects his masterly skill. One quickly imagines the Western influence at a glance; however, this work is not definitely Western. Among his works of Chinese motifs, we can see a somewhat Western or oil-painting-like minute expression. Examples of such paintings are *Fukuroku Hoko zu* (Deer and Monkey, Tokyo National Museum), containing an inscription of 1822, and *Sōkei zu* (Hen and Cock, Nagasaki Museum of History and Culture) of 1841 (Fig. 22). However, his *Momo zu* (Peach, Nagasaki Museum of History and Culture) which

Fig. 23 若杉五十八 *Wakasugi Isohachi*, オランダ海港図 Oranda Kaikō zu (Dutch Port). The Museum Yamatobunkakan.

was probably painted between the above two works is closer to the *kara-e* style than the Western style, and may also be somewhat close to the Nanpin style. The works by Ishizaki Yūshi contain both *kara-e* and Western painting styles. Araki Jogen (1774–1824) was named after Araki Gen'yū, a *kara-e* connoisseur. Probably Jogen was also concerned with the *kara-e* connoisseurs. His works include oil paintings, such as *Oranda Kaikō zu* (Dutch Port, Museum Yamatobunkakan) (Fig. 23). He painted many Western-style paintings; however, he also painted works that should be categorized as *kara-e* connoisseur paintings. *Bankoku Jinbutsu zukan* (People of Foreign Countries, Nagasaki Museum of History and Culture) is an example of such. Similar to Jogen, Wakasugi Isohachi (1759–1805) is also a master of Western-style painting in Nagasaki. He was not a *kara-e* connoisseur, but a local official who was responsible for trade in Nagasaki.[28] His work, *Yōsen zu* (Foreign Ships, Imamiya Shrine, Kyoto), produced in 1791 is a highly sophisticated oil painting. As a local official, Isohachi had a connection with Dutch culture through his work as an office accountant. Both Araki Jogen and Wakasugi Isohachi used shadow with an implied light source in their work.

Conclusion

We examined the situation in eighteenth-century Japan in order to explore the Western and Chinese influences on Japanese paintings and the overlapping status of these influences at that time. As for realistic expression, the use of shadows with an implied light source, often seen in Western paintings, was mixed with the minuteness of Nanpin style paintings. As for the motifs, the painters only had access to a limited number of Western image sources. However, they also selected motifs depending on their own taste. An example of such a motif is the lion. This motif was directly taken from the imported illustrated books authored by Johnston; but the selection of this motif must also have been inspired by *karajishi*, the artistic portrait of a lion as a symbol of power, which had been traditionally used in Chinese paintings.[29] As for perspective, the Western linear perspective technique was first brought to Japan via China and was welcomed as a novelty. Perspective was also brought to Japan through illustrations in Dutch books. This helped the painters of that time to deepen their understanding of perspective and they subsequently began to use the technique more accurately in their works. As a result, many images were created based on perspective and the novelty faded away. Although painters increased their understanding of spatial expression, the use of perspective finally settled into differences in size, as in the *ukiyo-e* works of Hiroshige and Hokusai.

Nagasaki opened up the door to foreign cultures. Many cultures simply passed through Nagasaki. We can imagine that many Dutch books came to Nagasaki but they were actually used in Edo. Shen Nanpin came to Nagasaki; however, his style was much more popular in Edo. The painting market at that time differed in size and tendency between Nagasaki, Edo and Kamigata. In Nagasaki, Western-style painting began full-scale with the works of Wakasugi Isohachi and Araki Jogen. It was rather a late start. Kōkan had already started working on Western style paintings before them. Isohachi only engaged in Western-style painting in earnest when Kōkan visited Nagasaki. Interpreters and translators only dealt with Chinese or Dutch languages; however, the *kara-e* connoisseurs covered both cultures. We may be able to detect in the works of Ishizaki Yūshi the transition from paintings dominated by the Chinese-style and those dominated by the Western-style that occurred among the *kara-e* connoisseurs of Nagasaki. However, the Chinese and Western styles co-existed before Jogen and also continued to co-exist after him. Even after the Nagasaki painters started Western-style paintings full-scale, few Nagasaki painters practised the Western-style. There were also painters, such as Tetsuō Somon (1791–1871, the head priest of Shuntoku-ji Temple and an official book inspector), who adopted the Chinese literati style of painting, and Kinoshita Itsu'un (1800–66, a painter from a family of Yawata city officials), who often visited Chinese residences and was also able to gather information about Dutch culture. In particular, even after Japan emerged from its period of isolation and opened up its ports to foreign countries at the end of the Edo Period, and even after Nagasaki was no longer the only channel to Western culture, the connection with China was maintained. One of the reasons for this was that China was geographically close to Nagasaki.

In the mid-Edo Period, Chinese and Western influences sometimes co-existed in Japanese paintings. The main reasons for this co-existence were probably the facts that China was not completely foreign to Japanese people, even though it was a foreign country, that the dominance of Chinese culture declined due to the entry of Holland as the third country, and that there were, temporarily, conflicts between the Japanese, Chinese, and Dutch cultures.[30] In the eighteenth century, at first, the Japanese painters only absorbed the Chinese, Dutch, and Western cultures selectively, according to their tastes. Most of the people who were enthusiastic about Dutch and Western paintings were deeply interested in not only the paintings but also its whole culture. And they were deeply interested in Chinese culture, too. However, these cultures, that had been absorbed selectively and partially, gained popularity, became normal to Japanese people, and ultimately brought about a fundamental change in Japanese paintings. At first, linear perspective was only applied to the expression of indoor structures because the effective use of the technique was relatively easy. However, it eventually came to dominate the whole picture plane. Paintings that demonstrated the technique of perspective itself gradually shifted to those that used perspective as a technique to support the landscape composition in the background. This brought logical spatial expression to landscape prints. The Nanpin style remained relatively popular into the late nineteenth century. (Painters such as Watanabe Kazan and Tsubaki Chinzan, the famous Japanese literati painters of the nineteenth century, also painted some works in the Nanpin style.) Even though the popularity of the Nanpin style gradually faded away, a few painters who participated in the *Naikoku Kaiga Kyōshinkai* Exhibition of 1884 called themselves Nanpin or Shen Quan style painters (Shen Nanpin was also called Shen Quan). I believe that minute and realistic representation took root in Japanese paintings as the Nanpin style gained in popularity and spread, together with natural history books that contained illustrations of animals and plants.

Notes

1. See Ito Shiori, "Ikoku to daimyō:Edojidaichukikaiga no ikokusyumi (Foreign Lands and the Daimyo: The Fascination with Foreign Cultures Found in Mid-Edo Period Painting)", in *Edo no ikokusyumi: Nanpinfūdairyukō* (*The Nanpin School: The Fascination with the Exotic in Edo-period Painting*) (Exhibition Catalogue, Chiba: Chiba City Museum of Art, 2001). I would like to add that some Chinese paintings were imported via Ryūkyū and Satsuma too. I received many ideas for this presentation from conversations with Mr. Tsukahara Akira. I appreciate his cooperation. I also thank Ms. Iwasa Yuri, who proof-read my English text.
2. I have mentioned this topic before. See Ito Shiori, "Edojidai no Ikokusyumi (The Fascination with the Exotic in the Edo-period)", in *Nihon ni okeru gairaibijyutsu*

no jyuyō ni kansuru chōsa kenkyū houkokusyo (Research report: Study of the acceptance of Foreign Arts in Japan) (Tokyo: Tokyo kokuritsu bunkazai kenkyūsyo (Tokyo Independent Administrative Institution National Research Institute for Cultural Properties), 2006.

3. See Kyoto kokuritsu hakubutsukan (Kyōto National Museum), *18seiki no nihonbijyutsu* (*Japanese Art in the Eighteenth Century*) (Exhibition Catalogue, Kyoto: Kyoto National Museum, 1990). Also, see the recent exhibition catalogue, Asian Art Museum of San Francisco, *Traditions Unbound: Groundbreaking Painters from Eighteenth Century Kyoto* (Exhibition Catalogue, San Francisco: Asian Art Museum of San Francisco, 2005).
4. For Ōbaku portraits and *Kara-e* painting of this period, see Narusawa Katsushi "Monohayari no keifu; Ōbakugakaryakuden (Genealogy of Fashion: Short Biographies of Ōbaku Painters)", in Kobe City Museum, *Ingenzenshi to Ōbakushu no kaiga* (*Priest Ingen and Paintings of the Ōbaku Zen Sect*) (Exhibition Catalogue, Kobe: Kobe City Museum, 1991), Kyoto National Museum, *Ōbaku no bijutsu;edojidai no bunka o kaetamono* (*The Art of Ōbaku*) (Exhibition Catalogue, Kyoto: Kyoto National Museum, 1993).
5. For relations between Ōbaku painting and western realistic representation, see Nishigori Ryosuke, *Ōbakuzenrin no kaiga* (*The Painting of Ōbaku*) (Tokyo: Chuō Kōron Bijutsu Shuppan, 2006).
6. *Kara-e* originally meant paintings imported from China, but, at that time, it included Japanese paintings, the style of which was influenced by Chinese paintings.
7. See, Koga Jūjiro, *Nagasakikaigazenshi* (*The History of Nagasaki Painting*) (Tokyo: Kitamitsu Shobo, 1944), pp. 93–6.
8. Ibid., pp. 100–3.
9. For Shen Nanpin, see Etchū Tetsuya, Tokuyama Hikaru, Kimura Shigekazu, *Nagasakiha no kachoga;shen nanpin to sonoshuhen* (*The Flower and Bird Painting of Shen Nanpin and his followers*) (Tokyo: Fuji Art Shuppan, 1981) and Zhou jiyin, Kondo Hidemi *Shen Quan yanqiu* (*The Study of Shen Quan*) (Jiangsu, Jiangsu Meishu Chupanshe, 1997).
10. Ishida Mikinosuke, "Rouseinei den ryakukou" (*A Short Biography of Lang Shining*), *Bijutsu Kenkyū*), no. 10 (1932). If we can find a Western influence in Nanpin works, it is not directly from Ran Shining, who employed the Western style of painting without using oil paint. Interestingly, this mode is parallel to the Japanese Western-style painters who also painted Western-style paintings without oil paint.
11. Etchū Tetsuya, "Nagasaki ni okeru Nanpinha no shiso Yūhi (Kumashiro jinzaemon) ni tsuite (The Founder of Nanpin School at Nagasaki; Yū-Hi, also known as Kumashiro Jinzaemon)", *Nagasaki Dansō*, no. 48 (1969).
12. Takeuchi Misako, "Owarihan goyōeshi to Nanpinha; Imamura Zuigakuto Sō Shikō" (The Official Painter of the Owari Clan and the Nanpin School: Imamura Zuigaku and Sō Shikō), *Nagoyashihakubutsukankenkyukiyō* (*Annual Bulletin of Nagoya City Museum*), no. 13 (1989).
13. This lion's face bears a slight resemblance to that in Johnston's book, but only in parts. Shiseki copied animal images from Johnston's book directly in his book

entitled *Kokongasō go Hasshu*. If he painted this lion after Johnston's book, the two lions should appear more similar, so we also examine other sources.

14. This "*Shishi Giji zu*" is difficult to identify as a genuine work by Shen Nanpin. Whether genuine or not, it is important that there are some works describing lion(s) and attributed to Shen Nanpin. I believe that their characteristic of realistic representation was accepted by Nanpin's repertoire. In my opinion, all historical works bearing the signature of Nanpin are useful for our understanding of what the Japanese painters of the Edo period recognized as Nanpin.
15. There is another important work by Sō Shiseki in the Western-style. It is "*Kujyaku Hi'inko zu* (The Peacock and the Red Parrot)" (Itsukushima Shrine in 1777), which was influenced by one of the oil paintings that arrived in 1726. For this work, see Kojima Kaoru "Bakumatsu meiji no kachōga ni tsuite no ichi shiron (An Essay on Bird and Flower Paintings from Bakumatsu to Meiji)", *Jissen zyoshi daigaku bungakubu kiyō* (*The Faculty of Letters in Jissen Women's College Annual Reports of Studies*), no. 43 (2001). This work is too damaged to determine its original style. It might be understood that the composition was from the oil painting and the style was from the Nanpin school, but this composition is possibly from the Nanpin school as well.
16. For Akita Ranga, in English, see Hiroko Johnson, *Western Influences on Japanese Art: The Akita Ranga Art School and Foreign Books* (Amsterdam: Hotei Publishing, 2005). Regretfully, it lacks some very recent Japanese study in this field.
17. Chinese painters already used aerial perspective with light and dark shades of colour in the eleventh century. Aerial perspective is not only a Western influence but also the oriental tradition, although the Japanese Western-style painters accepted it as a technique from Western painting. For example, Satake Shozan, an important painter of Akita ranga, wrote in his art theory work, *Gazu Rikai* (Understanding Painting), as follows: "We see trees closer to us darker green, and further from us lighter green", (translated by Hiroko Johnson, ibid., p. 160).
18. It is possible that Akita ranga had an influence later on the Nanpin school. Sō Shizan, the son of Sō Shiseki, also painted a flower and bird motif in front of a distant landscape; see Yamaguchi Yasuhiro "Mashiyama Sessai hitsu kinkeichō zu(Golden Pheasants by Masiyama Sessai)", Kokka, no. 1181 (1994).
19. For Kōkan's study of Dutch books in order to create copper etchings, see Isozaki Yasuhiko, *Edojidai no ranga to ransyo kinsei nichiranhikakubijyutsushi* (*Ranga, Dutch paintings and Ransyo Dutch Books in the Edo period*) (Tokyo: Yumani Syobo, 2004), pp. 368–96.
20. For Kōkan's dedications of landscape oil paintings at temples and shrines, see Tsukahara Akira, "Syaji hounou youfu fukeizu ni okeru Shiba Kōkan no seisaku ito (Shiba Kōkan's Artistic Intention as Reflected in his Dedications of Western-style Landscape Paintings at Shrines and Temples)", *Bijutsuhsi* (*The Bijutsushi Journal of the Japan Art History Society*), no. 135 (1994).
21. Kōkan himself wrote that his artist's name "Kōkan" was the Chinese mode; see Shiba Kōkan *Shunparōhikki* (*Notes by Shunparō*). "It seemed to me that it would be more refined to have Chinese sounding names to sign under my poems, so

I chose Shun, Shiba, Kungaku and Kōkan" (translated by Calvin L. French; see Calvin L. French, *Shiba Kōkan* (New York and Tokyo: Weatherhill, 1974)).

22. The familiar beauties motifs were composed with a Western perspective landscape in Harushige's works. This composition is somewhat similar to Akita ranga. Akita ranga artists arranged flowers and birds before a distant landscape, copying copperplate prints. I would like to propose that shows the influence of Harushige (Kōkan) on the Akita ranga artists.
23. See Yamaguchi Yasuhiro, "Gaikō hyōgen no yūgisei (Playfulness in the Representation of Light in Edo-period Yohga)" in Tsuji Nobuo sensei kanreki kinenkai, *Nihon bijutsushi no suimyaku* (*Currents in Japanese Art History*) (Tokyo: Perikansha, 1993) and Uchiyama Jun'ichi, *Edo no kōkishin* (*Curiosity in the Edo period ranga*) (Tokyo: Kōdansha, 1996). Uchiyama points out that painters did not always paint shadow and they painted it effectively for representation (ibid., p. 146).
24. See Kishi Fumikazu, *Edo no enkinhō uki-e no shikaku* (*Perspective in the Edo period*) (Tokyo: Keisō Shobō, 1994), pp. 4–5 and pp. 43–7. This *uki-e* painting, called *Ichimuraza Jyōnai no zu* (*Inside the Ichimuraza Theatre*), disappeared, and is only known through photographs now.
25. See Oka Yasumasa, *Megane-e shinkō* (*A New Study of Peep-show Pictures*) (Tokyo: Chikuma Shobō, 1992), pp. 66–70.
26. For peep-show pictures, see ibid.
27. For *Kara-e* mekiki official painters and connoisseurs of foreign paintings, see Koga ibid. and Nagasaki kenritsu bijyutsu hakubutsukan (Nagasaki Prefectural Art Museum), *Kara-e mekiki to dōmon* (*Kara-e Mekiki and Related Painters*) (Exhibition Catalogue, Nagasaki, Nagasaki Prefectural Art Museum, 1998). Kōkan wrote in his *Saiyū nikki* (*Diary of a Western Journey*) as follows: "I called on Araki Tamenoshin at Kajimachi. As the official connoisseur of pictures, he is somewhat capable of drawing but is not a good artist" (translated by Calvin L. French; see French, ibid). Araki Gen'yū was the adopted child of Araki Genkei, whose real father was one of the Dutch Interpreters.
28. For Wakasugi Isohachi, see Katsumori Noriko "Wakasugi Isohachi kenkyū (A Study on Wakasugi Isohachi, an Artist of Western-style Paintings in Nagasaki)", *Kōbeshiritsuhakubutsukankenkyukiyō* (*The Bulletin of Kobe City Museum*), no. 21 (2005).
29. I think that the horse subject is similar to the lion's case. Based on the engravings in the album of Johan Elias Riedinger, artists of Western-style painting painted horses frequently, but the Nanpin school painters also painted many horses, copying Nanpin's subject. Horses provided a suitable subject representing massiveness and texture, and, at that time, the horse was a very popular and important animal.
30. For the conflict and co-existence between Japanese, Chinese, and Dutch cultures at that time, see Timon Screech *Edo no shikōkūkan* (*Thought Space in the Edo Period*) (Tokyo: Seidosha, 1999).

CHAPTER 5

Jingdezhen and *imari*: Communication and Competition between Chinese and Japanese Porcelains in the Seventeenth and Eighteenth Centuries

Liu Zhaohui

I. Introduction

The seventeenth century marked a milestone in the history of Japanese ceramics. The story goes that Nabeshima Naoshige, the daimyo for the Kyūshū, took some captive Korean potters back to Japan after his participation in Bunroku Keichō no eki led by Hideyoshi. One of those potters, named Ri Sanpei, discovered large deposits of porcelain clay near Arita and, in the 1610s, he established the Tengu-dani kiln at the place where the town of Arita, Saga Prefecture, is now located, thus initiating the firing of Arita porcelain. Clues and evidence from a close analysis of documents and literature, the archeological excavation of the Tengu-dani kiln and the inscription on a tombstone in Shirakawa cemetery all testify to the credibility of this account.[1] Since most of the porcelain produced in Arita was exported to the outside world from Port Imari, the porcelain dealers and consumers then named this porcelain after the port, hence popularizing another name for Arita porcelain: imari. From then on, imari flourished rapidly under the influence of Chinese porcelain.

Although, at the beginning, Japanese porcelain borrowed techniques from Korea, the shape and decoration of early imari were affected by Chinese porcelain. The influence of Jingdezhen ware on seventeenth-century imari has been widely acknowledged by academic circles in Japan. Articles devoted to this specific subject have already been published by scholars such as Yabe Yoshiaki[2] and Murakami Nobuyuki.[3] Based on the previous researches, the present paper seeks to reanalyze the relationship between Jingdezhen porcelain and imari ware from the perspective of the Chinese ceramic history. Furthermore, by comparing woodprints illustrating *Tangshi Huapu*, a popular book introduced into Japan during the late Ming period, with decorations on Chinese and Japanese porcelain of the same period, this chapter examines the special role woodblock prints played as a medium for the ceramic art exchange between China and Japan.

The 1650s witnessed a turning-point in the development of imari. With a sharp decrease in volume of Chinese export porcelain, imari took over the European market and then grew in popularity through its creative Kakiemon ware. By comparing export imari with the Jingdezhen ware that was exported to Europe in the seventeenth and eighteenth centuries, this chapter examines how Japanese export porcelain was modeled on Chinese ceramics and also introduced its own innovations, as well as how the Chinese export porcelain absorbed imari styles and decorations later in order to win back the European market.

II. The Ceramic Trade between China and Japan from the End of the Ming to the Early Qing Dynasties

The export of Chinese porcelain reached a new peak in the period between the end of the Ming and the early Qing Dynasties. Japan was one of its most important overseas markets.

During the early phase of the Ming Dynasty, there was officially sanctioned (tribute) trade between China and Japan, which was suspended later partly because of the attacks by Japanese pirates along the Chinese east coast. However, after the middle period, with the development of the commodity economy in China, private overseas trade between China and Japan began to increase. Although the Ming government had banned maritime trade with foreign countries since the very beginning of its reign, there were countless violating cases of smuggling. Confronted with various protests and attacks against the prohibition, the Ming government eventually agreed to lift the ban by opening up Port Haichengyuegang in Zhangzhou, Fujian Province, to overseas trading, which led to the rapid boost of private overseas trade in the late Ming dynasty. To guard against the Japanese pirates, the Ming government still banned Sino-Japanese trade. However, since doing business with Japan meant traveling only a short distance yet obtaining fat profits, smuggling was prevalent. As some documents put it, "the profits those unscrupulous merchants got from smuggling goods to Japan were twice as great as what could be made through normal trade with the Philippines",[4] so "the harsh prohibitory regulations did not work well in banning all business with Japan".[5] Besides, the coastal defenses were relatively lax at the end of the Ming period, so the merchants in the southeastern coastal areas, "for the sake of money, took the opportunities to make frequent business trips between China and Japan, as if they were walking to visit an intimate next-door neighbour, totally ignoring the risks of sailing".[6] As for Japan, the Edo bakufu encouraged Sino-Japanese business by granting a special red-seal license to Chinese ships and providing protection for them. Therefore, the number of Chinese ships bound for Nagasaki was increasing every year and rose to several dozens per year at that time. A Japanese book entitled *Tsūkō-ichiran*, recorded that "many Chinese ships gathered together at Nagasaki and Hirado during the Keichō and Kan'ei periods" (early seventeenth century). In 1639, Japan adopted a closed-door policy and shut the country off from all international intercourse. Japanese ships were forbidden from sailing to other countries. However, as an exception, Chinese and Dutch ships were given access to the port of Nagasaki for trade, which caused non-governmental Sino-Japanese business to prosper to an unprecedented degree.

The porcelain trade between China and Japan was mainly conducted by private dealers. At that time, goods from China were very popular in Japan. "The demand for silk was the greatest, followed by the need for porcelain, while the demand for medicine was the most urgent. These goods were introduced and shipped to all parts of the country. From north to south, people appreciated them and could not get too much of them."[7] Since "Jingdezhen ware was especially cherished by the Japanese", porcelain constituted a large part of the cargos. Dr. Matsuura Akira quoted *Ikoku Nikki* to illustrate the situation: in 1609, ten ships from China arrived at Satsuma, and the cargo lists for three of them were recorded. Porcelain appeared on all three lists. There were "bowls" on Xuerongju's ship, "bowls and small cups for drinking" on Chenzhenyu's ship, and "bowls, small dishes and vases" on Hexinyu's ship. Huge amounts of porcelains and raw materials for porcelain-making were shipped to Japan, which made it the second largest overseas market for Chinese porcelain in the late Ming-early Qing period. A detailed record of the exact quantity can be found in the *Catalogue of Imports and Exports in Chinese Trades 1637–1833*, compiled by Nagazumi Yoko.[8]

Besides Chinese ships, ships from Portugal, Japan and the Netherlands also conducted porcelain trade between China and Japan in the early seventeenth century. According to the statistics in T. Volker's book, *Porcelain and the Dutch East India Company*,[9] China exported more than 16 million porcelain wares to Japan between 1602 and 1682. The Dutch East India Company began to ship Chinese porcelains to Japan in 1613, soon after the establishment of its factory in Hirado. Documents in the Netherlands reveal that, during the few years leading up to 1638, the Dutch East India Company shipped thousands or even tens of thousands of porcelain wares to Japan almost every year. In 1635, 135,905 pieces were shipped, while, in 1637, the volume was still as large as 39,075 pieces. However, after 1638, the volume decreased sharply, and only a very small amount of Chinese porcelain wares was shipped to Japan, whether by the Dutch East India Company, or by Chinese merchants.[10] Nevertheless, from the 1652 onwards, there had been a huge increase in the Japanese importation of raw materials for porcelain-making, while there were rare cases of shipping porcelain to Japan from China. This had much to do with the circumstances of the porcelain industry in both countries. During the 1650s, China was in turmoil because of the change of dynasty from Ming to Qing, so its porcelain industry stagnated, resulting in a sharp decrease in porcelain exports. At the same time, Japanese porcelain began to mature. Since Europe had a constant demand for Chinese porcelain, Japanese ware was exported to Europe as a substitute. That was why Japan imported so many raw materials for porcelain making from China at that time.

III. The Influence of Jingdezhen Porcelain on *imari* in the Seventeenth Century

(i) The Influence on Decoration

Many patterns on early blue-and-white imari were derived from decorations on Jingdezhen ware. Such patterns include figures, landscapes, animals, plants, etc., and their layout is similar also. Examples are provided below to illustrate the similarities.

(a) The Design of Human Figures

The figures painted on early imari are Chinese rather than Japanese. For example, the decoration of the imari blue-and-white plate with a human figure (Fig. 1) is relatively simple, with only one blue figure contrasting against the white plate. The design of an old man holding a bamboo stick was quite common on Jingdezhen ware at the end of the Ming dynasty. A similar design can be found in the Jingdezhen blue-and-white bowl with the decoration of the God of Blessing (Fig. 2). One can easily detect the similarity in composition between the two pictures.

Another example is the blue-and-white bowl with a painting of Old Man Longevity. Both Jingdezhen (Fig. 3) and imari (Fig. 4) produced such bowls and their designs are almost identical. There is an Old Man Longevity depicted at the centre of the inner base, with a circle of waves and flowers around the inside wall of the mouth rim. Eight Immortals of Daoism within the round reserved panels are painted on the exterior, and the Chinese character "Shou" 寿 (meaning longevity) appears outside the panels as a background pattern.

Fig. 1 Blue-and-white plate with human figure, imari, 1610–30s (*Early Imari*, ill. 38, Tokyo: NHK, 2004)

Fig. 2 Blue-and-white bowl with human figure, Jingdezhen, 1573–1628 (*Chinese ceramics: The Blue-and-white Porcelain of Jingdezhen Civilian Kilns* 中国陶瓷•景德镇民间青花瓷器, ill. 173, Shanghai: Shanghai People's Fine Arts Publishing House, 1994)

Fig. 3 Blue-and-white bowl with the decoration of Old Man Longevity, imari, 1660–70s (A *Cultural History of Ceramic Ware,* 陶磁器の文化史, p. 58, ill. 123, National Museum of Japanese History, 1998)

Fig. 4 Blue-and-white bowl with the decoration of Old Man Longevity, Jingdezhen, 1600–40s (A *Cultural History of Ceramic Ware,* p. 58, ill. 124, National Museum of Japanese History, 1998)

In terms of decoration, the imari bowl is almost an exact reproduction of the Jingdezhen one.

(b) The Design of Landscape

The landscapes on early imari are obviously influenced by Jingdezhen ware. Most landscapes on imari at that time have certain distinctive characteristics. The layout is spare, the brushwork is simple and there is a considerable amount

Fig. 5 Blue-and-white plate with landscape design, imari, 1630–40s (*Early Imari*, ill. 38, Tokyo: NHK, 2004)

Fig. 6 Ko-sometsuke square plate with landscape design, Jingdezhen, 1621–28 (*Ko-sometsuke and Shonzui* 古染付 祥瑞, ill. 33, Tokyo: Heibonsha, 1972)

of white space remaining (Fig. 5). It is clear that these landscapes were derived from the Jingdezhen Ko-sometsuke ware, which was especially made for the Japanese market, otherwise the style of early imari could not be so close to that of the Ko-sometsuke's (Fig. 6). There is another category of landscape on early imari, which is painted carefully and precisely with a delicate style; however, the influence of Jingdezhen ware can still be detected from the motifs and

Fig. 7 Blue-and-white plate with landscape design, imari, 1640–50s (*Early Imari*, ill. 99, Tokyo: NHK, 2004)

Fig. 8 Blue-and-white plate with landscape design, Jingdezhen, 1628–44 (Collection of the Tokyo National Museum, *Special Exhibition of Chinese Ceramics* 特別展 中国の陶瓷, ill. 304, Tokyo: Tokyo National Museum, 1994)

border decorations (Figs. 7 and 8). Furthermore, the eroded limestone pattern, which was common on Jingdezhen blue-and-white ware during the Ming dynasty, was also frequently used by imari, sometimes slightly simplified.[11]

(c) The Design of Animals

There is a unique rabbit design on imari (Fig. 9) which is blown onto the porcelain body. Fragments of this kind can be found at kiln sites in Arita. The pattern and method of blowing cobalt onto the porcelain body were influenced by the Ko-sometsuke ware (Fig. 10). Fragments of Jingdezhen wares decorated using this method were unearthed in Japan (Fig. 11). Besides, there is a plum blossom and oriole design on Ko-sometsuke ware. During the 1630s and 1640s, imari

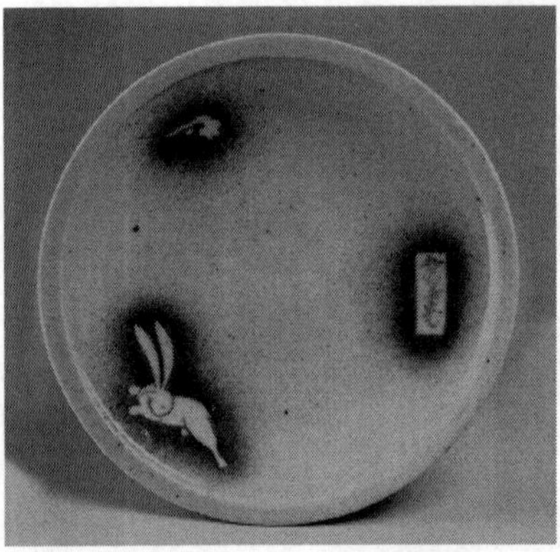

Fig. 9 Blue-and-white plate with rabbit design, imari, 1620–30s (*Early Imari*, ill. 32, Tokyo: NHK, 2004)

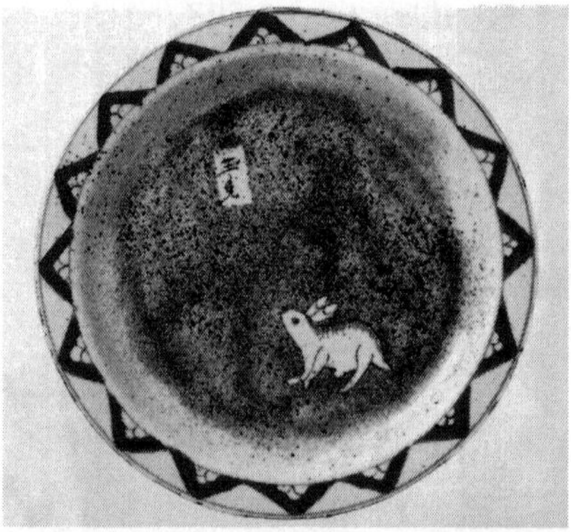

Fig. 10 Blue-and-white plate with rabbit design, Jingdezhen, 1610–20s (*A Cultural History of Ceramic Ware,* p. 51, ill. 112, National Museum of Japanese History, 1998)

Fig. 11 Fragments of late-Ming Jingdezhen blue-and-white wares unearthed at Kaga-han Maeda-ke Edo-yashiki site 加贺藩前田家江户屋敷 (Exhibit in the Tokyo National Museum)

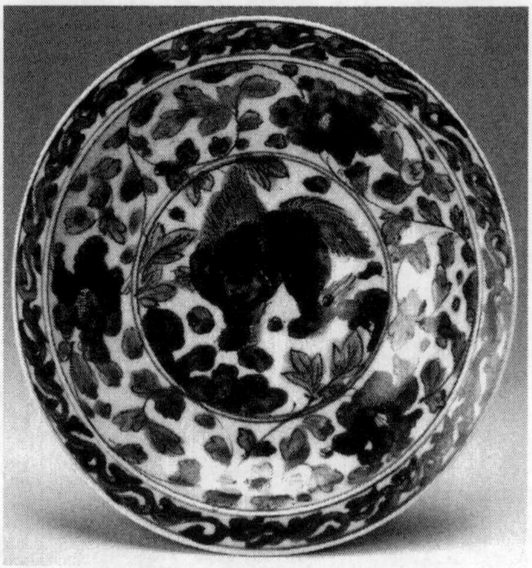

Fig. 12 Plate with flower and lion design, imari, 1630–1940s (*Early Imari*, ill. 42, Tokyo: NHK, 2004)

Fig. 13 Jar with flower and lion design, Jingdezhen, 1573–1628 (*Chinese ceramics, the Blue-and-white Porcelain of Jingdezhen Civilian Kilns*, ill. 165, Shanghai: Shanghai People's Fine Arts Publishing House, 1994)

used it as a model for imitation. Fragments of this kind were unearthed at the Kama-no-tsuji kiln site in Kineshima-gun, Yamauchi-cho, Saga Prefecture.[12]

Apart from that, the decoration of flowers and lions on imari (Fig. 12) is also a popular Chinese pattern of the civilian kilns at Jingdezhen (Fig. 13).

(d) The Design of Plants

Designs of plants such as peonies, chrysanthemums, grapes, interlocking sprays, plum blossoms, orchids, etc., are common in early imari. However, on Jingdezhen ware, we can find quite a few similar patterns, which are possibly the origins of the plant designs on imari. It is possible that the imari design of grapes, illustrated in Fig. 14, is copied from the Ko-sometsuke design shown in Fig. 15. The fragments of imari plates with the design of interlocking sprays of peonies, unearthed at the Kama-no-tsuji kiln site, Saga Prefecture,[13] remind us of a similar design on the blue-and-white porcelain that was prevalent during the mid- Ming period. Again, this is an imitation of the popular design of blue-and-white Ming porcelain.

(e) Imitation of a Popular Chinese Motif

During the period between the end of the Ming and the early Qing dynasties, Chibifu, a famous piece of rhyming text written by Sushi, an eminent poet of

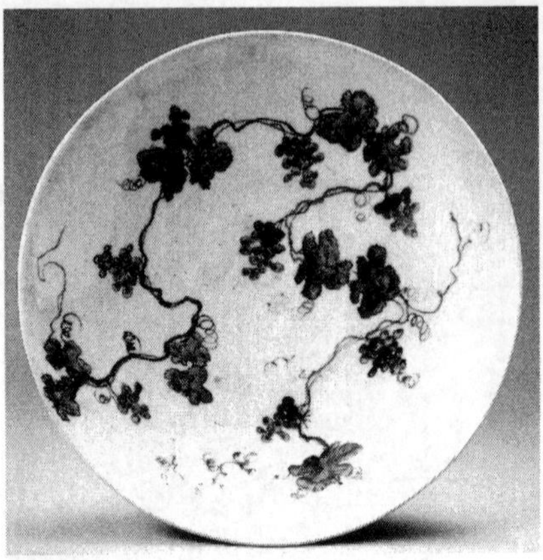

Fig. 14 Plate with the design of grapes, imari, 1610–1930s (*Early Imari*, ill. 42, Tokyo: NHK, 2004)

Fig. 15 Jar with the design of grapes, Jingdezhen, early seventeenth century (Collection of the Idemitsu Museum of Arts, A *Cultural History of Ceramic Ware*, p. 161, ill. 47, National Museum of Japanese History, 1998)

the Northern Song Dynasty, became a popular subject matter for the paintings on Jingdezhen ware. The scene of Sushi sightseeing on a boat at Chibi in the evening was frequently painted on porcelain (Fig. 17). Imari borrowed this motif from Jingdezhen ware (Fig. 16).

Fig. 16 Plate with the decoration of Sushi sightseeing at Chibi, imari, 1630–1940s (A *Cultural History of Ceramic Ware*, p. 50, ill. 111, National Museum of Japanese History, 1998)

Fig. 17 Plate with the decoration of Sushi sightseeing at Chibi, Jingdezhen, 1610–1930s (A *Cultural History of Ceramic Ware*, p. 50, ill. 110, National Museum of Japanese History, 1998)

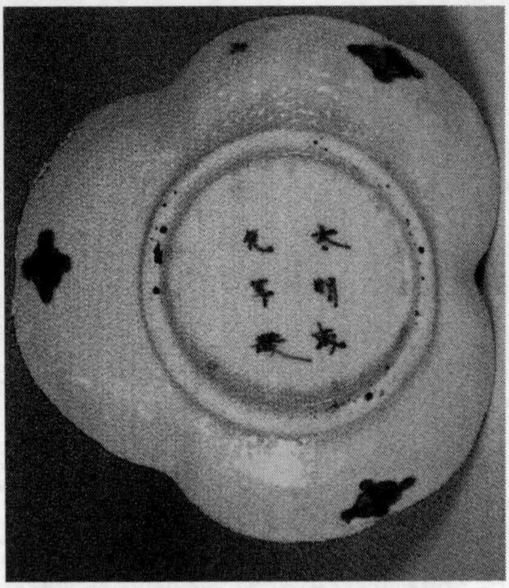

Fig. 18 Imari inscription of "Tai Ming Chenghua Nianzhi" 太明成化年制 (A *Cultural History of Ceramic Ware*, p. 50, ill. 114. Left, National Museum of Japanese History, 1998)

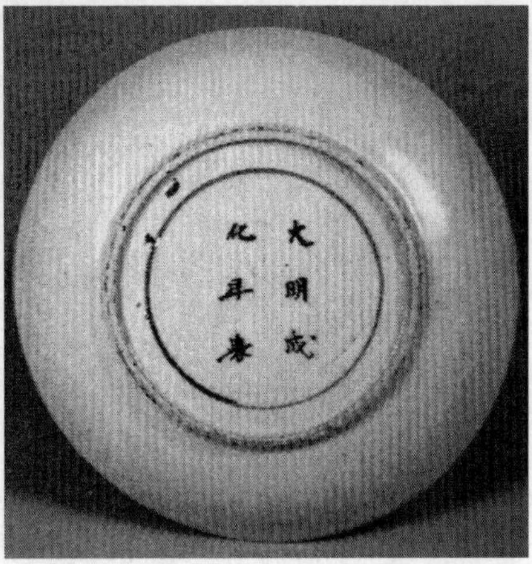

Fig. 19 Jingdezhen inscription of "Da Ming Chenghua Nianzhi" 大明成化年制 (*Polychrome Porcelain in the Late Ming-Early Qing Period: Iroe-Shonzui•Nanking-Akae•Koki-gosai* 明末•清初の五彩磁器 色絵祥瑞•南京赤绘•康熙五彩, p. 48, ill. 11, Kyoto: Kyoto National Museum, 1993)

(f) Border Decoration

In addition to motifs, imari borrowed border decorations from Jingdezhen ware. Designs of plantain leaves, the headpiece of Ruyi-sceptre (Fig. 5), crenelated bands, brocade and other popular border decorations in Jingdezhen can be found on imari too.

(ii) Imitation of Inscriptions

Imari also imitated the inscriptions on Jingdezhen porcelain.[14] At that time, there was a trend for the Jingdezhen civilian kilns to forge the reign marks of preceding dynasties, among which the inscriptions of "Da Ming Chenghua Nianzhi" 大明成化年制 (Made in the Chenghua Reign, Ming Dynasty) (Fig. 19) and "Da Ming Xuande Nianzhi" 大明宣德年制 (Made in the Xuande Reign, Ming Dynasty) were the most popular. The Japanese followed suit, using inscriptions like "Da Ming Chenghua Nianzhi", "Xuande Nianzhi", etc. Sometimes, there were incorrect characters or slight differences, such as "Tai Ming Chenghua Nianzhi" 太明成化年制 (Fig. 18) ,"Da Ming" 大明, "Tai Ming" 太明, "Da Ming Cheng" 大明成, etc. Furthermore, apart from reign marks, auspicious phrases were also popular inscriptions among civilian kilns in

Fig. 20 Imari inscription of "Fu" 福 (*Early Imari*, ill. 44, Tokyo: NHK, 2004)

Fig. 21 Jingdezhen inscription of "Fu" 福 (*Polychrome Porcelain in the Late Ming-Early Qing Period: Iroe-Shonzui•Nanking-Akae•Koki-gosai*, p. 48, ill. 11, Kyoto: Kyoto National Museum, 1993)

Jingdezhen. For example, the inscription "Fu" 福 (Fig. 21), (meaning good fortune) was adopted by imari (Fig. 20). After a close analysis of the inscriptions on vessel bases in the seventeenth century, Murakami Nobuyuki concluded that, during the first phase (roughly from 1610 to 1650), imari mainly imitated the Ming inscription of "Fu" with double square outlines while, during the second phase (from 1640 to 1690), in addition to the "Fu" inscription, there were inscriptions such as "Da Ming", "Tai Ming Nianzhi", "Tai Ming Chenghua Nianzhi", "Tai Ming Jiajing Nianzhi", "Xuande Nianzhi", "Wuliang Dafu" 五良大甫, cursive script "Fu" with double square outlines, and so on. Furthermore, according to Murakami Nobuyuki, some popular Jingdezhen "hall name" inscriptions, such as "Yuxiang Zhai" 雨香斋, and "Zhushi Ju" 竹石居 can also be found on imari ware of the second phase.[15]

(iii) Imitation of Ko-sometsuke and Shonzui Porcelain

Among the Jingdezheng porcelain exported to Japan in the late Ming period, there are two unique types, called Ko-sometsuke and Shonzui, which were made to the special orders of Japan, probably for use during tea ceremonies. They catered to the Japanese aesthetic taste and were deeply appreciated by the tea masters in Japan. Therefore, imari imitated both types.

Ko-sometsuke is a kind of blue-and-white porcelain produced by Jingdezhen civilian kilns and was exported to Japan during the Tianqi reign. It has a naïve, simple, spontaneous and free style. The blue-and-white colour smacks of grey and the glaze is tinted with blue, with occasional spots cause by the shrinkage of the glaze. The most distinctive characteristic of Ko-sometsuke ware is that on its mouth rim and edges there are certain peeling traces as if the porcelain has been nibbled by worms (known as "moth-eaten" edges in Japan). There are mukouzuke (dishes), tebachi (dishes with a handle), kougou (incense containers), mizusashi (fresh water jars), hanaike (vases) and mizutsugi (ewers), especially designed for use during tea ceremonies. There are various shapes designed according to Japanese tastes and styles, some of which resemble plants and animals in nature, such as fish, shrimps, mandarin ducks, horses, lions, camels, butterflies, cicadas, leaves, peaches, fans, rivers (resembling the Chinese character "人"), drums, etc. A certain kind of Ko-sometsuke ware is even moulded into the shape of Fuji Mountain, which fills it with distinctive Japanese characteristics. In fact, wooden models with painted patterns were furnished in Japan first and then sent to kilns in China for the potters to copy. Furthermore, some of the Ko-sometsuke patterns follow the Japanese style also. The patterns mainly include: (1) figures: arhat, immortals, children at play; (2) animals: tigers, deer, eagles, elephants, crabs and shrimps; (3) landscapes; (4) plants: cherry blossom, maple leaves and grapes; and (5) others: umbrellas, the eight divinatory trigrams, netlike designs, circles, and geometric designs. Sometimes, there are even poems written on this porcelain. Only a very small number of such vessels are preserved in China now. Ko-sometsuke had a great impact on the style of early imari. A detailed comparison between the two was made by Yabe Yoshiaki, who found more than twenty similar patterns between Ko-sometsuke and imari, and made a clear chart to illustrate these similarities. To name just a few of the identical patterns pointed out by Yabe Yoshiaki, there are landscapes, fishing scenes, scenes of going to town, pine trees, plum blossom, the eight divinatory trigrams, dragons, phoenixes, etc.[16]

Shonzui got its name from the eight-character inscription, "Wuliang dafu Wuxiangrui Zao" (Made by Wuxiangrui), found on some of the vessels of this type. Shonzui ware can be divided into two groups: underglaze blue and polychrome. Most Shonzui ware is blue-and-white. It is painted in a bright, rich blue color, and there is differentiation between thick and thin, and deep and shallow washes. The paintings are naturalistic and fresh, and are often accompanied by poems. The glaze around the mouth rim is brown. Obviously, all of these characteristics mentioned above are typical of the transitional porcelain produced during the Chongzhen reign. Therefore, generally speaking, Shonzui ware was also produced during that period. Polychrome Shonzui refers to similar vessels decorated in underglaze blue and overglaze enamels. Most Shonzui ware was used during tea ceremonies and kaiseki ryōri. There are small boxes, jars, bowls for drinking tea, tokkuri (vases), sara (plates), patras and cups, most of which differ from the vessels used in China. Their border decoration has

Fig. 22 Shonzui bowl unearthed at Bunkyou-ku in Toukyou-to (Exhibit in the Tokyo National Museum)

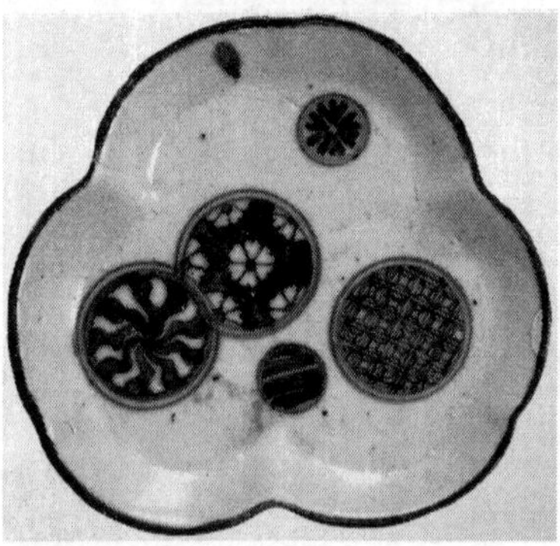

Fig. 23 Shonzui plate, imari, 1640s (A *Cultural History of Ceramic Ware,* p. 51, ill. 114 Right, National Museum of Japanese History, 1998)

Fig. 24 Shonzui fresh water jar, Jingdezhen, early seventeenth century (*Ko-sometsuke and shonzui,* ill. 21, Tokyo: Heibonsha, 1972)

a distinctive Japanese style too: there are linked geometric patterns and small round panels with geometric patterns, landscapes or figures inside. Shonzui ware constitutes a considerable proportion of the seventeenth-century Chinese porcelain unearthed in Japan. Fig. 22 is a Shonzui bowl unearthed at Bunkyō-ku in Tokyo-to don. On its base is inscribed, "Wuliang Dafu Wuxiangzhui Zao". Shonzui ware was relished by the Japanese tea masters, and was imitated by imari. For instance, the round panels on the imari blue-and-white plate in Shonzui style (Fig. 23) resemble those on the Jingdezhen porcelain (Fig. 24). Besides, the glaze around its mouth rim is brown too. It should be noted that, in the 1740s, imari developed a new style by imitating Polychrome Shonzui. Figs. 25 and 26 show two polychrome plates with the decoration of landscapes, birds and flowers. The two plates were among the collection of Nabeshima Katsushige, the daimyo of Saga, and were kept in the same case.[17] The imari

Fig. 25 Polychrome plate with the decoration of landscape, birds and flowers, imari, 1640s (*Early Imari*, ill. 89, Tokyo: NHK, 2004)

Fig. 26 Polychrome plate with the decoration of landscape, birds and flowers, Jingdezhen, 1620–40s (*Early Imari*, ill. 88, Tokyo: NHK, 2004)

Fig. 27 Bottom of the polychrome plate with the decoration of landscape, birds and flowers, imari, 1640s (*Early Imari*, ill. 89, Tokyo: NHK, 2004)

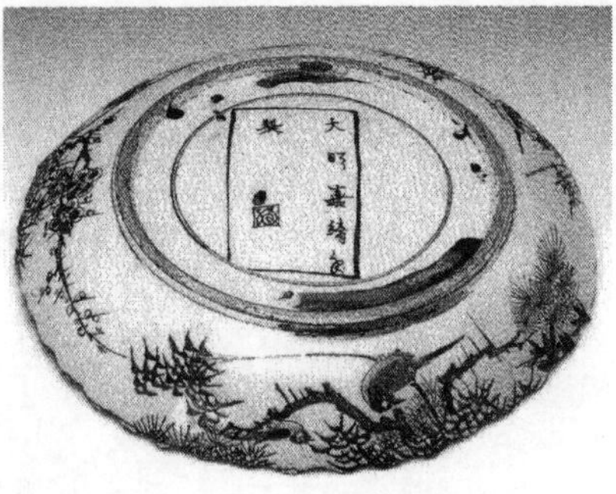

Fig. 28 Bottom of the polychrome plate with the decoration of landscape, birds and flowers, Jingdezhen, 1620–40s (*Early Imari*, ill. 88, Tokyo: NHK, 2004)

polychrome plate (Fig. 27) copied the exact shape as well as the interior and exterior decoration of the polychrome Shonzui. Only the inscriptions on their bottoms differ.

(iv) Imitation of the Imperial Porcelain from Jingdezhen

It is interesting that imari copied faithfully the early-Ming imperial porcelain in terms of both its shape and decoration. The gourd-shaped pilgrim flask with

Fig. 29 Gourd shaped pilgrim flask with ribbon handles, imari, 17th century (*Ceramic Art of the World Volume 8: the Edo period III* 世界陶磁全集8 江户 (三), p. 161, ill. 109, Tokyo: Shōgakkan, 1978)

Fig. 30 Gourd shaped pilgrim flask with ribbon handles, Jingdezhen, Yongle (Exhibit in the Shanghai Museum)

ribbon handles (Fig. 30) was popular during the Yongle and Xuande reigns. Its shape originated from Islamic gold and silver ware, and imari adopted the shape in the seventeenth century (Fig. 29).

IV. *Tangshi Huapu* 唐诗画谱 (the Tang Poetry Painting Manual): A Medium for the Ceramic Art Exchange between China and Japan in the Seventeenth Century

(i) *Tangshi Huapu* and the Transitional Porcelain in Jingdezhen

With the decline of the imperial kilns in the late Ming/early Qing periods, the kiln workers could no longer copy the Imperial ware designs, so they turned to woodblock prints and painting manuals for inspiration, employing them as new models for porcelain painting. Thus, *Tangshi Huapu* became an important source of porcelain designs at that time. *Tangshi Huapu*, also known as *Jiya Zhai Huapu*, *Bazhong Huapu*, was compiled by Huang Fengchi, the master of Jiyazhai Studio in Xin'an, at the end of the Ming period. *Tangshi Huapu* consists of a total of eight volumes: namely, *Wuyan Tangshi Huapu* 五言唐诗画谱 (A Painting Manual illustrating Tang Poems with Five Characters to a Line); *Liuyan Tangshi Huapu* 六言唐诗画谱, *Qiyan Tangshi Huapu* 七言唐诗画谱, *Mei Lan Zhu Ju Sipu* 梅竹兰菊四谱 (A Painting Manual of Plum Blossoms, Orchids, Bamboo and Chrysanthemums); *Tang Xieyuan Fanggujin Huapu* 唐解元仿古今画谱 (A Painting Manual of Tang Bohu's Imitation of Antique and Present Paintings); *Zhangbaigong Xuan Minggong Shanpu* 张白云选名公扇谱 (Zhangbaigong's Selection of Fans painted by Celebrities): *Muben Huaniao Pu* 木本花鸟谱 (A Painting Manual of Wood Flowers and Birds); and *Caoben Huashi Pu* 草本花诗谱 (A Painting Manual of Herbaceous Flowers Accompanied by Poems). The format is as follows: there is a painting on one page, and, on the reverse side, a poem is printed. The painting and the poem supplement and enrich each other, creating a perfect match. Published in the first half of the seventeenth century, it was widely applauded by the literati.

The merit of *Tangshi Huapu* is that it provides the reader not only with Tang poems for chanting, but also with the poems' artistic moods reflected in the accompanying illustrations for a fuller enjoyment, which will doubtless bring the reader much artistic gratification. This characteristic had a fundamental influence on the decoration of the transitional porcelain in Jingdezhen at the end of the Ming and early Qing dynasties. The practice of combining poetry, calligraphy, painting and seals in the decoration on transitional period porcelain was inspired by *Tangshi Huapu*. Some designs on porcelain were directly borrowed from the painting manuals. For example, Wang Qingzheng once pointed out that the poetry and the painting (Fig. 32) depicting the Tang poetry mood on a blue-and-white vase (Fig. 31) with a high ring foot and a long neck in the collection of the Shanghai Museum were based on the illustration of Wangwei's poem, *Zhu li Guan* (The Inn among the Bamboos) in *Tangshi Huapu* (Figs. 33 and 34).[18] Another example is a plate salvaged from the Hatcher Junk. It is blue-and-white with the design of human

Fig. 31 Blue-and-white vase reflecting Tang poetry moods (Exhibit in the Shanghai Museum)

Fig. 32 A part of the blue-and–white vase reflecting Tang poetry moods (Exhibit in the Shanghai Museum)

Fig. 33 Illustration for *Zhu li Guan*, *Tangshi Huapu* (Huang Fengchi, *Tangshi huapu* 唐诗画谱, Shanghai: Shanghai Chinese Classics Publishing House, 1982)

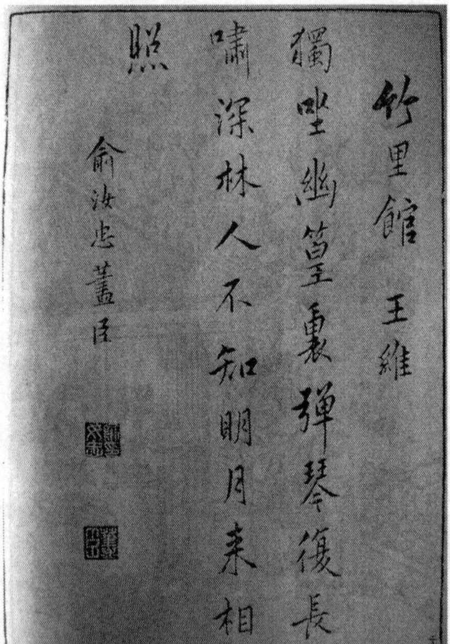

Fig. 34 *Zhu Li Guan* poem (Huang Fengchi, *Tangshi huapu*, Shanghai: Shanghai Chinese Classics Publishing House, 1982)

Fig. 35 Blue-and-white plate with the design of human figures in a snowy landscape (Richard Kiburn, "The Hatcher Junk (1643–46)", p. 53, pl. 65, The Hatcher Porcelain Cargoes, Phaidon: Christies' Limited, 1988)

Fig. 36 Illustration for "Lodging on Hibiscus Mountain after Encountering Snow" *Tangshi Huapu* (Shanghai: Shanghai Chinese Classics Publishing House, 1982)

figures in a snowy landscape (Fig. 35). The painting depicts a literatus dressed in white riding a horse slowly along a mountain path covered with snow, with a young male attendant leading the way. This is the same scene as illustrated in "*Lodging on a Hibiscus Mountain after Encountering Snow*" 逢雪宿芙蓉山 (Fig. 36). The content is the same as that of the woodblock print, which was probably used as a model.

Tangshi Huapu produced not only new models for decoration, but also a fresh style with literati taste to the transitional porcelain.[19]

(ii) *Hasshu gafu* and imari

As noted before, during the late Ming-early Qing period, *Tangshi Huapu* and other painting manuals prevailing in the late Ming dynasty became the models for paintings on civilian porcelain in Jingdezhen. However, these painting manuals were introduced into Japan during the Kan'ei reign (1624–44). In the twelfth year (1672) of the Kanbun reign, *Hasshu gafu* was first block-printed and published in Japan, and a copy of the first edition, published by Karahonya in Kyoto, is still kept in Aizu-bunko at Waseda University in Japan. *Hasshu gafu* had a widespread influence in Japan. Some painting manuals were deliberately copied by literati painters, like Hattori Nangaku (1683–1759),

Fig. 37 Plate of a shepherd boy playing the flute with Chuimo method, imari, 1610–30s (*Early Imari*, ill. 6, Tokyo: NHK, 2004)

Fig. 38 *Mushu* 牧竖 (shepherd boy) *Tangshi Wuyan Huapu* (Shanghai: Shanghai Chinese Classics Publishing House, 1982)

Ikeno Taiga (1723–76). Occasionally, these painters made innovations based on imitation. The painting manuals were the models for various handicraft articles, such as ceramics, textiles, handiwork inlaid with mother-of-pearl and sculpture. Pictures on imari absorbed the content and subject matter of *Hasshu gafu* or imitated its paintings directly. As noted previously, from the late Ming to the early Qing periods, there was a prevailing custom among Jingdezhen potters to use woodblock paints as their models for porcelain decoration. Although, at present, we cannot allege that it was this custom in Jingdezhen that eventually affected the practice of Japanese porcelain making, the phenomenon that the same painting manuals were used as models for both Chinese and Japanese porcelain in similar periods should be carefully examined.

The relationship between *Hasshu gafu* and Japanese porcelain was mentioned by a Japanese scholar, Saito Kikutaro, as early as the 1960s.[20] In recent years, Arakawa Masaaki has published several papers analyzing the impact of *Hasshu gafu* on Hizen porcelain.[21] He carefully compared the pictures in the painting manual with the designs on the porcelains and found several similarities, three of which were on early imari. (1) Plate of a shepherd boy playing the flute using Chuimo method (a method of painting by blowing cobalt onto the porcelain body) (Fig. 37) using *Mushu* 牧竖 (the shepherd boy) (Fig. 38) in *Tangshi Wuyan Huapu* as a model. (2) Plate with human figure and pavilion

Fig. 39 Plate with human figure and pavilion design imari, 1610–30s (*Early Imari*, ill. 4, Tokyo: NHK, 2004)

Fig. 40 *Xiju* 溪居 (pavilion along the riverside) *Tangshi Wuyan Huapu* (Shanghai: Shanghai Chinese Classics Publishing House, 1982)

design (Fig. 39) using *XiJu* 溪居 (pavilion along the riverside) (Fig. 40) in *Tangshi Wuyan Huapu* as a model. (3) Plate with human figure and zigzag bridge design (Fig. 41) using *Chunye* 春夜 (the spring night) (Fig. 42) in *Tangshi Wuyan Huapu* as a model. As for polychrome imari, there are 7 examples: (1) Polychrome plate with the decoration of human figure under a pine tree (collection of the British Museum) using *Chunye* in *Tangshi Wuyan Huapu* as a model. (2) Polychrome plate with the decoration of human figure on a bridge using *Jiangcun Yegui* 江村夜归 (returning home at night from a river village) in *Tangshi Wuyan Huapu* as a model. (3) Polychrome plate with human figure and pavilion design using *Shijia Ren* 示家人 (message to family members) in *Tangshi Wuyan Huapu* as a model. (4) Patra decorated with underglaze blue and overglaze enamels of human figures in the boat design (Fig. 43) using *Songren You Hunan* 送人游湖南 (farewell to a friend setting out for Hunan) (Fig. 44) in *Tangshi Wuyan Huapu* as a model. (5) Polychrome plate with the decoration of a human figure (Fig. 45) using *Jiachuan Dufan* 葭川独泛 (boating alone at Jiachuan) (Fig. 46) in *Tangshi Wuyan Huapu* as a model. (6) Polychrome plate with the decoration of human figure in reserved panels using *Ou You Zhuren Yuan* 偶游主人园 (an occasional visit to the master's garden) in *Tangshi Wuyan Huapu* as a model. (7) Polychrome plate with the decoration of human figure under a pine tree using *Youren Yefang Ren* 友人夜访 (a night visit from a friend) in *Tangshi Wuyan Huapu* as a model.[22]

Fig. 41 Plate with human figure and zigzag bridge design, imari, 1640–50s (*Early Imari*, ill. 94, Tokyo: NHK, 2004)

Fig. 42 *Chunye* 春夜 (spring night), *Tangshi Wuyan Huapu* (Shanghai: Shanghai Chinese Classics Publishing House, 1982)

Fig. 43 Patra decorated in underglaze blue and overglaze enamels with human figures in the boat design imari, 1640s (*Early Imari*, ill. 96, Tokyo: NHK, 2004)

Fig. 44 Songren You Hunan 送人游湖南 (farewell to a friend setting off for Hunan), *Tangshi Wuyan Huapu* (Shanghai: Shanghai Chinese Classics Publishing House, 1982)

Fig. 45 Polychrome plate with the decoration of human figure, imari, mid-seventeenth century (Arakawa Masaaki, *Hizen Porcelain and the Hasshu gafu*, ill. 2 on colored plates, Tokyo: Idemitsu Museum of Arts, *Journal of Art Historical Research*, Vol. 5, 1999)

Fig. 46 Jiachuan Dufan 葭川独泛 (boating alone at Jiachuan), *Tangshi Wuyan Huapu* (Shanghai: Shanghai Chinese Classics Publishing House, 1982)

Being the common origin of paintings on both Chinese and Japanese porcelain in the seventeenth century, *Hasshu gafu* played a unique role as a medium in the ceramic art exchange between China and Japan.

V. Export Imari's Imitation of Chinese Porcelain

Because of the change of dynasty from the Ming to Qing, the export of Chinese porcelain came to a halt, but the demand for porcelain from China remained strong in the European market. Imari, with its similar style to Jingdezhen ware, was chosen by the Europeans as a substitute, which gave imari an opportunity to gain historical significance. The first recorded purchase of Japanese porcelain by the Dutch East India Company was in 1650, and the volume was relatively small: only 145 pieces. Nevertheless, the company ordered large quantities of Japanese porcelain (up to 56,700 pieces) in 1659. In the 1660s, the export of Japanese porcelain flourished, and from 1673 to 1683, the output of imari porcelain ordered by the Dutch reached its peak. Spurred by extensive exportation, imari developed rapidly.

The need for exportation inspired imari to learn from Jingdezhen. The export imari imitated Jingdezhen Kraak porcelain and the European-style ware among the transitional porcelain.

Fig. 47 Plate decorated with flowers and panels, imari, 1680–1710s (*Exhibition of Export Ko-imari* 《海を渡った古伊万里展》, ill. 52, Fukuoka: Nishi-Nippon shinbunsha, 1993)

Fig. 48 Plate decorated with flowers and panels, Jingdezhen, 1573–1620 (Collection of the Hayashibara museum, Okayama Japan *Special Exhibition of the Chinese Ceramics* 特別展 中国の陶瓷, ill. 303, Tokyo: Tokyo National Museum, 1994)

(i) Export Imari's Imitation of Kraak

Kraak is characterized by its division of the surface into certain panels as a decoration. Most Kraak ware is blue-and-white, and only a small proportion of it is polychrome. There are plates, bowls, vases, Kendi, etc., among which large plates are the largest in quantity and the most typical in style. The characteristic of their decoration is distinctive: generally, the motifs on the central field are flowers, flower baskets, birds and animals. Occasionally, human figures are used as motifs. The wide sloping rim is usually divided into eight, ten or twelve fan-shaped or oval panels. The panels are filled with flowers, miscellaneous treasures and other patterns, which are arranged one after another. The panels are separated by columns of brocade design. The outlines of petals or panels on some plates are moulded as a further decoration. The exterior of most of the plates are decorated with corresponding panels too. The layout is complex, with a full and dense decoration, but the effect is harmonious.

Kraak is called huyō-de in Japan, because it looks like a lotus in full blossom. Kraak was a primary type of export porcelain in the late Ming-early Qing period, and was an important kind of commodity sold to Europe by the Dutch East India Company. Kraak ware is found in large quantities not only in Japan, but also in Southeast Asia and Europe. Imari imitated Kraak too. The imari plate with a flower design (Fig. 47) looks like a duplicate of the Kraak ware made in Jingdezhen (Fig. 48). The flower basket motif on the

Fig. 49 Plate decorated with flowers and panels, imari, 1660–80 (*Porcelain in Palaces* 宮廷の陶磁器, p. 94, ill. 32, Kyoto: Dōhōsha Shuppan Co., 1994)

Fig. 50 Blue-and-white Kendi decorated with flowers and panels. Left: imari, Right: Jingdezhen (*The Inter-influence of Ceramic Art between the East and the West* 陶磁の東西交流, ill. 34, 33, Tokyo: Idemitsu Museum of Arts, 1984)

central field and the eight panels filled with flowers and miscellaneous treasures are extremely alike. The mark "VOC", which stands for the Dutch East India Company, can be found on some Kraak-style ware made in Arita (Fig. 49). In addition to imitating the typical Kraak plate, imari copied some unique shapes, like Kendi (Fig. 50).

(ii) Export Imari's Imitation of the Transitional Porcelain

In the late Ming and early Qing period (from the end of the Wanli reign of the Ming dynasty to the early Kangxi period of the Qing), changes occurred in the Jingdezhen blue-and-white porcelain produced by civilian kilns. Porcelain appeared with a relatively fine body and fresh, naturalistic paintings in a bright, rich blue. Such porcelain is referred to in ceramic circles abroad as "Chinese porcelain of the transitional period" and is known for its fine quality. The transitional porcelain had a large overseas market and was especially popular in Europe. Imari copied the Jingdezhen transitional ware in various ways. For example, in imitation of the transitional porcelain, imari produced pitchers in the European style, which were manufactured in Jingdezhen during the transitional period. Imari pots of this kind were manufactured for the overseas market, and the decoration on the pots was borrowed from Jingdezhen too. The tulip, the national flower of the Netherlands, is painted on both Jingdezhen and imari blue-and-white pitchers (Fig. 51). Besides, the motifs on both pots are human figures, which is possibly a deliberate choice. Imari also copied some typical vessels of the transitional period, such as bottle with a bulbous mouth (Fig. 52) and the rolwagen (Fig. 53). The rolwagen, popular in Jingdezhen

Fig. 51 Pitcher with the decoration of human figures and tulips. Left: imari, Right: Jingdezhen (*The Inter-influence of Ceramic Art between the East and the West,* ill. 26, 25, Tokyo: Idemitsu Museum of Arts, 1984)

Fig. 52 Blue-and-white bottle with a bulbous mouth. Left: imari, Right: Jingdezhen (*The Inter-influence of Ceramic Art between the East and the West,* ill. 21, 20, Tokyo: Idemitsu Museum of Arts, 1984)

Fig. 53 Blue-and-white rolwagen with human figures, imari, 1660–80 (*Porcelain in Palaces,* p. 97, ill. 38, Kyoto: Dōhōsha Shuppan Co., 1994)

Fig. 54 Blue-and-white bottle with a bulbous mouth, Jingdezhen, 1628–44 (Exhibit in the Shanghai Museum)

Fig. 55 Kakiemon polychrome pot with a flower design, end of the seventeenth century (*The Kyushu Ceramic Museum Collection*, ill. 68, Saga: Saga Prefectural Museum of Kyūshū Ceramic Arts, 1987)

Fig. 56 Polychrome pot with a flower design, Jingdezhen, 1690–1700 (*Porcelain in Palaces*, p. 234, ill. 252, Kyoto: Dōhōsha Shuppan Co., Ltd, 1994)

during the transitional period, is a rare type in imari. It can be inferred that the imari rolwagen was a special kind of export porcelain produced in imitation of the Jingdezhen ware.

VI. Kakiemon Ware and the Chinese imari: the Influence of Japanese Porcelain on Chinese Ceramics

The 1640s witnessed the emergence of polychrome imari and, in the 1670s, a new colouring type called Kakiemon appeared. The porcelain known by this name is distinctive of the Japanese style and aesthetic: brightly coloured decorations are painted onto the white glaze, and the effect of the white space is emphasized. From the end of the seventeenth into the eighteenth centuries, another type of imari porcelain, Somenishiki-de, was manufactured. Somenishiki-de is noted for its luxurious and gorgeous style with underglaze blue, overglaze enamels and gold decoration. Kakiemon-style porcelain and Somenishiki ware were popular in Europe and were imitated by European porcelain factories like Meissen in Germany and Worcester in Great Britain. In the eighteenth century, Jingdezhen ware began to be exported to Europe again. To meet the needs of the European market, Chinese porcelain imitated the polychrome imari, and a type called "Chinese imari" was manufactured. For instance, in the ceramic collection of the Queen of Great Britain, there is a Jingdezhen polychrome pot fired during the Kangxi reign (Fig. 56).[23] There are eight panels filled with flowers on the body of the pot, and the spout and handle are decorated with interlocking sprays. As far as the shape, the flower design and the colour are concerned, the pot is an exact reproduction of the Kakiemon pot shown in

Fig. 57 Polychrome chrysanthemum plate with petal rim, imari, eighteenth century (*The Inter-influence of Ceramic Art between the East and the West*, ill. 125, Tokyo: Idemitsu Museum of Arts, 1984)

Fig. 58 Polychrome chrysanthemum plate with petal rim, Jingdezhen, eighteenth century (*The Inter-influence of Ceramic Art between the East and the West*, ill. 126, Tokyo: Idemitsu Museum of Arts, 1984)

Fig. 55. Among the Somenishiki ware popular in the eighteenth century, there is a kind of flower plate with a petal rim (Fig. 57). The petal-shaped panel on the central field is painted with chrysanthemums. The wide sloping rim is decorated mainly with a brocade design, and there are a few chrysanthemums and plum blossoms on the rim also. Both the brocade design and the flowers are enriched with gold traces, which make the plate look luxuriously gorgeous. The decoration of chrysanthemums on the wide rim as a method for adding some white space to the dense decoration is a typical Japanese touch. This kind of plate was imitated both by the Jingdezhen kilns and the Worcester kiln in the Great Britain, but the Jingdezhen products are closer to the originals in all aspects except for the fact that they are slightly larger.[24]

It should be noted that both Chinese and Japanese export porcelains were affected by the tastes of their overseas consumers in the eighteenth century. The emergence of "Chinese imari porcelain" was spurred on by the requirements of the European market. There was a special kind of custom-made ware in both Chinese and Japanese export porcelains. They were made according to the sample manuscript provided by the European buyers. The well-known "Parasol Design" provides us with a good example of this. The design of the Jingdezhen plate (Fig. 59) is based on a European sample manuscript (Fig. 61), as is the case with the imari piece (Fig. 60). Nevertheless, as far as the style of painting is concerned, there are some slight differences between the three. The ladies on the original manuscript have a touch of the Indian style, but they are localized

Fig. 59 Polychrome plate with the Parasol design, Jingdezhen, 1730–40s (*A Cultural History of Ceramic Ware*, p. 62, ill. 136, National Museum of Japanese History, 1998)

Fig. 60 Polychrome plate with the Parasol design, imari, 1730–40s (*A Cultural History of Ceramic Ware*, p. 62, ill. 135, National Museum of Japanese History, 1998)

Fig. 61 Sample manuscript by the European purchasers, 1734 (*A Cultural History of Ceramic Ware*, p. 62, ill. 136, National Museum of Japanese History, 1998)

on the Chinese and Japanese plates. Competition between Chinese and Japanese export porcelain could hardly be avoided, and I leave the relevant questions for further discussions later.

VII. Conclusion

In the seventeenth century, Chinese porcelain was exported to Japan in large quantities, and then exerted a deep influence on early imari blue-and-white ware. Imari learnt its decoration, inscriptions, etc. from Jingdezhen porcelain. Ko-sometsuke and Shonzui porcelain, which were exported to Japan in large volume and were deeply appreciated by the Japanese, influenced the styles of the early blue-and-white and polychrome imari respectively. In the ceramic art exchange between China and Japan, *Tangshi Huapu*, being the common origin of both Chinese and Japanese porcelain decorations, played a unique role as a medium during that period.

During its process of development, imari seized an opportunity of historical significance. In the 1650s, there was a sharp decrease in the volume of export Chinese porcelain. Chosen as a substitute for Chinese porcelain, imari took over and came to dominate the European market. This further inspired the export Japanese porcelain to imitate Kraak ware, the transitional porcelain and other export porcelains produced in Jingdezhen. In the late seventeenth century, imari won the European market with its creative porcelain, such as Kakiemon and Somenishiki ware. The end of the seventeenth and the beginning of the eighteenth centuries witnessed the revival of export Chinese porcelain. Hence began the Sino-Japanese competition over porcelain exportation. To win back the European market, Jingdezhen porcelain absorbed the painting style of polychrome imari, and porcelain of this kind is known as Chinese imari. The mutual influence and competition between Chinese and Japanese porcelains in the seventeenth and eighteenth centuries reflect not only the ups and downs of the porcelain industry in both countries, but also the international business circumstances of that time.

Acknowledgements

Miss Sugitani Kayoko, a Ph.D candidate at the University of Tsukuba, helped to purchase and copy the relevant source materials for me, and Ms. Chenjie of Fudan University translated this paper into English. I would like to pay tribute to both of them.

Notes

The research is funded by the 2006 Social Science Project of the State Ministry of Education (06JA770010 History).

1. See Xie Mingliang, "*Record of Imari in the Collection of the National Palace Museum*" 记故宫博物院所藏的伊万里瓷器, *Trade Ceramics and Cultural History* 贸易陶瓷与文化史, pp. 139–41, Yuncheng Culture Co. Ltd 允晨文化实业股份公司, Taibei, 2005, for a comprehensive account and discussion in Chinese.
2. Yabe,Yoshiaki, "*The Origin and Development of Early Imarii Blue-and-white Porcelain in Connection with Chinese Ceramics*" 初期伊万里染付の起源と展开一中国陶磁との关联から, *Ceramic Art of the World: Volume 8: the Edo period III* 世界陶磁全集8 江户 (三), Shogakukan Inc., 1978.
   Yabe, Yoshiaki, "*Jingdezhen and Imari Porcelains in the Seventeenth Century: On the Relationship between their Styles*", 17 世纪の景德镇と伊万里——その作風の関連, *Jingdezhen and Imari Porcelains in the Seventeenth Century* 17 世纪の景德镇と伊万里, Saga Prefectural Museum of Kyushu Ceramic Arts, 1982.
3. Murakami Nobuyuki, "The Impact of Ming and Qing Ceramics in Hizen" (肥前における明•清陶磁の影响), *Trade Ceramics Study*, no. 19 (1999).
4. *Ming Shenzong Shilu* 明神宗实录 (Record of the Shenzong, Ming Dynasty), juan 476, the entry of *"Wanli Sanshiba Nian Bingxu"* 万历三十八年十月丙戌条, collated and published by the Institute of History and Philology.
5. Gu Yanwu 顾炎武, "Fujian San, Yangshui" (福建三•洋税), in *Tianxia Junguo Libinshu* (天下郡国利病书), no. 93.
6. Xie Zhaozhe 谢肇淛, "Dibu Er" (地部二) (Earth, part two), 《五杂俎》, no. 4.
7. Xu Guangxi "Haifang Yushuo" (海防迂说) (On Coastal Defence), *The Collected Works of Xu Guangqi* 徐光启集, vol. 1.
8. Nagazumi Youko, *Catalogue of Imports and Exports in Chinese Trades 1637–1833* (Tokyo: Sobunsha, 1987).
9. T. Volker, *Porcelain and the Dutch East India Company* (Leiden: Brill, 1954).
10. Maeyama Hiroshi, "*Ceramic Trading between China and Japan in the Seventeenth Century*" (17 世纪における日本・中国陶磁の贸易), *Jingdezhen and Imari Porcelain in the Seventeenth Century*, pp. 87–90 (Saga Prefectural Museum of Kyushu Ceramic Arts, 1982).
11. Ohashi Koji, *Decorative Patterns of Ko-imari* (古伊万里の纹样) (Tokyo: Rikogakusha Publishing Co., 1994), p. 192 ("eroded limestone").
12. Ohashi Koji, *Decorative Patterns of Ko-imari* "Oriole" (Tokyo: Rikogakusha Publishing Co., 1994), p. 140.
13. Ohashi Koji, *Decorative Patterns of Ko-imari* (Tokyo: Rikogakusha Publishing Co., 1994), p. 76.
14. Ohashi Koji, *Inscriptions on Hizen in the Latter Half of the Seventeenth Century* (十七世纪后半における肥前磁器の铭款にっぃて), *TOYO TOJI* (Oriental Ceramics) no. 17.
15. Murakami Nobuyuki, "The Impact of Ming and Qing Ceramics in Hizen" (肥前における明•清陶磁の影响), *Trade Ceramics Study*, no. 19 (1999): 67, 71–2.
16. Yabe Yoshiaki, A Comparative Table of Early Imari and Chinese Blue-and-white Porcelain (初期伊万里染付•中国青花対照), Ceramic Art of the World: Volume 8: the Edo period III, pp. 182–3 (Tokyo: Shogakukan, 1978).
17. See the descriptions of Illustrations 88 and 89 in *The Exhibition of Ko-imar* (初期伊万里展), p. 185, 2004.

18. Wang Qingzheng, "*Major Changes in the Porcelain Industry at Jingdezhen in the Late Ming-early Qing Periods*" (明末清初景德镇制瓷业的重大转折), *Shanghai Museum Journal* (上海博物馆集刊), no. 7 (Shanghai: Shanghai Calligraphy and Painting Publishing House (上海书画出版社), 1996).
19. See Liu Zhaohui, "Paintings on Porcelain, Woodblock Prints and Literati Taste — A Study of the Decoration on Transitional Blue-and-white Porcelain and the Prevailing Social Customs" *Zhongguo Gutaoci Yanjiu* (中国古陶瓷研究), no. 5, Zijin Cheng Publishing House, 1999, for a detailed analysis.
20. Saito,Kikutaro, "Landscape Paintings on Kokutani and Hasshu gafu (I), (II)" (古九谷山水图と八種画譜), *TOSETSU*, no. 186–187 (1968); "A New Analysis of Kokutani" (古九谷新論), *Kobijutsu*, no. 25 (1969).
21. Arakawa Masaaki, "Characteristic Features of Kokutani Type Ceramic Designs", *MUSEUM*, no. 485 (1991).
    Arakawa Masaaki, "Hizen and Hasshu gafu" (肥前磁器と--[八種画譜」), *Idemitsu Museum of Arts Journal of Art Historical Research*, no. 5 (1999).
    Arakawa Masaaki, *"Chinese Patterns on Early Imari — Landscape Design and Hasshu Gafu* (初期伊万里にみえる唐様の意匠--[八種画譜」と人物図を中心に), *Early Imari: the Origins of Underglaze Cobalt-blue and Overglaze Polychrome Enamels* (初期伊万里展 染付と色絵の誕生), 2004.
22. See Arakawa Masaaki, "Hizen Porcelain and the Hasshu Gafu", *Idemitsu Museum of Arts Journal of Art Historical Research* 5 (1999), for a detailed account.
23. The Oriental Ceramic Society, *Porcelain in Palaces* (宮廷の陶磁器) (Kyōto: Dohosha Shuppan Co., 1994), p. 234.
24. *The Inter-Influence of Ceramic Art between the East and the West* (陶磁の東西交流), p. 39, ill. 125–127 (Idemitsu Museum of Arts, 1984).

Chapter 6

On the Waterfront: Life and Labour Around the Batavian Roadstead

Leonard Blussé

Fig. 1 View on the Batavian Roadstead by Johannes Rach (1720–83). J. de Loos-Haaxman, *Johannes Rach en zijn werk* (Batavia, 1928).

Introduction

In 1619, when Governor-General J.P. Coen informed the directors of the Dutch United East India Company (VOC) that he had conquered the Kingdom of

Jayakarta in western Java and had started to build the new headquarters of the company in Asia from its ashes, he was instructed to name this new city Batavia after the putative valiant ancestors of the Dutch, the tribe of the Batavi who had rebelled against Roman hegemony. The Dutch Republic was, after all, celebrating the fiftieth anniversary of its revolt against the Spanish king, a state of war which would only be ended by the concluding of the Treaty of Munster in 1648.

The new town was to serve as a rendezvous point, as a staple port in the Company's trading network but also as the military headquarters in the struggle against the Portuguese and Spanish colonial empires in Asia. Many of the bricks for the construction of the new castle and the town which was to be built behind it were brought from Holland as ballast in the holds of the Dutch East Indiamen. Even the arches of the city gates were prefabricated in Europe, evidence of which has been provided by the recently retrieved cargo of the *Batavia*, a VOC ship which was tragically shipwrecked on the Abrolhos Reefs off the west coast of Australia in 1629.[1]

Built from scratch in the tropics, the colonial port town of Batavia stirred the imagination of its European visitors. To the sailor who had been at sea for seven months or longer, the walled town, resplendent in its fresh, neat appearance, did indeed present an amazing sight, as suggested by Woodes Rogers' exclamation that he 'was perfectly surprised [...] to see such a noble city and Europeans so well settled in the Indies', when he cast anchor in the city's roadstead in 1710.[2]

Morphology

The Gentlemen Seventeen sent their Governor-General a city plan, designed by the famous mathematician and surveyor, Simon Stevin, in accordance with which they wished him to lay out the new urban settlement in the tropics.[3] The internal lay-out of this city may have been new, as I shall point out, but, by building a castle town close to the shore, Coen emulated the Portuguese pioneers who always chose strategic locations for their colonial settlements. Creating a string of castle towns along the monsoon shipping routes of the millennia-old Asian trading world, the Estado da India sought to control the shipping networks which connected such populous Oriental empires as Safavid Persia and the Mughal Empire in west and south Asia with the many port principalities of the Southeast Asian island world and, from there, with China and Japan in the Far East. The Portuguese deliberately constructed their settlements on small islands or peninsulas so that they could defend themselves against attack by numerically superior forces from the shore. The profiles of these fortified settlements depict castle-like settlements housing *soldados* and *casados* together with their dependents. The Iberians ensured that they lived separately from the surrounding settlements or *kampongs* of Asian traders of many different nationalities, admirably demonstrated by Portuguese Malacca, which controlled the thoroughfare between the Indian Ocean and the South China Sea, and also the Spanish Manila, in which what was known as the Parian or China town was situated *extramuros*, which served as the terminus for the Mexican galleon trade.

Batavia, situated at the mouth of the Ciliwong on the shore of a well-sheltered bay, was criss-crossed by rectangular canals and streets and surrounded by a wide, deep moat and sturdy walls, reinforced with bulwarks constructed of coral stone. The cannons placed on top of these bulwarks faced outwards but could easily be turned around so that they also could rake the main streets of the town in the event of popular unrest or rebellion. The river running in the north-south direction dissected the town and was intersected by canals. Most of the streets and canals were straight, forming a grid-like pattern. The town hall and the main church fronted onto a large city square and a parade ground that connected the town with the entrance to Batavia Castle, which was situated between the sea and the town. Across the river, opposite the castle, were located the company's ship wharves and godowns, and a specially dug basin provided a mooring-place for native craft and the rowboats and lighters which sailed to the ships anchored in the roadstead via the harbour canal.[4]

According to François Valentijn (1666–1727), at the end of the seventeenth century, Batavia had a surprisingly pleasant climate for a town so close to the equator. A refreshing sea breeze arose around ten in the morning and continued to blow until dusk, when, after a short intermission, the land wind would start to pick up. The in-coming and out-going traffic of fishing boats and the native trading craft would exploit these land and sea breezes, leaving in the evening and returning on the morning breeze. Johan Nieuhof, who lived in Batavia in the early 1660s, likewise commented that the climate of Batavia was "as temperate and healthy as any place in the Indies" [...] "the most agreeable season begins in May, which continues with continual breezes from the east, and a very serene sky till November; when the winter season [is] approaching, it rains sometimes continually for three or four days without ceasing, which sets all the low grounds under water. This however has the convenience that it kills and washes away all insects, which otherwise would prove very noxious to the fruits."[5]

Special Features

What set Batavia apart from its Iberian sisters was the fact that it was founded and ruled by a large mercantile corporation, which, by a special charter or *octrooy*, had acquired a monopoly over the trade in Asia from the States-General of the Dutch Republic. This commercial link was evident in the extraordinary amount of space allotted to the warehouses for storing trade goods and the wharves for building and repairing ships. On the island of Onrust, a few miles off the coast of Batavia, some 200 skilled craftsmen and several hundred slaves toiled in a shipyard with repair facilities for the large East Indiamen or *retour schepen*. These would arrive weather beaten and very much the worse for wear after the long six month voyage from home and had to be careened, patched up and re-rigged. In all, the company was served in Batavia by some 4,000 personnel (both civil and military).

Another characteristic feature of the walled town of Batavia, built adjoining the castle in which the merchant elite of the company were lodged, was the fact that it also included the ethnic groups on whose military assistance and industry its very survival depended: the so-called "Mardijkers" (*orang merdeka*), free Christian burghers of Asian and mestizo extraction, and the industrious Chinese. In contrast to Manila, where the Spaniards and Chinese sojourners were strictly segregated, the Dutch and Chinese townspeople of Batavia lived within the walls of one and the same town, served by large numbers of domestic slaves from all around the Indonesian Archipelago and even the Indian Sub-Continent. In the so-called "Ommelanden" or environs/surrounding districts of the city, the company granted tracts of land, where the Indonesian 'martial nations' were concentrated in *kampong* of their own. The Balinese, Bugis, Madurese and Ambonese who lived here provided — when called upon — manpower and troops for military campaigns elsewhere in the Archipelago.[6] Around 1700, about 20,000 people resided within the walls and another 50,000 outside the city. About 5,000 Europeans and Christian mestizos and 3,500 Chinese lived in the town and, of course, large numbers of sailors lodged in the inns or on the ships in the roadstead.

In their overseas possessions, the Dutch replicated all of the municipal institutions of the burgher society of their home country and carried out such typically Dutch public construction works as the canal systems lined by rows of trees and neatly-built town houses. A town hall, two hospitals, a plague house/hospital for contagious diseases, a Court of Justice and several churches, as well as the usual institutions of correction for "drunk and adulterous women", "rasphouses" or gaols, and the urban almshouse, all contributed to the familiar Dutch Calvinistic atmosphere. In one respect, however, Batavia was very different from its free-trading sister cities in the Dutch Republic: it was ruled by one, large business corporation which jealously guarded its own monopolies of trade in Monsoon Asia.

The Lifecycle of an Urban Settlement

The extraordinary, commerce-oriented character of the town, its strong defences, its curious multicultural mixture of citizens, and, finally, its civic architecture,

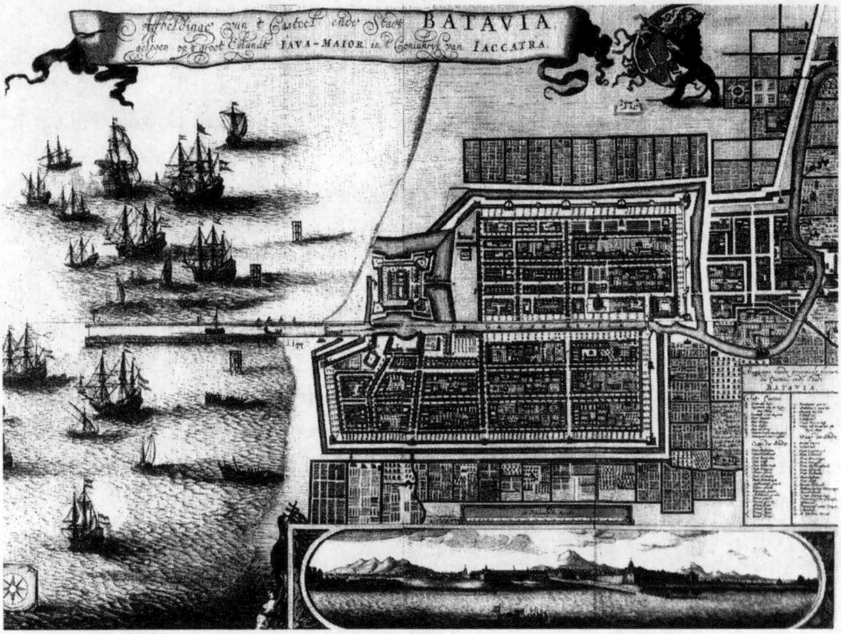

Fig. 2 Map of Batavia, circa 1660. F. de Haan, *Oud Batavia*, Vol. 2, enclosed map (Bandoeng, 1935).

made Batavia appear, in the eyes of its visitors, as a "Holland in the tropics". All of these features were mentioned in the various descriptions by visitors from abroad, whether European or Asian, although it is interesting to note that they often observed that, beneath the veneer of the male Dutch society operated an altogether different "Oriental" female society, which corrupted the so-called frugal Dutch traits. The sense of an embarrassment of riches simply did not exist in Batavia, but when opulence, pomp and circumstance became a typical feature of Batavian life in the tropics in the course of the eighteenth century, such excesses were stigmatized as typical adaptations to "corrupt oriental standards".[7] In the latter days of the company, this ostentatious behaviour was derided as evidence of the corruption which would soon drive the company to bankruptcy: VOC, "*Vergaan Onder Corruptie*" (perished under corruption).[8]

Seventeenth century visitors were overawed by the military and commercial supremacy of the Dutch in the Indonesian Archipelago. With its large fleet and numerous trading factories, the VOC was by far the greatest maritime power in Asia of that age, overshadowing all of its European and Asian rivals. However, by the middle of the eighteenth century, these roles had been reversed. Not only had the Dutch Republic dropped down in the pecking order of the family of nations in Europe, but the rival English East India Company was actually overtaking its Dutch counterpart in Asia. After the Battle of Plassey (1757), after which the English emerged victorious as the dominant power-brokers in Bengal, the EIC soon eclipsed Dutch trading interests in the Indian Ocean.

Living organisms, real or imagined, as do cities or nations, tend to pass through lifecycles. Urban settlements, like Goa and Batavia, shed their skins like snakes when their city centres succumbed to the unhealthy local conditions. In 1684, the Viceroy of the Estado da India, Francisco de Távora, decided to abandon Goa, the "Pearl of the Orient" and move the capital to a more salubrious location.[9] Batavia had become so unhealthy by the end of the eighteenth century that most of its Dutch citizenry, of their own free will, had moved *extramuros*, preferring the fresh air of the more elevated hinterland to the stench of the port city's stagnant canals. Various explanations have been posited to explain why this comparatively healthy town had, within only a few decades, degenerated into an insalubrious urban settlement. Contemporaries believed that the volcano, Mount Salak, which had erupted in 1702, was the principal culprit. Its debris turned the Ciliwong, or Great River, which flowed through the centre of the town, into a sluggish, muddy stream. Inevitably, the river's arteries became clogged with silt and were transformed into malodorous pools, providing the perfect breeding ground for the anopheles mosquito, although, at the time, the connection with infectious insect bites had not yet been made. It was generally believed that illness was caused by the stinking miasma, *malaria*. Truly high mortality rates only occurred after 1733. Personally, I believe that the first outbreak of malaria was caused by the digging of a new canal, the Mokervaart, when hundreds of navvies working on the project all suddenly died of high fever. A very convincing alternative, or rather additional, explanation, has been advanced by Peter van der Brug. He blames the fish ponds that were sited along the silted up river mouth of the Ciliwong, and must have served as breeding grounds for teeming colonies of mosquitoes.[10]

The VOC was liquidated in 1795 and nationalized lock, stock and barrel, including its remaining possessions in Asia, by the Batavian Republic, which was proclaimed immediately after the French invasion of Holland. Its charter was formally terminated in 1800. Governor-General Daendels, who was sent to Java in 1807 by King Louis Napoleon to carry out reforms and strengthen the defences against an imminent British attack, decided to move the administrative centre from downtown Batavia to the higher land of Weltevreden and dismantled Batavia Castle altogether. By that time, almost all of the Dutch possessions in Asia were in English hands, with the exception of Java and, of course, the factories in Canton (Guangzhou) and Nagasaki, which were operating under the jurisdiction of the mighty empires of China and Japan.

Batavia, the one-time rendezvous of the VOC commercial web spread out over Monsoon Asia, was now transformed into the administrative centre of a territorial colony which focused on the optimal production of such tropical agricultural and horticultural products as sugar, coffee, indigo, pepper and tea. Today, only a few buildings in downtown Jakarta survive to remind us of the port town which was first adored as the "Queen of the East", and later cursed as the "Cemetery of the Orient". It is telling that the lifecycle of Batavia *intramuros* was so closely tied to that of the East India Company itself. When the company went bankrupt, so did its headquarters in Asia, although not altogether for the same reasons.

Eyewitnesses

Many adventurers jotted down their experiences in Asia on their return home. The number of German travel writers who served in the VOC army is particularly high.[11] For all of these authors, Batavia served as the point of departure, point of repose or point of return in their stories, and is often described by them in glowing, somewhat sentimental terms. Many visitors borrowed freely from the writings of their predecessors when describing Batavia and it is easy to discern certain *topoi* in their accounts, which are always stressed. Among the most frequent are its spick and span appearance, its strict organization, its industrious Chinese citizens and its lazy housewives surrounded by flocks of slaves. At this point, I shall mention only a few people who have left us pictures of the town as they saw it. In the 1660s, Johan Nieuhof drew many pictures of the public buildings of Batavia and an interesting map of the town. Thanks to him, we can envisage what the walled town must have looked like in its heyday. During the second half of the eighteenth century, when the elite of the town had moved out of the city into beautiful country mansions, artists like the German, Johann Wolfgang Heydt (c. 1705–after 1750), and the Dane, Johannes Rach (1720–83), were there to document this exodus into the countryside with stylish drawings.[12]

It is curiously that very little was written by these visitors about the port function of the town, even though this was its *raison d'être*.[13] Batavia, after all, was built as the trade emporium for VOC shipping in Asia; that is, as the staple port for the intra-Asian trade and as the terminus for the trade with Europe. Not only did visitors pass over the port in their writings, but the same can be said of the various historians of the town, who, surprisingly, studiously ignored that subject. There is an abundance of material on shipping movements in the published *Generale Missiven* (General Missives) sent by the Governor-General and Council to the Netherlands, and the *Dagregisters van het Casteel Batavia* (Journals of Batavia Castle).[14] The incoming and outgoing freights traded by the company in Batavia can be traced in the *negotie journalen* (ledgers) in the VOC archives of the Hague, but it is difficult to find information about the organization of the logistics in the port. What follows here is a sketch of some of the main features of the organization of the port of Batavia. Let us first focus on the particular layout of the port and its geographic situation in Monsoon Asia before turning to the policy and management of trade during the VOC period.

Geographical Position

Located only a hundred sea miles from the Sunda Strait, one of the two main thoroughfares between the Indian Ocean and the South China Sea, Batavia catered to an extraordinarily widespread network of shipping, which extended in a westerly direction via the Bay of Bengal, the Indian Ocean and the Arabian Sea to Mocha on the Red Sea, eastwards via the Java and Banda Seas to Maluku (the Spice Islands), and northwards via the South and East China Seas to Ayutthaya in Siam, Tonkin in North Vietnam, Guangzhou (Canton) in South China, the island of Formosa (Taiwan), and finally the man-made island of Deshima in the bay of Nagasaki. In contrast to most other ports in Monsoon Asia, Batavia with its sheltered bay was an all-weather port, accessible throughout the year. During the dry season between May and October, steady winds blew from the east, and, after the monsoons in November, wet westerly winds began to blow in December, generally lasting until the end of March. The monsoon set the rhythm for all of the shipping movements of the Dutch East India Company from and to its headquarters in Asia.

The VOC, which was served by 25,000 military and civil personnel in the Netherlands and abroad, annually sent an average of some twenty-five ships to and from Asia and had about another forty ships sailing along the Asian monsoon trading routes at any one time. Three fleets were sent to the East every year: the fleet which left in September, when the *Amsterdamse Kermis* (Amsterdam Fair) was held, was called the Kermis fleet; in December and January, the *Kerstmisvloot* (Christmas fleet) followed; and, in April or May, the *Paasvloot* (Easter fleet) weighed anchor. After a voyage of 120–200 days, these ships, which sailed in convoy, arrived at the Sunda Strait, from where they would be escorted to the Bay of Batavia.

The Bay of Batavia was a large cove between Krawang and Ontong Java, which provided an ideal anchorage for both trans-oceanic and local shipping because the many surrounding islands (Pulau Seribu or Duizend Eilanden) guaranteed calm waters with almost no swell. In what was known as the inner anchorage close to shore were moored the Chinese junks and such smaller craft as the privately-owned vessels from Macao and Manila, while the large East

Fig. 3 View on Batavia's inner harbor. Johan Nieuhof, *Voyages and Travels to the East Indies 1653–1670* (London, 1703).

Indiamen of the VOC anchored in the outer roads, where the depth exceeded six fathoms. Foreign square-riggers were directed to a specially designated area in the Eastern Outer Roadstead. Johan Nieuhof described the harbour as follows:

> Both within and without this bay lie about 17 or 18 islands, upon which the violence of the winds and waves being broken and check'd, this renders the road of Batavia one of the safest harbours of the whole world, being able to contain above 1000 vessels at once; small vessels and barks lie commonly close under the banks of the river, where they may lie without anchors in a muddy bottom; the river is lined with stones on both sides as far as the boom, which is shut up every night at nine a clock, and guarded by a good number of soldiers. Besides which, there is cut a channel out of the main river, for the reception of smaller vessels; no vessel passes the boom without paying a certain custom, every vessel that fetches salt pays a *real*, and those that carry stones two *reals*.[15]

All of the large square-riggers in the roadstead were directed to their anchorage by the personnel of the *shahbandar* or harbour master. The admiral ship or 'ship of the watch' flew a large flag from the main mast and surveyed everything that happened in the roadstead from its station at the eastern end of the anchorage. The commander of the anchorage was not stationed on the ship herself but on the shore wharf. The ship basically served as a depot for the ships' crews and bore the curious name *Mits desen* (because of), the opening words of the form required for the transfer of personnel. An oared *chaloupe*, with the no less curious name of *Labberlot*, served as a means of transport for the harbour authorities.[16]

As the morning reveille was sounded from Batavia Castle, a shot was discharged from the watch ship, and, at sunset, the beating of the tattoo on the castle parade ground was likewise echoed by a gunshot. Incoming foreign shipping from east and west was signalled respectively from the islands of Edam and Onrust, whereupon the watch ship would fire salutes. In his *Oost-Indische voyagie*, Wouter Schouten, gives a precise account of his arrival at the roadstead:

> Upon arrival the *fiscal* (public prosecutor) and his entourage immediately came on board to check ship and cargo for possible (forbidden) private merchandise. When nothing of this kind was discovered, the party returned to the shore. Thereupon a great number of Chinese came to the ship to see whether there were any Dutch peddlers' wares on board, which they could resell to a third party with much profit. Instantly the chests and boxes of the crew were opened, because here there was a chance for making money! They started to barter with looking-glasses, needles, knives, hats, English caps, yes even woollen clothing was offered for sale to the cunning Chinese and indeed sold because these curious merchants could purchase these commodities at a really cheap price. Thereupon, many peddlers, Moors, Javanese, Mestizos and Dutchman came to the ship in their bumboats to offer the crew all kinds of Indian fruits, food and refreshments… gluttons who could not control themselves, soon fell ill: high fevers, diarrhoea and other illness. Some of them died.[17]

Once these peddlers had left, affairs more or less returned to normal. Soon, the ship was unloaded and, if it had come from Holland, its cargo was often awaited with eager anticipation because these ships brought "all kinds of provisions from home such as bacon, salted meat, cheese, butter and alcoholic beverages, of which Batavia had a need and consequently were warmly welcomed".[18]

Every ship in the roadstead was served by its own selected Chinese prahu, the so-called *biermaat* or "beer buddy", which brought provisions and transported passengers and crews between ship and shore. These bumboats required a licence. All boats reaching the shore passed by the boom or *Pabejan*, as Nieuhof already pointed out, where incoming and transhipment goods and passengers were examined by the customs officials.[19] Smaller native craft were allowed to pass through the piers/breakwaters of the harbour canal and moor in the inner basin outside the city walls. Here, there was also a ship wharf, where small yachts and lighters, "such as are used only in the road for the loading and unloading of ships", were built .[20] On the western side of the town was the rope-walk. In its vicinity stood the *Prauwenhuis*, where small *prahu* were built. The larger, seagoing ships were built and repaired on the isle of Onrust in the bay. On Onrust, as in the Ambachtsquartier or Artisans Quarter, there were foundries, where all the ironwork needed for the shipping was forged.

A typical characteristic of a port city like Batavia was that it had to provide foodstuffs for a far larger number of people than the actual sum of its own inhabitants: it had to supply food and provisions for the sailors of the ships in the roadstead, not only to meet their daily needs while they were anchored offshore, but also to sustain them on the often long voyages on which they were embarking. Consequently, in addition to the warehouses where the grain was stored, there were also large food markets in town: the rice or corn market, a fruit market and a poultry market where dried fish could also be purchased. The fruit was mostly cultivated by the Chinese and the local inhabitants in gardens around the town, while the poultry was the speciality of the Mardijkers and Topasses, who "kept pigs, pigeons, fowl and other sorts of poultry" at the rear of their dwellings.[21] Near the mouth of the river, the Pasar Ikan or Fish Market was situated, where fishmongers sold sea and river fish or shellfish on their stalls from 10 a.m. until 4 p.m.

Nieuhof devotes several pages to the description of the various fruits and their wholesome effects on the consumer, and, here, was obviously referring to the health of the well-fed inhabitants of the town rather than the vitamin-starved sailors, to whom Wouter Schouten referred as a high-risk group. In other words, in contrast to the industrial surroundings of today's seaports, crammed with refineries, large industrial complexes and container storages, the Asian port cities of the past were located amidst bucolic greenery: extensive fruit gardens and rice-fields, which all catered for the incoming and outgoing seaborne society. Traditional Asian emporia were markets for trading both commodities and large quantities of foodstuffs and victuals for sailors.

The Management of Trade

The overseas possessions of the Dutch East India Company in Asia were ruled by a Governor-General and the Council of the Indies, consisting of the Director-General and five ordinary Councillors who met on Tuesday and Friday afternoons. All shipping movements of the company in Asia were directed by the

Directeur-Generaal, the second-in-command at Batavia Castle. He was in charge of all of the loading and discharging of the ships, provisioning the vessels, examining all ledgers, and supervising the chiefs of all the factories scattered over Monsoon Asia. As all of these tasks could not possibly be carried out by one man, he was soon assisted by a staff, consisting of the *Visitateur-Generaal* and various experts in trade.[22] This management team co-ordinated all of the shipping of the company from its headquarters in Batavia Castle. Early in the morning, the front portal of the office of the Director-General was thronged with ships' captains, assistants, junior merchants and merchants who waited upon him to have their papers signed or to speak to him in person. He also had to be present at all of the meetings of the Council of the Indies, supervise the incoming and outgoing shipping, and take care of the correspondence with the factories elsewhere in Asia. No wonder, Valentijn remarks, that this official often looked slighlty dazed on public occasions; he was the hardest working man in Batavia.[23]

Because all of the shipping movements were closely interrelated, a well thought-out master plan was put into practice. This made it possible to dispose of the goods at the right moment in time, an indispensable precondition for price-fixing in the intra-Asian and inter-continental trade of the VOC. François Valentijn, who marvelled at the ingenuity of this business and trade model, had this to say about it:

> Because Batavia is the centre and the heart of the Company, through which pours the blood and all the juices which keep the veins and sinews of this large body operating… the biggest task for the management is to ensure on a daily basis that the ships are sent in time with the requisite and ordered cargoes to all *comptoirs*, or to deal with the streams of goods received from abroad item by item in such a way that they are dispatched to destinations where they are most required and where the highest profits can be obtained, because this is the general entrepôt of the Indies, where it is possible to find storehouses filled with all kinds of spices, textiles, grains, drinks and so on for all of Asia.[24]

Intra-Asian Trading Patterns

The departures and arrivals of the ships were inexorably governed by the rhythm of the monsoon winds but were, nevertheless, closely attuned to the arrival of goods which had to be transhipped to other destinations in Asia or were prepared for the homeward voyages, which generally departed between November and February, so that they could discharge their costly cargoes at the Dutch ports in the summer. The logistics involved in setting up the VOC shipping network in Asia has been recently studied in detail by Robert Parthesius.[25] He

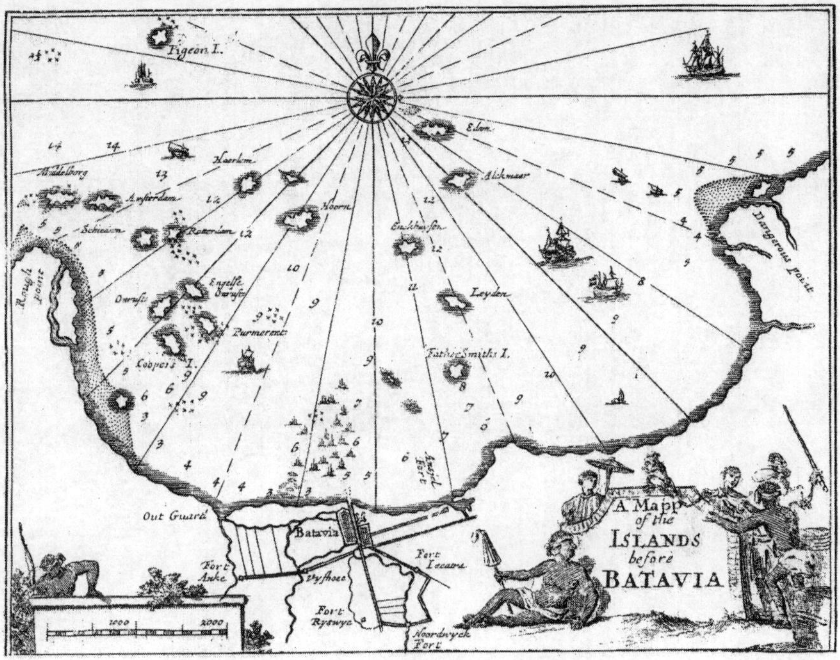

Fig. 4 View on the Bay of Batavia. Johan Nieuhof, *Voyages and Travels to the East Indies 1653–1670* (London, 1703).

posed the question: how successful was the VOC in adjusting its fleet to the demands of both the overall organization of trade and defence and unfolding events in its efforts to conduct its Asiatic operations? He reached the conclusion that particular types of ship were used for each task, and he distinguishes eight different ship types, each of which can be further divided into classes for certain purposes.

The actual number of voyages which were made between the Dutch Republic and the Indies in the period 1595 and 1660 and the number of voyages within the intra/Asian network varied considerably: while some 1,368 voyages were made around the Cape of Good Hope, no less than 11,507 voyages were undertaken in the Eastern Seas. We should take into consideration here that not until the establishment of the transhipment port of Batavia were the intra-Asian shipping routes consolidated and finely tuned. Between 1610 and 1620, about 1,000 shipping movements in Asia were recorded. By the 1650s, this number had stabilized at about 2,800 shipping movements per decade. The following schematic survey is largely borrowed from Valentijn's description of the annual pattern of VOC trading movements.[26]

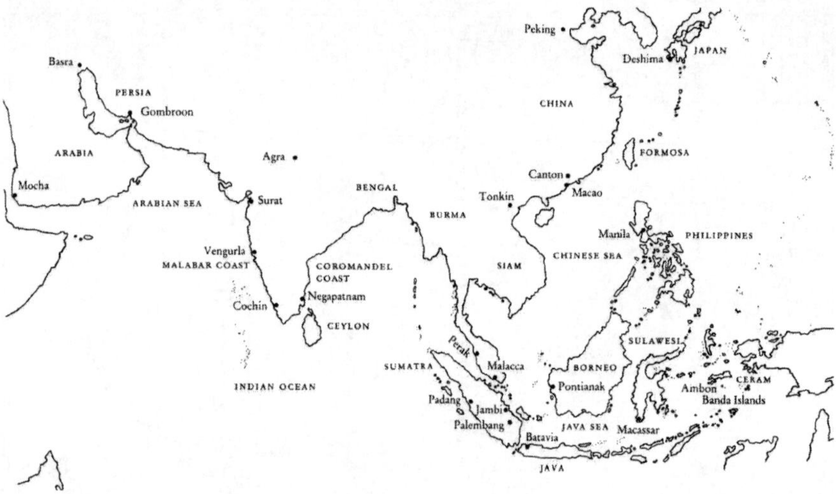

Fig. 5 Maritime network of the VOC.

Japan

In May, June or early July, the so-called *Japanvaarders*, ships for Japan, were sent to Nagasaki bearing Dutch and Indian textiles, rayskins, spices, and so on. These ships would depart from Japan at some time in October or November, with cargoes of gold *koban* (coins), lacquer ware, porcelain, silk, copper staves, tea and some products imported by Japan from China. Part of this cargo, combined with goods received in Batavia from China and complemented with tin from Malacca, would be shipped to Bengal or Persia for arrival in February. The ships would return from these *Westerkwartieren* with textiles for Batavia just in time to set sail again on the next Japan voyage.

Coromandel (East coast of India)

Ships destined for Coromandel were dispatched between April and August, passing by Jaffna in Ceylon, heading for Nagapattinam and from there up to Pulicat, where they would load stone slabs — often used for tombstones in Batavia — as ballast, and all sorts of textiles, indigo, saltpetre and diamonds. They returned to Batavia in September after this round-trip voyage of about two and a half months.

Ceylon, Surat (North-west Coast of India) and Persia

At the beginning of September, the ships left for Galle in Ceylon with a cargo of spices and locally ordered wares. From there, the ships continued to follow the north-easterly wind in October, sailing to the Malabar ports of Cochin and

Wingurla. From there, areca, pepper, cowries, and coconut husks (for rope-making) were transported to Surat and then onwards to Persia. Ships were also sent directly to Persia and Surat from Ceylon, bearing cargoes of spices, cardamon, pepper, copper and tin. Ceylon ships were also occasionally sent directly to the Netherlands in December. In February and March, the goods were prepared for the destination of Batavia: textiles, jewels, as well as Persian silks, Shiraz wines, fruits, armosins, brocades, and horses from Persia. In May, Ceylon would send two more ships to Batavia filled with cinnamon.

Bengal (North-east Coast of India)

In July and August, ships were sent to Bengal bearing Japanese copper to purchase silk for Japan and cotton textiles and opium for Java.

The West and East Coast of Sumatra

Ships were sent to Western Sumatra in April and May to purchase gold and pepper from various locations. They returned in August or September, although more favourable winds for the voyage home could be found in December and January, if there were no particular hurry. The same schedule was maintained for the east coast of Sumatra, where textiles and pieces of eight were exchanged for pepper in Palembang, gold and pepper in Jambi, and gold in Indragiri. These ships also returned in October, just in time to transfer their cargoes to the fleet in the roadstead waiting for the order to sail home to the Netherlands.

Malacca (Melaka)

In May, Batavia supplied this factory with necessities in exchange for tin and pepper from the "Tin Kingdoms". In September or October, other ships were sent to the Malacca Straits to await and transfer goods from the ships that sailed directly from Japan to Bengal without calling at Batavia.

Siam

In June, July and August, ships were sent to Siam. Sailing with the west-south-west winds along the coast of Johor and Ligor, they arrived in Ayutthaya in September, carrying the special goods ordered by the Siamese king, such as arms and clothing. The cargo for the trip home to Batavia consisted of tropical timber, hides, rayskins, wax, elephant tusks and other forest products. The ships set sail again with the north- easterly wind at the beginning of November. En route to Batavia, they called at Ligor to collect tin.

China and Tonkin

Ships sailed to these destinations in May, June and July, but, by the end of the seventeenth century, all of the VOC vessels on this route had been replaced by private shipping run by Batavian *free burghers*, merchants from Macao, and Chinese *yang hang* traders.

Arakan (Burma)

Voyages to this *comptoir*, which was served from Coromandel (on the opposite side of the Bay of Bengal) also commenced in August of September. Here, the company purchased rice, slaves and elephants, and the ships would return in November via the Malacca Straits, or occasionally sail south, skirting the coast of Western Sumatra via the Sunda Strait.

Maluku or de Grote Oost (Spice Islands)

All shipping to the eastern part of the Indonesian Archipelago departed between December and February loaded with such ample provisions as rice, wheat, bacon, oil, beer, wines and vinegar for the various strongholds manned by company soldiers to preserve the VOC's spice monopoly. Between June and September, the ships from Maluku would return filled with spices, nutmeg, mace, sandalwood, caret, bird's nests and birds of paradise, just in time to liaise with the homeward bound fleet waiting at anchor in the Batavian roadstead.

The Cape of Good Hope

Special shipments of rice and textiles were sent to the Cape in August or September. On their return to Batavia, the VOC ships also called at Mauritius to load ebony until the island became completely denuded of this timber by the end of the seventeenth century.

The Significance of Batavia

These dovetailing shipping movements and trading patterns demonstrate clearly that the months of the dry period between May and August were a particularly busy time for equipping ships for intra-Asian trade. The period from September to November were the months in which most shipping arrived back just in time for the transhipment to the *retour* fleets heading for the Netherlands. With the exception of occasional direct shipments from the Netherlands to Ceylon, all goods were first cleared through the Batavian roadstead, demonstrating the central position of Batavia in the intra-Asian shipping network of the Dutch East India Company.

Not until the middle of the eighteenth century were questions raised about the indispensable role of the town in the successful management of the company. The first grumblings could be overheard in connection with the high cost of the upkeep of the town and its unhealthy climate. The high mortality figures forced the company management to send ever greater numbers of personnel to the East. In 1756, the Gentlemen Seventeen took the momentous decision to establish the *China Comité* (Chinese Committee), which was ordered to reorganize the direct tea trade between the Netherlands and China in such a way that the position of Batavia would be reduced to that of an auxiliary port. By that time, the company's intra-Asiatic shipping network was gradually disintegrating due to the strong British competition, and Batavia's status was reduced to that of a regional trading centre in the Indonesian Archipelago. Even within the South-east Asian region, that position was challenged by the expanding networks of the English traders, the Chinese junks and the Bugis shipping, all of which were looking for new entrepôts close to the Malacca Straits, the most convenient route between the Bay of Bengal and the South China Sea. That search initially favoured such islands as Penang and Riau, but finally culminated in the establishment of the freeport of Singapore in 1819.

Epilogue

Today, very little is left of Old Batavia. Downtown, close to the sea, far away from the contemporary bustling city centre, a couple of badly neglected eighteenth-century town houses still stand along the once again heavily polluted Kali Besar. The mansion of Governor-General Reinier de Klerk, where the colonial and, later, the National Archives of Indonesia were kept until the 1980s, has been carefully restored and is now a popular venue for wedding receptions. Plagued by a leaking roof and struggling against badly neglected maintenance, the original town hall of 1710, now the city's historical museum, is a disgrace to the Archaeological Service of Indonesia. Most of the town's canals have been filled in, and those remaining are probably just as murky and smelly as they were at the end of the eighteenth century.

At Pasar Ikan, where the old harbour canal that leads to the sea originates, the curious tourist may still encounter a few of the surviving former warehouses of the VOC and a tower, the *Uitkijk* or 'Look Out', which was built in the early nineteenth century on the site of the original location of the *Pabejan* or customs house. It is a miracle that these sturdy buildings, often sadly neglected, have survived the onslaught of time as well as they have. The old inner city of the company period has largely disappeared because the *intramuros* town crept out of its shell at the beginning of the nineteenth century and moved several kilometres inland to be transformed into a garden city.

There is a certain irony in all of this. With the construction of the seaport of Tanjung Priok at the end of the nineteenth century, all ocean-going shipping moved away from the roadstead to the new docks, although the Buginese lumber schooners, which still bring timber from the outer islands, continue to ply the original channel of Old Batavia and moor at Pasar Ikan. Inadvertently, their strangely shaped hulls remind us of the situation as it must have been a few hundred years ago.

Notes

1. Mike Dash, *Batavia's Graveyard* (New York: Crown Publishers, 2002).
2. F. de Haan, *Oud Batavia* (Bandoeng: Nix, 1935), p. 710.
3. H.A. Breuning, *Het voormalige Batavia. Een Hollandse stedestichting in de tropen. Anno 1619* (Amsterdam: Allert de Lange, 1954), p. 125; J. van Leur-de Loos, *Het ontwerp van het kasteel te Batavia, Tijdschrift voor Ind. Taal-, Land-, en Volkenkunde*, vol. LXXXIII 2–3 (1949): 194–8. For Dutch colonial town building, see also Ron van Oers, *Dutch Town Planning Overseas During VOC and WIC Rule (1600–1800)* (Zutphen: Walburg Pers, 2000).
4. For a general bibliography of Batavia, see Ewald Ebing and Youetta de Jager, comp., *Batavia-Jakarta, 1600–2000, A Bibliography* (Leiden: KITLV Press, 2000).
5. Johan Nieuhof, *Voyages and Travels to the East Indies 1653–1670* (Singapore: Oxford University Press, 1988), p. 264.
6. Remco Raben, "Round about Batavia, Ethnicity and Authority in the Ommelanden, 1650–1800", in *Jakarta-Batavia, Socio-cultural Essays*, ed. K. Grijns and P. Nas (Leiden: KITLV Press, 2000), pp. 93–107, and Remco Raben, "Batavia and Colombo: the Ethnic and Spatial Order of Two Colonial Cities, 1600–1800", unpublished PhD thesis, Leiden University, 1996. For a fine social history of Batavia in the seventeenth century, see H.E. Niemeijer, *Batavia. Een koloniale samenleving in de 17de eeuw* (Amsterdam: Uitgeverij Balans, 2005).
7. Jean Gelman Taylor, *The Social World of Batavia European and Eurasian in Dutch Asia* (Madison: University of Wisconsin Press, 1983).
8. Leonard Blussé, *Strange Company, Chinese Settlers, Mestizo Women and the Dutch in VOC Batavia* (Dordrecht: KITLV Press, 1986), p. 33.
9. Michel Chandeigne, *Goa 1510–1685, L'Inde Portugaise, Apostolique et Commerciale* (Paris: Editions Autrement, 1997), p. 207.
10. P.H. van der Brug, *Malaria en Malaise. De VOC in Batavia in de Achttiende Eeuw* (Amsterdam: De Bataafsche Leeuw, 1994).
11. R. van Gelder, *Het Oost-Indische avontuur. Duitsers in dienst van de VOC (1600–1800)* (Nijmegen: SUN, 1997).
12. J.W. Heydt, *Allerneuester geographisch- und topografischer Schauplatz* (Willhermsdorff, 1744); J. de Loos-Haaxman, *Johannes Rach en zijn werk* (Batavia: Bataviaasch Genootschap, 1928).
13. The monograph by Gerrit Knaap and Heather Sutherland on the organisation of shipping in eighteenth century Makassar, *Monsoon Traders, Ships, Skippers and Commodities in Eighteenth Century Makassar* (Leiden: KITLV Press, 2004) shows what can be done in this respect. See also my own study entitled "The VOC and the Junk Trade of Batavia: a Problem in Administrative Control", in *Strange Company*, pp. 97–155.
14. W.Ph. Coolhaas *et al.*, eds., "Generale Missiven van Gouverneurs-Generaal en Raden aan Heren XVII der Verenigde Oostindische Compagnie 1610–1761", *'s-Gravenhage, Rijksgeschiedkundige Publicatien* 1–13 (1960–2007); J.A. van der Chijs *et al.*, eds., *Dagregister gehouden int Casteel Batavia vant passerende daer ter plaetse als over geheel Nederlandts-India 1624–1682* (Batavia, 's-Gravenhage, 1887–1928),

21 vols. The remaining unedited manuscript diaries may be consulted in the Arsip Nasional in Jakarta.

15. Johan Nieuhof, *Voyages and Travels to the East Indies 1653–1670* (Singapore: Oxford University Press, 1988), p. 266.
16. J.A. van der Chijs, ed., *Nederlandsch-Indisch Plakaatboek* (Landsdrukkerij: Batavia, July 3, 1743).
17. Wouter Schouten, *De Oost-Indische voyagie van Wouter Schouten*, ed. Michael Breet (Zutphen: Walburg Pers, 2003), p. 45.
18. Schouten, *Oost-Indische voyagie*, p. 427.
19. De Haan, *Oud Batavia*, p. 191; François Valentijn, *Oud en Nieuw Oost-Indien*, Vol. 4, p. 230.
20. Nieuhof, *Travels*, p. 271.
21. Ibid., p. 272.
22. Pieter van Dam, *Beschryvinge van de Oostindische Compagnie*, Vol. 3 ('s-Gravenhage, Rijksgeschiedkundige Publicatiën, 1943), p. 65.
23. Valentijn, *Oud en Nieuw Oost Indië*, Vol. IVa, p. 352.
24. Ibid., p. 257.
25. Robert Parthesius, "Dutch Ships in Tropical Waters, The development of the Dutch East India Company (VOC) shipping network in Asia 1595–1660", Unpublished PhD thesis, University of Amsterdam, 2007.
26. Valentijn, *Oud en Nieuw Oost-Indien*, Vol. IVa, pp. 256–61.

References

Abeyasekere, Susan, *Jakarta: A History* (Singapore: Oxford University Press, 1987).

Blussé, Leonard, *Strange Company. Chinese Settlers, Mestizo Women and the Dutch in VOC Batavia* (Dordrecht: Verhandelingen KITLV 122, Foris Publications, 1986).

Breuning, H.A., *Het voormalige Batavia: Een Hollandse stedestichting in de Tropen. Anno 1619* (Amsterdam: Allert de Lange, 1954).

van der Brug, P.H., *Malaria en Malaise. De VOC in Batavia in de Achttiende Eeuw* (Amsterdam: De Bataafsche Leeuw, 1994).

Chandeigne, Michel, *Goa 1510–1685, L'Inde Portugaise, Apostolique et Commerciale* (Paris: Editions Autrement, 1997).

van der Chijs, J.A., *Nederlandsch-Indisch Plakaatboek 1602–1811* (Batavia: Landsdrukkerij, 17 vols., 1885–1900).

van der Chijs, J.A. *et al.*, eds., *Daghregister gehouden int Casteel Batavia vant passerende daer ter plaetse als over geheel Nederlandts-India 1624–1682* (Batavia: 's-Gravenhage, 21 vols., 1887–1928).

Coolhaas, W. Ph. *et al.*. eds., *Generale Missiven van Gouverneurs-Generaal en Raden aan Heren XVII der Verenigde Oostindische Compagnie 1610–1761* ('s-Gravenhage, Rijksgeschiedkundige Publicatiën, 13 vols., 1960–2007).

van Dam, Pieter, *Beschryvinge van de Oostindische Compagnie*, ed. F.W. Stapel ('s-Gravenhage, Rijksgeschiedkundige Publicatiën, 7 vols., 1927–54).

Dash, Mike, *Batavia's Graveyard* (New York: Crown Publishers, 2002).

Ebing, Ewald and Youetta de Jager (comp.), *Batavia-Jakarta, 1600–2000, A Bibliography* (Leiden: KITLV Press, 2000).

van Gelder, Roelof, *Het Oost-Indische Avontuur. Duitsers in dienst van de VOC* (Nijmegen: SUN, 1997).

Grijns, Kees and Peter J.M. Nas, eds., *Jakarta, Socio-cultural Essays* (Leiden: Verhandelingen KITLV 187. KITLV Press, 2000).

de Haan, F., *Oud Batavia* (Bandoeng: A.C. Nix & Co., 1935) .

Heydt, J.W., *Allerneuester geographisch- und topografischer Schauplatz* (Willhermsdorff, 1744).

Knaap, Gerrit and Heather Sutherland, *Monsoon Traders, Ships, Skippers and Commodities in Eighteenth Century Makassar* (Leiden: KITLV Press, 2004).

van Leur-de Loos, J., "Het ontwerp van het kasteel te Batavia", *Tijdschrift voor Indische Taal-, Land-, en Volkenkunde*, vol. LXXXIII 2–3 (1949): 194–8.

de Loos-Haaxman, J., *Johannes Rach en zijn Werk* (Batavia: Bataviaasch Genootschap, 1928).

Niemeijer, H.E., *Batavia: Een koloniale Samenleving in de 17de Eeuw* (Amsterdam: Balans, 2005).

Nieuhof, Johan, *Voyages and Travels to the East Indies* (Singapore: Oxford University Press, 1988).

van Oers, Ron, *Dutch Town Planning overseas during VOC and WIC Rule (1600–1800)* (Zutphen: Walburg Pers, 2000).

Parthesius, Robert, "Dutch Ships in Tropical Waters: The Development of the Dutch East India Company (VOC) Shipping Network in Asia 1595–1660", Unpublished PhD thesis, University of Amsterdam, 2007.

Remco Raben, "Batavia and Colombo, the Ethnic and Spatial Order of two Colonial Cities, 1600–1800", Unpublished PhD thesis, University of Leiden, 1996.

________, "Round about Batavia, Ethnicity and Authority in the Ommelanden 1650–1800", in *Jakarta-Batavia: Socio-cultural essays*, ed. K. Grijns and P. Nas (Leiden: KITLV Press, 2000), pp. 93–107.

Schouten, Wouter, *De Oost-Indische Voyagie (Amsterdam 1676)*, ed. Michael Breet (Zutphen: Walburg Pers, 2003).

Taylor, Jean Gelman, *The Social World of Batavia, European and Eurasian in Dutch Asia* (Madison: University of Wisconsin Press, 1983).

Valentijn, François, *Oud- en Nieuw Oost-Indiën* (Dordrecht/Amsterdam: Van Braam, 1724–26).

CHAPTER 7

Dutch Interaction with Siamese Law and the City Rules of Ayutthaya in the Seventeenth and Eighteenth Centuries*

Bhawan Ruangsilp

Introduction

The Thai Kingdom of Ayutthaya (c. 1350–1767) was one of the most prosperous port-polities in Southeast Asia. Its capital city derived its cosmopolitan character from its dual function as a political and a commercial centre. This is made evident from the many eyewitness accounts that state that Ayutthaya, usually referred to as Siam in contemporary foreign documents, was swarming with foreign settlers and sojourners. The Dutch merchant, Joost Schouten, who lived there for several years during the 1620s and 1630s, wrote that this port city "by reason of its great traffick, is frequented by several Nations, as the *Indians*, the more Western *Asiaticks*, Europeans, Moors, and Christian Merchants".[1]

Ayutthaya's foreign population consisted not only of multi-ethnic trading communities but also of many other categories, such as war captives, political and religious refugees, mercenaries and experts in other fields, missionaries, and merchants. The ethno-cultural diversity of Ayutthaya's foreign populace, which indicates the very active participation of this Siamese port polity in the global process of migration, raises the question of how the indigenous administration maintained peace and order in this socio-culturally mixed milieu.

The interactions between the Siamese state and its people, especially in the capital city, on the one hand, and the residing and visiting foreigners, on the other, have been considerably studied from the various aspects of commerce, politics, diplomacy, society and culture.[2] The legal element of the contacts, however, has been insufficiently investigated, mostly because of the paucity of primary sources. The most important indigenous source for the pre-modern legal history of Thailand, the *Kotmai Tra Sam Duang* (The Three Seals Laws), fails to offer substantial information about the laws pertaining to foreigners in Ayutthaya, and what it offers does not reflect the changes that must have occurred over time.[3] Therefore, historian tends to make use of foreign documents, especially published travelogues and treaties. Correspondingly, only a few works fully commit to this topic. Having combined all of the fragmented information in the *Kotmai Tra Sam Duang*, Manop Thavornwatsakul suggested that, according to Siamese law, foreigners were to be watched closely, and all of them were bound by the local law as much as the indigenous population.[4] In an earlier work, Robert Lingat drew attention to the French-Thai treaties of 1685 and 1687, according to which France attempted to obtain legal privileges for her subjects in Siam.[5]

The aforementioned Joost Schouten was one of the many Dutch/European men who served the Dutch East India Company (Verenigde Oostindische Compagnie – VOC) in Siam between 1604 and 1765. In sending the first group of its employees to initiate contact with the Siamese court, the company hoped to gain access to the attractive Chinese market through Siam's commercial connection with the Middle Kingdom. However, the Dutch soon discovered the real benefit of Siam: it provided highly desired commodities for the Japanese market. These products, especially sappanwood and animal skins, were used to barter for Japanese bullion which the VOC needed for the purchase of Chinese silk and Indian textiles. In short, the VOC policies towards Siam were based upon the significance of the kingdom in the overall scheme of the company's intra-Asian trade, particularly its operations in East Asia. Although the company's Japan trade had declined around the turn of the century, the Dutch remained in Siam until 1765 — less than eighteen months before the kingdom ultimately fell at Burmese hands — although for a strategic reason (to secure a position on Mainland Southeast Asia and rice supply), rather than for real profit. In the absence of colonial bias, the diplomatic approach ruled its relationship with the Siamese court in general.[6]

It was true that the VOC, on the whole, dealt with the court of Ayutthaya with the confidence born of its commercial and military strength. However, its employees in Siam had a different negotiating power in relation to that court. They were not only bound to the guidelines and regulations of their superiors in Asia and the Dutch Republic,[7] but also obliged to obey Siamese rules. As far as the daily contacts were concerned, it was these men-on-the-spot who played a crucial role in intermediating between the two powers of relatively equal position and different cultures. Their own behaviour was responsible for the fate of the Dutch community as well as the success or failure of the company's business in Siam.

Following the monopolistic trading system of the Siamese Government, the VOC employees were required to maintain direct contact with the king and his court members. When engaged with the Siamese elite, the Dutch merchants fittingly assumed the roles of diplomatic representatives of the VOC and the Dutch Republic. For the sake of formality, the VOC *Opperhoofd* (trade director) commenced his term of office armed with a written accreditation from the High Government in Batavia, and would usually be granted a welcome and a farewell audience by the King, or the *Phrakhlang* (Minister of External Relations and Maritime Trading Affairs).[8] He would expect to be integrated into the Siamese administrative hierarchy and conferred with a court rank and title, together with "a royal gift in accordance with his rank — a plot of land, a golden betel-nut box and a sword".[9] That plot of land was more of a symbolic gift, but the latter two were regarded as insignia, which he was obliged to carry with him when presenting himself at court.[10] Above all, most of the daily activities of the Dutch centred on the company's lodge, where they pursued their business transactions and conducted their day-to-day lives through interactions with the officials, the local people, and other foreign communities.

The presence of the VOC employees in Siam posed questions to both the Siamese authorities — regarding how to deal with them — and the men themselves — regarding how to negotiate between the two different cultural and legal traditions — their own and that of their host. This article is a study of the status of the VOC employees and the company settlement in Siamese law and social organization. Due to the limited number of Thai sources, the reconstruction of the Dutch legal status in Siam is based overwhelmingly on Dutch records — two in particular. The first document, the Dutch-Siamese Treaty of 1664, not only clarified the commercial privileges of the VOC, but also established a clear legal protection, the "extraterritorial rights", for the Dutch and European employees of the company in Siam.[11] This makes the Dutch presence a special case in Siam. The second document, the *Memorie van Overgave* (Instructions for his Successor), of 1720 composed by VOC's *Opperhoofd*, Wijbrand Blom, provides exceptional information about how the Dutch managed and protected their settlement in practice.[12]

Extraterritoriality: The VOC Men and Siamese Jurisdiction

While the Dutch understood that Siam had a well-established law,[13] their general attitude towards the legal practices in the kingdom was entirely negative. They neither trusted the Siamese judicial system, believing that the Siamese were almost ubiquitously corrupt,[14] nor appreciated the sadistic methods of physical punishment and trials by ordeal commonly practised in Siam. In his "Description of Siam", Schouten drew the attention of his superiors and other readers to the kingdom's judicial process, especially the customs of punishment and ordeal: "Cashiering, banishments into Desart [deserted places], slavery, confiscations, mutilation of hand or foot, burning in oyl, quartering, and other severe executions … by ducking under water, holding their hands in boyling oyl, to go bare-foot upon hot coales, or to eat a mess of charmed rice."[15]

Not only were the general attitudes of the Dutch towards the legal and judicial practices in Siam negative, it was their direct experiences of being under threat by the Siamese authorities that compelled the company servants to seek immunity from the local jurisdiction. In 1634, when the VOC was reluctant to give King Prasatthong (r. 1629–56) the assistance demanded for his troops in his attempt to suppress Patani, the rebelling vassal state in the south, its employees in Ayutthaya were forbidden by the Siamese court to leave their lodge. Only after Schouten, who had led the company's armed ships to Patani, had managed to prove that his superiors had indeed rendered military assistance to the Siamese troops were the Dutch allowed to resume their business. Similarly, in 1640, the king's dissatisfaction with the Dutch, fuelled by further accusations made by their enemies at court, led to another siege of the VOC lodge and a threat to have the Dutch trampled to death by elephants. The Dutch were reportedly saved by the intercession of their friends at court.[16]

The decisive turning-point for the future legal status of the Dutch in Siam was the incident in 1636, termed by Ten Brummelhuis and Kleinen the "Dutch Picnic in Ayutthaya", which almost caused the deaths of a few Dutchmen in the Thai kingdom.[17] In December of that year, while enjoying some leisure in Ayutthaya, two VOC employees, under the influence of alcohol, attacked the servants of the king's brother and consequently were arrested and brought to the prince's court. The other employees who came to secure the release of their compatriots became embroiled in a fight with the courtiers, but were outnumbered and compelled to surrender to the Siamese. Outraged, King Prasatthong (r. 1629–56) was on the verge of having these Dutchmen executed, in addition to restricting Dutch trade and stationing armed guards at their lodge.

In the end, King Prasatthong stayed the intended execution of the Dutchmen and lifted the ban on VOC trade. Instead, he compelled Jeremias van Vliet, as the Chief of the Dutch in Siam, to perform before him a ritual which the *Opperhoofd* painfully recognized as an "admission of guilt",[18] as well as to accept, in a written declaration, his responsibility for any mistakes committed by the VOC men in Siam in the future. This declaration also required the Dutch to conform to the laws and customs of the kingdom.[19] In short, it was an attempt to subject the Dutch to the local legal procedures and punishments and to the power of the Siamese King — who promulgated Siamese law.

Prasatthong's act was certainly unacceptable to the company, which alone, as a rule, administered justice to its own servants and the Dutch free burghers in Asia. Batavia had since attempted to rescind this clause. Between September 1663 and February 1664, the VOC enforced a naval blockade at the mouth of the Chao Phraya River (selectively capturing junks sailing to Siam from China and Japan) in an attempt to restrict the expansion of Siam's trade to East Asia. The conflict was settled with the signing of the first, unequal Dutch-Siamese Treaty of 1664. The VOC finally managed to use its advantageous situation to force the Siamese court to place its employees outside Siamese jurisdiction. Incorporated into this Treaty, the following clause provided the VOC with what Robert Lingat defines as a *système des capitulations*, and Smith and Ten Brummelhuis labelled extraterritorial rights; namely, the privilege of immunity from local law enforcement for company employees and Dutch subjects.[20]

> Should (God forbid!) any of the Company's residents commit a grave crime in Siam, neither the King nor the Siamese courts shall judge him, but he shall be delivered to the chief of the Honourable Company, in order to be punished according to Dutch law; and in case the said chief himself commit a capital crime, His Majesty shall have the power to place him under arrest until notice shall have been given of the same to the Governor-General.[21]

Hence, the extraterritorial rights, according to the 1664 Treaty, in effect, abolished the force of the declaration of responsibility of 1636.

In 1685, King Narai (r. 1656–88) refused to grant exemption from local jurisdiction to the Portuguese who sent an embassy from Goa to Ayutthaya to request this but apparently lacked the influence to convince the monarch.[22] However, the king agreed to grant the French, his close allies, this privilege, as stated in the Franco-Siamese Treaties of 1685 and 1687.[23]

The first Franco-Siamese Treaty of 1685 reveals the intention of the French to propagate the Roman Catholic faith in Siam, for it envisaged the freedom for French missionaries to preach and provided indigenous converts with certain privileges. The local Christians were to be exempt from the royal *corvée* on Sundays and holy days, were completely liberated from that service in old age, and were allowed their own system of justice. The subsequent Treaty of 1687 gave the French East India Company (*Compagnie des Indes Orientales* – CIO), established in 1664, the right to prosecute any of its employees who committed crimes against other employees in Siam, in its own way. If the matter should entail a CIO employee and a person outside the company service, of any nationality, the employee should appear before a Siamese court, which would then include one or more company officials. In the end, the fact that these French officials would actually give a verdict made this "international court"[24] merely a formality. In effect, France requested extraterritorial rights not only for its own subjects but also for the Roman Catholic community under its protection — which included converted subjects of the Siamese King. In contrast to the French, the VOC excluded any possibility of its employees undergoing the Siamese judicial procedure, even should they have inflicted injury on a Siamese. Although it seems that the Dutch Company, according to the Treaty of 1664, humbly limited the scope of extraterritoriality to cover only its employees and subjects, like Dutch free burghers, and obviously had no intention of propagating religion, it actually did, in certain cases, offer protection against Siamese law enforcement to the local people who lived within its settlement, as we shall see in the following paragraphs.

In the end, all of the agreements between the French and the Siamese court became null and void immediately upon the demise of King Narai in 1688 and did not protect the French from the anger of his successor, Phetracha, and his followers, who resented the French attempts to impose their political and religious agendas on Siam. Apparently, the Dutch had learnt that the ruler could reverse or modify the law promulgated by his predecessors at any time. Therefore, they constantly strove to renew the Dutch-Siamese Treaty at the beginning of every reign in order to reconfirm their commercial and legal privileges.

Order and Protection: The VOC Settlement in Siam

As mentioned earlier, the Siamese King allowed many foreign communities in his realm to administer their own settlements and peoples, assuredly on condition that they observed the common order of society. The report on the company's property of 1731, which included a list of the legal papers held at the lodge, reveals some of the rules which governed the daily life of foreigners in Ayutthaya. One particular document is an order prohibiting all foreigners in Ayutthaya to make an appearance without advance permission at and around the royal court or in any place where the king and the members of the royal family might happen to be present. Another was an order to maintain a night watch to prevent fire, theft and other disorders in all districts of Siam. The last order concerned a prohibition on firing canon or any ammunition, or letting off fireworks without the permission of the court.[25]

The status of the VOC trade director in Siam was complicated not only by his duty to lead the company employees but also by his obligation to govern the indigenous inhabitants of the settlement. In accordance with the Siamese concept of social organization, the Dutch settlement was categorized as a *ban* (village or community), with the *Opperhoofd* as a *nai* (head of the community) who, like the heads of other foreign communities, answered to the *Phrakhlang* Minister through the *Syahbandar* (harbour master) and via the interpreters.

The VOC settlement in Ayutthaya was established under conditions and in a way which reflected the importance of Siam to the company, the dependency of the Dutch upon the Siamese court, and, at the same time, a certain degree of autonomy to handle their own affairs. To put this in perspective, first of all, the *comptoir* (VOC local office) in Ayutthaya must be seen as part of the broad network of the VOC settlements that stretched from South Africa to East Asia. There were three basic types of settlement: unfortified trading-posts in the domains of powerful rulers; fortified bases; and smaller forts that controlled vast areas and island groups. The features of the Ayutthaya factory placed it in the first category, which also included such VOC establishments as Deshima in Nagasaki, and those in Canton and in Surat — places where the Dutch had submitted to the local rulers and lived under their protection.[26]

Like other foreign communities in Ayutthaya, the Siamese authorities dictated to the Dutch, deciding where they should live and trade. When King Ekathotsarot (r. 1605–1609/10) permitted the VOC to establish a trading office in his capital in 1608, this company lodge was located in a Muslim quarter within the city walls. Later, in 1634, King Prasatthong granted the Dutch a plot of land on which to build a new lodge, which became the place where VOC servants and their families were to live until the company's final withdrawal from the kingdom. This new settlement was situated south of Ayutthaya proper on the east bank of the Chao Phraya River. It was closer to the river bank, larger than the previous lodge and, therefore, more convenient for loading and unloading goods. Fortunately, situated on a high islet, it was not easily flooded.[27] Gijsbert Heeck, the company surgeon who visited Ayutthaya in 1655, described the main building as being:

> a sturdy and excellent building, rather large and high, with airy lofts and spacious, proper warehouse space below [the dining hall and offices]. Two of its sides are of white brick, with many door frames and window casings, most of them trellised and barred. The walls are built entirely of brick and plastered with good lime.

The lodge was protected by a bamboo fence and surrounded by a moat on the northern, eastern, and southern sides. A small bridge on each side connected the lodge with its main storehouse in the east and with the community surrounding it. The whole compound consisted of the main building, smaller storehouses, a garden, a cemetery, and a prison. It was spacious enough to accommodate up to forty permanent employees as well as some sojourning sailors.[28]

In the beginning, the Siamese Government allowed the Dutch to build the main edifice of the lodge as they preferred, merely stipulating that it should not be too close to the river bank and not too high, thereby complying with the kingdom's custom.[29] This was probably connected to the security of the royal water procession, which would sail down the river, passing in front of the lodge. Indubitably, it was also linked to the idea that a foreign settlement should not compete with the magnificence of the palace and temples in the city. Despite these restrictions, the French priest, Nicholas Gervaise, confirmed Heeck's aforementioned impression of the lodge, describing it as "one of the most beautiful and most spacious houses in the kingdom".[30] This quality of the building reflected the determination of the company in the 1630s that Siam trade was worthy of investment, which signalled a long stay. This two-storey building in the European style was one of the first structures to be observed by visitors entering the city of Ayutthaya via the river and must have made them aware of the Dutch presence there.

The VOC compound sometimes gave the Siamese court cause for dissatisfaction with the Dutch. In early 1636, some opponents at court — apparently trying to arouse the King's suspicions of the Dutch — told King Prasatthong that the VOC lodge had been extended to resemble a fort rather than a house, and that there were too many company men in Ayutthaya. The Dutch protested but complied with the subsequent inquiry by submitting a plan of the building and a list of the present employees, which satisfied the king.[31] In 1732, King Thaisa's interest in the VOC settlement unfortunately transformed into irritation about it. In appreciation of the company surgeon's role in the attempts to cure a sore in his mouth — which turned out to be terminal cancer — the monarch expressed an interest in finding out more about the Dutch settlement. Therefore, the court sent two servants to make drawings of the VOC lodge and its surroundings. Having seen the drawings, Thaisa became disturbed by the tombstones in the Dutch cemetery, probably because they resembled Thai pagodas. The *Phrakhlang* consequently recommended that the Dutch should tear down these "pagodas". Digging in their heels, the Dutch resisted, claiming that it was beyond the authority of the current *Opperhoofd* and council to remove the tombstones which the families of the deceased had erected using their own money.[32]

The VOC had certain other properties, besides the lodge in Ayutthaya, which were established by royal permission and also reflected the range and nature of Dutch activities within the kingdom. Most important was the company warehouse called "Amsterdam" and a smaller office in Ligor (Nakhon Srithammarat). "Amsterdam" was situated in the village of Ban Chao Phraya (often called the "Sea Village" in the VOC records) at Pak Nam, the mouth of the Chao Phraya River, which is connected to the present-day Gulf of Thailand. It was the place into which the East Indiamen called. The transportation between the warehouse and the lodge in Ayutthaya was performed by vessels — small enough to sail the river — owned by the Siam *comptoir* or local people. When Commissioner Rijckloff van Goens proposed its construction in 1650, he argued that the warehouse would protect the stored goods from the elements and facilitate the loading of the company's ships, and its supervisor would prevent the other employees from smuggling their own goods via the ships.[33] The Ligor office was operated by a few VOC residents, focusing especially on the procurement of tin. Over time, like the settlement in Ayutthaya, it developed into a mixed community of VOC personnel and local people.

Admittedly, by dividing the foreign communities in Ayutthaya into *ban* according to nationality, the Siamese authorities intended to keep them apart from the (majority of the) indigenous society, thereby making them easier to control.[34] It would be misguided, however, to regard each foreign *ban* as a unit that was completely isolated from either the other foreign communities or the indigenous people.

By the seventeenth century, there were a considerable number of foreign communities residing outside Ayutthaya proper, especially the trading communities established along the Chao Phraya River. These foreigners regularly interacted with each other. As a rule, the retiring VOC *Opperhoofd* recommended that his incumbent successor should maintain daily contact with the other nations trading in Ayutthaya. Across the river, opposite the Dutch lodge, lived the Portuguese. As Heeck observed, the relationships between the Dutch and the Portuguese living in Siam were rather amicable, for pragmatic reasons.[35] The Portuguese delivered local goods to the company besides offering a translation service because their language, besides Malay, often served as the lingua franca between the Dutch and the Siamese court.[36] To the south of the VOC settlement lay the English and Japanese *ban* as well as the Peguan (Mon) and Malay communities. The Dutch often hired the Japanese to pack the animal skins that they were exporting to Japan; they obtained these services through a contract with one of the local Japanese *nai*.[37] The contacts between these communities were not purely commercial, however; they were social and cultural as well. In the absence of Dutch clergymen from Ayutthaya, the mainly Protestant Dutch often sought out the services of the Portuguese Roman Catholic priests. In order to maintain peace with the host society and to save unnecessary costs, the VOC supported the missionary activity of the Dutch Reformed Church only to a limited extent. Clerics were appointed to reside and serve in only major Dutch settlements, especially Batavia and Colombo.

The Dutch cemetery also accommodated some Englishmen after their death as fellows in faith.[38] It was reported that, in 1730, together with "people of other religions", the VOC *Opperhoofd* and his assistant attended the burial of René Charbonneau — a former medical attendant in the French missionary hospital and later the Governor of Phuket under King Narai — in the French settlement, after which the Dutch paid a visit to the French Bishop.[39] In 1733, the Roman Catholic "Sinhora Donna Louisa Faulcon" — daughter-in-law of the late infamous grandee of Greek origin Constantine Phaulkon — appeared as a witness of the union between a VOC employee, Paulus Scheeper, and a

Eurasian woman, Maria Wens.[40] Such events reflect the cosmopolitan and almost ecumenical daily life of the foreign population in Ayutthaya, which was sometimes overshadowed by the hostile rhetoric spouted against each other, especially among the Europeans, in their written accounts.

George Vinal Smith has presented Ayutthaya as an example of a place where "the Dutch community interacted with, but was not integrated into" the local society.[41] The living conditions for the Dutch in sovereign Siam were different from such "transplanted" colonial towns in Asia as Batavia and Colombo. Above all, the VOC never considered Ayutthaya a place in which it wanted to settle a large number of Europeans; it was only a trading station. As elsewhere in Asia, the absence of European-Dutch women led to cohabitation and miscegenation between VOC men and local (Siamese, Mon, Lao, or mestizo) women. The VOC reports from the late seventeenth and early eighteenth centuries reveal that the Dutch settlement had evolved to include not only the company lodge but also an adjacent village, referred to by the Malay word *kampong*, where the population was composed of descendants of the VOC employees and the Dutch free burghers and, in a greater number, indigenous people who were attracted to live in the close vicinity because of the prospect of paid jobs and the protection which the company sometimes afforded.

In the 1720 instruction for his successor, the outgoing *Opperhoofd*, Wijbrand Blom (1717–20), reminded Hendrik Verburg that the administration of the Dutch settlement in Siam tended to be based on the oral tradition; hence, his instruction was based on experience gathered from his predecessors.[42] The content of this instruction, precisely the part which concerns the enforcement of law and order in the settlement, has four main points. Firstly, the document reveals how the VOC understood its jurisdiction over its settlement in Ayutthaya. Secondly, it issues an operational instruction to the trade director, informing him how to maintain order in the settlement. Thirdly, it suggests how to counter the local authority in the event of legal transgressions within the settlement or involving the residents of the settlement. Lastly, it instructs him how to behave in the presence of Siamese royalty.

Blom emphasized to Verburg that the VOC exercised full control over its lodge. No one was allowed to settle within the privileged terrain which had belonged to the company for almost a century without the permission of the *Opperhoofd*.[43] Although the Dutch jurisdiction over the settlement was not specified in the Dutch-Siamese Treaty, it was built upon a common understanding between the VOC and the Siamese authorities that both the terrain where the Company lodge was situated and its vessels were imbued with a kind of immunity from local law enforcement. This unwritten agreement appears to have been a precursor of diplomatic immunity.

Next, Blom pointed out that the company wanted to maintain good relations with such ordinary workers as carpenters, coolies, sailors (on inland routes), and the like, whom it regularly needed for all kinds of work. These local inhabitants of the settlement hoped to benefit from the privileges and protection which the Dutch offered to or even created for them — special rights which, in Blom's words, "could not be found outside the *kampong* other than through an almost daily practice of bribery".[44]

When the attempts of the *kampong* inhabitants to sell small commodities at the nearby bazaar next to Wat Phananchoeng (north of the Dutch settlement) were repeatedly obstructed by the bazaar master, Blom solved this problem by procuring a licence from the court which allowed the Dutch to establish a market in their settlement in the grounds behind the lodge. In return, the bazaar paid a tax of "four *taels* or 28.16 florins per year" to the Siamese Government. The *Opperhoofd* appointed a resident to collect the rent from the traders on a daily basis. Blom remarked that the market not only yielded a rather satisfying income, but also offered an impressively wide variety of goods. The Dutch certainly discerned the dynamics of the local economy and took advantage of the prospering domestic markets — which were evidently under royal control.[45]

With regard to the people in the settlement, Blom pointed out that no one had the power to arrest any inhabitant of the *kampong* except by the express instruction of the *Phrakhlang* or the court. To ensure that this was observed, the arrest warrant must be addressed first to the company interpreters, who would then communicate it to the *Opperhoofd*. Should someone insist on arresting a resident on his own authority and without the express instructions of the court, the company employees should either courteously escort him out of the *kampong*, or tell him to resubmit his demand via the *Phrakhlang*.[46]

The Dutch side also had obligations. Consequently, as a result of the prevailing Siamese law, in cases of manslaughter, creating an affray and the like, which caused injury or death, the perpetrator must immediately be arrested to prevent his escape. The case must be reported to the *Phrakhlang*. The company should attempt to secure a fair process in the court. Whenever a murder, manslaughter, serious physical assault, or theft had occurred, the local authority would draw a circle around the crime scene. For this purpose, a pole was planted on the spot where the crime had been committed, to which was tied a cord about thirty-six fathoms long. Using the pole as the centre, the cord was swung round to create a circle. Those who lived within the radius of this circle were to be arrested and interrogated to determine whether or not they had been complicit in the crime. If they were not involved, they still had to pay a fine of "no less than five *taels* or thirty-six florins" for failing to help to prevent the crime and to bear the further costs of the arrest. Blom warned that the employment of this local method could also affect the Dutch *kampong*, should a crime be committed in its vicinity.[47]

In the event of a fire within the settlement, the VOC should act according to the local law by arresting the head of the house in which the fire had broken out and immediately summon him to be tried in a criminal process. Blom actually considered this Siamese rule a "sound concept". Nevertheless, he emphasized that the VOC must act quickly to prevent the arrest of such an individual by the Siamese authorities and try him within the *kampong* or by their own Council of Justice, even without instructions from the *Phrakhlang* or the court. In this way, friction with the local government might be prevented.[48]

As a further precaution, the number of bamboo-built houses in the *kampong* must be limited because they were highly flammable. Fires caused by carelessness indeed broke out annually. To prevent a repetition of the great fire of 1718, Blom himself had ordered some houses to be torn down and others to be moved further away from the lodge, yet he admitted that it was rather difficult to exercise control over the way in which houses were constructed in the settlement. For example, when someone asked for permission to plant a garden on the northern side of the lodge, shortly afterwards a house also appeared there, followed by all kinds of other buildings.[49]

Apparently, the VOC tried to limit the number of residents in its settlement. Blom described the Siamese as a "quarrelsome nation" and, therefore, warned that the more of them lived in the lodge, the more problems they would cause, thereby bringing the Dutch chiefs into conflict with the local government. However much the VOC relied on the co-operation of the people in its settlement, in order to avoid conflict with the Siamese Government, the lodge authorities had to remove anyone from the *kampong* who misbehaved. Sometimes, as a warning, the trouble-makers could be gaoled for a few days and flogged in imitation of the Dutch custom of maintaining discipline on ships.[50]

According to the Dutch experience, some undesirable local types occasionally tried to move into the *kampong* on the pretext of being friends of the inhabitants, in order to escape the administration of punishment by the local government. In an attempt to prevent this kind of opportunism, Blom had ordered an annual census of the inhabitants, which was to be conducted in January of every year. The Dutch also intended to use this registration as evidence for convincing the local authorities of their good intentions, when they had to confirm or deny the residence status of the persons who might have been involved in legal problems.[51] Actually, the first survey had probably been conducted in January 1689, when, as a result of the unrest caused by the sudden presence of an unusual number of criminals in Ayutthaya, the VOC decided to compile a list, describing the inhabitants of its *kampong*. Although the *Opperhoofd* unfortunately decided not to include that list in his report, his excuse being that it was not worth reporting to Batavia because the inhabitants, especially the petty traders and coolies, constantly change, it also gives us a glimpse of the sort of people residing within the Dutch settlement.[52] The only surviving statistics of the local residents of the Dutch *kampong* date from 1732, listing 240 households consisting of 1,443 men, women, and children.[53]

Debt settlement was a logical exception to the attempted self-administration of justice by the Dutch, in the sense that the VOC entrusted this problem to the local law enforcement agencies. It was such an important a matter that it was included in the 1664 Treaty:

> In case … a debtor of the Honourable Company refuse [*sic*] the payment of his debt, His Majesty after being duly advised to that effect by Oya Berckelang … shall assist the Honourable Company to recover its claim by arresting the defaulter and keeping him in custody until the claim shall have been settled. If, however, the Honourable Company might fail to obtain in this way the full payment of its claim, the King or Oya Bercclang [*sic*] shall be bound to deliver the debtor to the said Company.[54]

Blom's instruction shows that the same procedure was to be applied to the local inhabitants of the Dutch settlement. If a resident had incurred a debt and refused to pay it, he should be referred to the *Phrakhlang*. His debt should be settled according to Siamese custom.[55] Since the Dutch were in great need of the assistance of the local government in this matter, they willingly reciprocated also.

From Blom's instruction, we can see that: firstly, the VOC chose to deal with cases of fire itself; secondly, it was willing to call in the local authority to solve matters arising from debt; and, lastly, it was obliged to trust the case of a murder or physical assault to the local justice system. However, Blom reminded his successor that, whenever a European employee was accused of being the offender, the *Opperhoofd* as well as the local authority must rule on the case in accordance with the extraterritorial clause in the Dutch-Siamese Treaty. By virtue of the said agreement and Dutch law, a European employee could not be arrested by the Siamese authorities, summoned to appear in a local court, interrogated, sentenced, or executed by the Siamese Government in cases of debt, physical assault, or manslaughter.[56]

In general, the VOC tried to retain its employees' affairs in its own hands. There was one exception, in 1713, when the Dutch sailor, Jodocus de Vries, was murdered by some Chinese, among them the servant of a Chinese official. Since the case involved two foreign parties, it required arbitration by the Siamese authorities. After a long struggle on the part of the Dutch, the Siamese judges sentenced the murderers only to life imprisonment, on the grounds that they were not subjects of the Siamese King and therefore could not be granted the death sentence in Siam. In the absence of legal evidence to prove the existence of this rule, we are compelled to resort to the explanation that the strong Chinese elements at King Thaisa's court may have intervened to protect their convicted compatriots.[57]

To return to the last point of Blom's instruction, another highly important matter to which he drew his successor's attention was the manner in which to prepare the VOC lodge and employees for any appearance of Siamese royalty. The mere presence of the Siamese King had legal implications in itself. The code of conduct was certainly known among the employees stationed in Siam.[58] However, Blom carefully instructed his successor, who was a newcomer, regarding which points of etiquette to observe whenever the King and his suite passed by the lodge. The Dutch were obliged to decorate the front fence of the lodge and company vessels with flags. The company's ceremonial barge also had to be manned with rowers. The company guards had to be relocated from in front of the gateway to behind the fence. The *Opperhoofd* and his assistant were to present themselves under a tent, waiting to greet the King in the Siamese way as he and his suite passed by. While the royal procession was passing, no one was allowed to traverse the riverbank in front of the lodge or to stare at the royals.[59] Any infringement of this rule was punishable by death.

Conflicts

In addition to the commercial disagreements which occurred almost daily, incidents involving the company settlement and its residents sometimes brought the Dutch into conflict with the Siamese authorities.

Despite the rising power of the VOC in Southeast Asia, at any time, the Siamese King could, in practice, pressurize the company employees residing in his realm through the very fact that, devoid of any substantial military capacity, their lives depended upon his mercy alone. Laying siege to the VOC lodge in Ayutthaya was one of the common ways in which the court expressed its dissatisfaction with the Dutch and by which it tried to force them to make concessions. Sometimes, the "immunity" of the VOC personnel and lodge was contested, which, in effect, meant that the degree of the 'immunity' tended to be dependent on the actual state of the relations between the company and the Siamese Crown. On one occasion, in early 1689, the Siamese Minister of Justice sent his men into the Dutch settlement to arrest some *kampong* inhabitants and carry them off to prison without informing the *Opperhoofd*. When the Dutch immediately protested to the *Phrakhlang*, on principle, to "preserve the privilege of the lodge" rather than in an attempt to defend the rights of the captives, the minister was forced to apologize for violating the company's immunity.[60] This happened at a time when the VOC enjoyed great favour with the newly crowned King Phetracha (r. 1688–1703). During the eighteenth century, the Siamese court increasingly resorted to inspections of the VOC lodge and ships. The search for contraband goods occasionally gave the Siamese officials a pretext for inspecting the Dutch settlement and vessels. In 1713, the officials raided the *kampong* searching for opium; the incident resulted in a scuffle and the death of the mestizo interpreter, Pieter Brochebourde.[61] In 1731, the Siamese wanted to search a company ship which allegedly bore a contraband cargo of elephant tusks. The Dutch vehemently argued that this action would conflict with the "long tradition" which gave them immunity. Eventually, both parties reached a compromise; the Dutch unloaded the suspected tusks from the ship and took them to the lodge for inspection by the officials.[62]

The Dutch and the Siamese jurisdictions did or would theoretically overlap each other on three counts: the local inhabitants of the Dutch settlement; the VOC employees who also accepted the service of the king; and the offspring of VOC fathers and indigenous mothers.

More minor conflicts may have appeared on a daily basis when the Dutch tried to take control of and provide protection for non-VOC employees. In some cases, the Dutch did no more than to attempt to prevent the *kampong* residents from being investigated by Siamese law enforcement. On occasion, they even attempted to free the residents from the labour recruitment by the court, as happened in 1731, although without success, when the men in the settlement were taken for the construction of a pagoda.[63] The recruitment of men by the Siamese authorities, whether for the preparation of a grand ceremony, war, or construction work, as in this case, deprived the VOC of labourers with whom to pursue its own business.

If we compare the number of the local (presumably indigenous as well as mestizo) residents of the Dutch settlement — the statistics for 1732 suggest about 1,500 persons — to the number of the population of Ayutthaya — Anthony Reid has suggested an estimation of 200,000 people for the late seventeenth century — the former appears insignificant, as it fails to constitute even one per cent of the latter.[64] Although the Dutch clearly had no intention of expanding their power in this matter, it remains the fact that, up until the early eighteenth century, as our sources reveal, at least some of these 1,500 people, who moved into the Dutch settlement for benefit and protection, simultaneously moved away from their original Siamese *nai* towards a foreign one. Therefore, the VOC in Siam also functioned under the Siamese model of the patron-client relationship, with a foreign body being the patron of the indigenous clients.

Our Dutch and French sources agree that a third of the estate of a deceased servant went to the king, and occasionally the whole of it.[65] Although the Dutch director enjoyed a ranking at court, the king did not claim his assets after his demise, which confirmed that his position at court was relatively superficial.

One extraordinary case was that of the VOC doctor of French Huguenot origin, Daniel Brochebourde, who was seconded in 1672, with the approval of Batavia, to attend King Narai in his medical capacity. He became the favourite of Kings Narai and Phetracha, and his mestizo descendants, including the aforementioned Pieter, continued to serve both the Crown and the company in Siam as court physicians and interpreters. After having served both the VOC and the Siamese court, however, when Daniel died in 1697, the money he left reverted to the Crown, on the grounds that it was the result of the king's generosity towards him and that his heirs, who were born of an indigenous woman and were therefore subjects of the king, were considered to be subject to the inheritance law of Siam and the royal jurisdiction, which authorized the king to become the heir of his deceased servants. In this case, the VOC *Opperhoofd* allowed the process of Siamese law to take its course without protest.[66]

As time passed, jurisdiction over the mestizo children became a regular source of conflict between the VOC and the Siamese court. One structural inadequacy of this port polity was manpower. It is thus understandable that, in Siam, natives and the children of natives, including those who were partly foreign, were automatically the subjects of the king. The laws of 1633 and 1663, promulgated by Prasatthong and Narai respectively, forbade Thai and Mon women to cohabit with foreign men, who held "erroneous beliefs", including Europeans, Javanese, and Malays. The kings were concerned that such unions and the resultant offspring would harm the Buddhist religion and the state, and that the manpower of Siam would become diluted by confusion about the children's identity.[67] Naturally, it proved impossible to uphold this law in the cosmopolitan society of Ayutthaya. The fact that each case concerning Dutch-indigenous children was treated differently reflects the state of Dutch-Siamese relations at that time. The matter was ever further complicated by the fact that the Siamese authorities, recognizing the weakness of the Dutch in their concern about the considerable number of their mestizo offspring in Siam, sometimes used the seizure of these children as a means of punishing the Dutch during the recurrent crises in their relations.

The VOC occasionally retrieved children from their Asian mothers when their European fathers had died or been repatriated.[68] It seemed that the Dutch would rather place these Eurasian offspring in the orphanage in Batavia than leave them in the care of their indigenous mothers to be brought up in a "heathen" way. In 1689, the Siam *comptoir* asked the Governor-General to consider taking the half-Dutch children born of local women to Batavia, or having an orphanage built in Ayutthaya.[69] This is an indication that the mestizo children — whose number unfortunately was not mentioned — had become a "problem" for the VOC office in Ayutthaya which required a solution from the High Government.

Whenever the VOC wanted to take the local or mestizo wives and/or children of its employees out of the country, it had to ask royal permission for each particular case, mostly not without trouble but with reasonable success. Despite their attempts to prohibit the cohabitation between indigenous women and non-Buddhist foreigners, Kings Prasatthong and Narai had allowed the Dutch to take some mestizo children out of the kingdom without much objection.[70]

Exceptionally difficult was the extrication of Van Vliet's children because their mother, Osoet, who was an influential Mon merchant, had successfully activated all of her contacts at court to prevent them from being sent to Batavia, until her death in 1658.[71] Another problematic case occurred when, around 1690–1, Daniel Brochebourde's son, Moses, wanted to leave the company's service. The *Opperhoofd*, Pieter van den Hoorn (1688–91), consequently threatened to send him to Batavia. The *Phrakhlang* took young Brochebourde under his protection, claiming that Moses was the king's subject, because he had been born to a local woman, and had entered royal service.[72] Finally, the Dutch considered the case unworthy of a legal wrangle and surrendered Moses Brochebourde. In 1706, when the VOC was temporarily withdrawing from Siam after a dispute with the Crown, the bookkeeper, Gerrit de Haas, asked for the court's permission to take his wife, who was a Dutch-Mon mestizo, and their children with him. King Süa (r. 1703–9) refused on the grounds that they were his subjects, but he was probably also acting out a grudge he bore against the company. Finally, in 1710, upon the plea of the Governor-General, the new king, Thaisa (r. 1709–33), granted permission for this.[73]

When the relationship between the company and the court was breaking down in 1740–1, the Dutch were faced with two additional problems. Firstly, some drunken company soldiers had assaulted some Siamese people, including monks, injuring one of them fatally. Insisting on their extra-territorial rights, the Dutch refused to hand over their compatriots to the *Phrakhlang* and were forced to pay compensation to the injured Siamese.[74] It was, however, the second case that the court seemed to take more seriously. Floris van Essen, the warehouse supervisor, attempted to smuggle his child born of a local woman out of Siam aboard a Dutch ship. The Siamese court demanded that the *Opperhoofd* should punish Van Essen; otherwise, the Siamese threatened, notwithstanding the extraterritorial rights of the Dutch, to take him to the Amsterdam warehouse and behead him there! Under pressure from the court, the company's council in Ayutthaya decided to flog Van Essen (which took place in the presence of the Siamese officials but without any European witnesses, in order to prevent any further humiliation for him), to suspend his salary, and to send him to Batavia immediately.[75]

Conclusion

One of the primary purposes of the Dutch-Siamese treaties securing was extraterritorial rights for VOC employees and Dutch subjects in Siam. This shows that, contrary to Manop Thavornwatsakul's conclusion, not all foreigners were bound by Siamese law. Although the company's naval blockade of 1663–4 and several threats to the Dutch by the Siamese authorities must have aroused a sense of caution on both sides, the limits of the relations between the VOC and the Siamese court were never put to the test. These measures served rather as a signal that the one party was seeking a concession from the other. Moreover, while the Dutch in Ayutthaya were privileged with their extraterritorial rights, in practice, they felt vulnerable and carefully avoided coming into any conflict with the Siamese authorities.

Furthermore, the study of our Dutch sources reveals that the VOC was required by the local authority to share responsibility for legal and social order of Siam. Han ten Brummelhuis has asserted that "[the] etiquette of the Siamese court also made the position of [VOC trade] director even more important than it already was in the company hierarchy".[76] Yet, it was not only his status in the hierarchy of the Siamese court but also his actual responsibility as the *nai* of the Dutch *ban* which made him very important in Siamese society. Life at the lodge reveals another obligation of the Dutch merchants towards the Siamese king: besides their roles as diplomats and courtiers, they were "administrative officials", a body governing a part of the population of Ayutthaya. In this sense, the Dutch were more deeply integrated into the Siamese system than George Vinal Smith has suggested: that the Dutch-Siamese interactions could be seen only at the higher level of Thai society, at court.[77]

Both the court of Ayutthaya and the High Government in Batavia allowed the multi-ethnic societies in the territories under their jurisdiction to exercise legal plurality; that is, they gave limited administrative and judicial autonomy to other ethnic groups.[78] The VOC in Siam made a tremendous effort to explore the possibility, which the Siamese legal plurality allowed, of ordering its affairs in its own way. The Dutch-Thai case was not unique in the whole context of the cross-cultural interactions between Asia and Europe in the early modern period. The plurality of the legal system did exist in practice in many places in Asia by the approval of the indigenous rulers as well as the overseas European authorities as a response to the cosmopolitan environment of its time, when a nation-state that enforced the monopoly of order and justice was still merely a concept.

Notes

* This chapter is a revised version of Chapter Two of my *Dutch East India Company Merchants at the Court of Ayutthaya: Dutch Perceptions of the Thai Kingdom,*

c. 1604–1765 (Leiden: Brill, 2007), pp. 35–54, and is published here with kind permission of Koninklijke Brill N.V.

1. Joost Schouten in: François Caron and Joost Schouten, *A True Description of the Mighty Kingdoms of Japan and Siam*, tr. Roger Manley, ed. C.R. Boxer (London: Argonaut Press, 1935), p. 108 (originally published in 1638; hereafter, Schouten, *Description of Siam*).
2. Only a few of those studies are to be named here. The major works on the commercial relations are Sarasin Viraphol, *Tribute and Profit: Sino-Siamese Trade 1652–1853* (Cambridge, Mass/London: Harvard University Press, 1977); George Vinal Smith, *The Dutch in Seventeenth-Century Thailand* (Northern Illinois: Centre for Southeast Asian Studies, 1977); Kennon Breazeale, ed., *From Japan to Arabia: Ayutthaya's Maritime Relations with Asia* (Bangkok: The Foundation for the Promotion of Social Sciences and Humanities Textbooks Project, 1999). The studies of the political, social and cultural interactions between Ayutthaya/Siam and the Europeans include Dirk van der Cruysse, *Siam and the West 1500–1700*, tr. (from French) Michael Smithies (Chiang Mai: Silkworm Books, 2002); Han ten Brummelhuis, *Merchant, Courtier and Diplomat: a History of the Contacts between the Netherlands and Thailand* (Lochem-Gent: De Tijdstroom, 1987).
3. The *Kotmai Tra Sam Duang* were compiled and revised, on the basis of the surviving laws of Ayutthaya, in 1805, at the behest of the founder of the Chakri Dynasty, King Rama I (r. 1782–1809).
4. Manop Thavornwatsakul, "kot mai keaw kab chao tang chat nai samai Ayutthaya" (Law Pertaining to Foreigners during the Ayutthaya Period), *ruam bot kwam prawatsat* 21 (1999): 96–112.
5. Robert Lingat, "La condition des étrangers au Siam au XVIIe siècle", in *Recueils de la Société Jean Bodin*, IX: *L'étranger*, ed. John Gilissen (Bruxelles: Editions de la librairie encyclopédique, 1958), pp. 255–66.
6. Smith, *The Dutch in Seventeenth-Century Thailand*, p. 111.
7. See, for example, the instructions to the VOC employees of 1607 and 1617, in Pieter van Dam, *Beschryvinge van de Oostindische Compagnie*, ed. F.W. Stapel (The Hague: Nijhoff, 1927), I, pp. 584–60. (Pieter van Dam is the author of this historical text written in the eighteenth century. The text is later edited for publication in the twentieth century.) These instructions gave direction to the trade directors and assistants about how to administer such company affairs as record- and bookkeeping, handling the VOC ships, and disciplining subordinates on the spot. The 1607 order was especially concerned with the behaviour of employees; for instance, it prohibited private trade, the conversion to Asian religions, the maintenance of a luxurious lifestyle, and courtship with local women. The first and the last were difficult to prevent.
8. See Kennon Breazeale, "Thai Maritime Trade and the Ministry Responsible", in *idem* (ed.), *From Japan to Arabia*, pp. 23–45.
9. Gijsbert Heeck, *A Traveller in Siam in the Year 1655: Extracts from the Journal of Gijsbert Heeck*, translated and introduced by Barend Jan Terwiel (Chiang Mai: Silkworm Books, 2008), p. 48 (hereafter, Heeck, *A Traveller in Siam*).

10. For the ranks, titles, and insignia which the Dutch *Opperhoofd* usually received, see Smith, *The Dutch in Seventeenth-Century Thailand*, p. 106.
11. The content of this Treaty appears in J.E. Heeres, ed., *Corpus Diplomaticum Neerlando-Indicum: verzameling van politieke contracten en verdere verdragen door de Nederlanders in het Oosten gesloten, van privilegebrieven aan hen verleend, enz* ('s-Gravenhage: Martinus Nijhoff, 1931), II, pp. 280–5 (hereafter *Corpus Diplomaticum*); Smith, *The Dutch in Seventeenth-Century Thailand*, pp. 138–41 (English translation).
12. VOC 1945, Memorie door genoemde heer Blom aan sijn vervanger ter naricht gelaten (Instruction by (Wijbrand) Blom to his successor), 22 Dec. 1720, pp. 30–92. The records of the Dutch East India Company referred to in this article are kept in the *Nationaal Archief* (NA), The Hague.
13. Schouten, *Description of Siam*, 100; Jeremias van Vliet, *Description of Siam*, in *idem*, ed. Chris Baker *et al.* (Chiang Mai: Silkworm Books, 2005), pp. 112, 153–4 (hereafter Van Vliet, *Description of Siam*).
14. Van Vliet, *Description of Siam*, p. 107.
15. Schouten, *Description of Siam*, pp. 100–1; see also Van Vliet, *Description of Siam*, p. 154. A person could prove his innocence by swallowing this charmed rice ball without spitting it out.
16. Dhiravat, *A Political History of Siam under the Prasatthong Dynasty, 1629–1688* (Dissertation, University of London, 1984), pp. 210–2.
17. Han ten Brummelhuis and John Kleinen, *A Dutch Picnic in Ayutthaya, 1636* (Amsterdam: University of Amsterdam, 1984). The incident was elaborately documented by Jeremias van Vliet in the form of a diary, first published in 1647. It has been translated into English as "The Diary of the Picnic Incident, 1636–7", with an introduction by Alfons van der Kraan, in Van Vliet in *Van Vliet's Siam*, ed. Baker *et al.*, pp. 37–88 (hereafter Van Vliet, "Diary of the Picnic Incident").
18. Van Vliet, "Diary of the Picnic Incident", pp. 86–8.
19. For the text of this declaration, see Van Vliet, "Diary of the Picnic Incident", p. 84. It is incorporated as "Copie van de acte door den Siamschen coninck den coopman Jeremias van Vliet afgedrongen te passeren ende nae te coomen" (Copy of the Act Forced by the Siamese King upon Merchant Jeremias van Vliet to issue and observe), 30 september [*sic*] 1636", in *Corpus Diplomaticum*, I, pp. 284–5.
20. Robert Lingat, "La condition des étrangers au Siam", pp. 255–6, 262; Smith, *The Dutch in Seventeenth-Century Thailand*, p. 38; Ten Brummelhuis, *Merchant, Courtier and Diplomat*, p. 38.
21. "The Dutch-Thai Treaty of 1664", in Smith, *The Dutch in Seventeenth-Century Thailand*, p. 139.
22. VOC 1415, Missive Johannes Keijts to Batavia, 17 Dec. 1685, fos. 896^r–897^v.
23. For the text of the Franco-Siamese Treaty of 10 Dec. 1685, see L. de Reinach, *Recueil des traités conclus par la France en Extrême-Orient*, I: 1684–1902 (Paris: Leroux, 1902), pp. 4–6; for the text of the Franco-Siamese Treaty of 11 Dec. 1687, see Reinach, *Recueil des traités*, I, pp. 8–13; see also Van der Cruysse, *Siam and the West*, pp. 346–7.

24. Lingat regards this as a remarkable suggestion from the French side, an anticipation of the International Court. See Lingat, "La condition des étrangers au Siam", pp. 261–2.
25. VOC 2193, Transport gedaen door het opperhooft Rogier van Alderwereld aen sijn vervanger Pieter Sijen, 1731, fos. 203–6.
26. Kees Zandvliet, "Vestingbouw in de Oost", in *De Verenigde Oost-Indische Compagnie tussen oorlog en diplomatie*, ed. Gerrit Knaap and Ger Teitler (Leiden: KITLV, 2002), pp. 151–80, esp. pp. 167–70.
27. Smith, *The Dutch in Seventeenth-Century Thailand*, 101; VOC 1118, Dagregister (Daily Report) Schouten, 10 July 1634, fo. 75[r], Missive Schouten to Batavia, 15 Nov. 1634, fo. 48[v]; VOC 3089, Missive Werndlij to Batavia, 31 Dec. 1763, fos. 12–4. Werndlij wrote that the islet remained dry, even when the neighbourhood lay three to four feet under water.
28. Heeck, *A Traveller in Siam*, pp. 54–7; Smith, *The Dutch in Seventeenth-Century Thailand*, pp. 54–7.
29. VOC 1118, Dagregister Schouten, 10 July 1634, fo. 75[r].
30. Nicholas Gervaise, *The Natural and Political History of the Kingdom of Siam*, tr. and ed. John Villiers (Bangkok: White Lotus, 1998), p. 48 (originally published in 1688).
31. VOC 1119, Dagregister Van Vliet, 6 Apr. 1636, fo. 1340[r].
32. VOC 2239, Dagregister Sijen, 18 July 1732, fo. 60. For a report about the VOC's participation in the attempts to cure King Thaisa's cancer, see Dhiravat na Pombejra, "The Last Year of King Thaisa's Reign: Data Concerning Politics and Society from the Dutch East India Company's Siam Factory *Dagregister* for 1732", in *Khwam yokyon khong adeet* (The Wilderness of the Past), ed. Winai Pongsripian (Bangkok, 1994), pp. 125–45.
33. Alfons van der Kraan, "On Company Business: The Rijckloff van Goens Mission to Siam, 1650", *Itinerario* 22/2 (1998): 42–84, esp. 68.
34. Dhiravat na Pombejra, "VOC participation in Siamese Society during the Late Ayutthaya Period, 1688-1767", in *idem*, *Court, Company, and Campong: Essays on the VOC Presence in Ayutthaya* (Ayutthaya: Ayutthaya Historical Study Centre, 1992), pp. 44–62, esp. p. 46.
35. Heeck, *A Traveller in Siam*, p. 61.
36. For example, the VOC used the local Portuguese to go upcountry — where the Dutch were not allowed to visit — to buy goods, such as deerskins. VOC 1119, Dagregister Schouten, 19 Sept. 1636, fo. 1303.
37. Smith, *The Dutch in Seventeenth-Century Thailand*, p. 101.
38. VOC 1458, Dagregister Pieter van den Hoorn, 5 Mar. 1689, fo. 501[r].
39. VOC 2193, Dagregister Van Alderwereld, 20 and 21 Nov. 1730, fos. 47–8; Dhiravat, "VOC participation in Siamese Society", p. 49. On René Charbonneau, see Dhiravat na Pombejra, "Towards a History of Seventeenth-Century Phuket", in *Recalling the Pasts: Autonomous History in Southeast Asia*, ed. Sunait Chutintaranond and Chris Baker (Chiang Mai: Silkworm Books, 2002), pp. 89–126, esp. pp. 120–1.

40. VOC 2286, Originele resolutie op 11 April 1732 rakende het huwelijk van de Barquir Paulus Scheper en de jonge dochter Maria Wens (Resolution concerning the marriage of Paulus Scheeper and Maria Wens), fo. 92.
41. Smith, *The Dutch in Seventeenth-Century Thailand*, p. 111.
42. VOC 1945, Memorie W. Blom, 22 Dec. 1720, fo. 68.
43. Ibid., fo. 69.
44. Ibid., fo. 73.
45. Ibid., fos. 72-3; see also Anthony Reid, *Southeast Asia in the Age of Commerce, 1450–1680*, II: *Expansion and Crisis* (New Haven: Yale University Press, 1993), pp. 90–3.
46. VOC 1945, Memorie W. Blom, 22 Dec. 1720, fo. 69.
47. Ibid., fos. 70–1.
48. Ibid., fo. 75.
49. Ibid., fo. 75.
50. Ibid., fo. 69.
51. Ibid., fos. 75–6.
52. VOC 1458, Dagregister Van den Hoorn, 19 Jan. 1689, fo. 465^{r}.
53. VOC 2239, Dagregister Sijen, 5 May 1732, fo. 39.
54. "The Dutch-Thai Treaty of 1664", in Smith, *The Dutch in Seventeenth-Century Thailand*, p. 139.
55. VOC 1945, Memorie W. Blom, 22 Dec. 1720, fo. 69.
56. VOC 1945, Memorie W. Blom, 22 Dec. 1720, fo. 70.
57. The case of the murder of De Vries is presented in Dhiravat, "VOC participation in Siamese Society", p. 57. VOC 1841, Missive Dirck Blom to Batavia, 15 Dec. 1713, fos. 29–30; Translaet vonnis van de Siamse Coning over de moordenaars van de matroos Jodocus de Vries (Translation of the verdict of the Siamese King on the murderers of the sailor Jodocus de Vries), 5 Feb. 1713, fos. 38–41.
58. For instance, as early as 1621, Van Nijenrode had written that everyone had to step outside their houses to lie prostrate and pay homage to the King's procession, and whoever failed to do so incurred heavy punishment, even death. Cornelis van Nijenrode, "Remonstrantie en verthoninge der gelegentheyt des coninckrijx van Siam mitsgaders haeren handel ende wandel ende waar de negotie meest in bestaet etc", *Kroniek van het Historisch Genootschap Gevestigd te Utrecht* 10 (1854): 176–91, esp. 181.
59. VOC 1945, Memorie W. Blom, 22 Dec. 1720, fos. 91–2.
60. VOC 1458, Dagregister Van den Hoorn, 19 Jan. 1689, fo. 467^{r-v}.
61. Dhiravat na Pombejra, "Ayutthaya as a Cosmopolitan Society: a Case Study of Daniel Brochebourde and His Descendants", in *idem*, *Court, Company, and Campong*, pp. 25–43, esp. p. 37; Ten Brummelhuis, *Merchant, Courtier and Diplomat*, p. 47.
62. VOC 2193, Dagregister Van Alderwereld, 30 Nov.-3 Dec. 1731, fos. 180–3.
63. Ibid., 25 & 26 June 1731, fos. 154–5.
64. Reid, *Age of Commerce*, II, p. 71.
65. Van Vliet, *Description of Siam*, pp. 164–5; Heeck, *A Traveller in Siam*, p. 61; Abbé de Choisy, *Journal of a Voyage to Siam 1685-1686*, tr. Michael Smithies (Kuala Lumpur: 1993), p. 190 (originally published in 1687).

66. Dhiravat, "Ayutthaya as a Cosmopolitan Society", pp. 35–6.
67. Dhiravat na Pombejra, "VOC Employees and their Relationships with Mon and Siamese Women: A Case Study of Osoet Pegua", in *Other Pasts: Women, Gender and History in Early Modern Southeast Asia*, ed. Barbara Watson Andaya (Hawaii: Center for Southeast Asian Studies, 2000), pp. 195–214, esp. pp. 209–11.
68. Jean Gelman Taylor, *The Social World of Batavia: European and Eurasian in Dutch Asia* (Wisconsin: The University of Wisconsin Press, 1983), pp. 43, 76.
69. VOC 1456, Rapport Keijts, 14 Feb. 1689, fo. 2012v.
70. For example, VOC 1139, Journaelsche aenteeckeninge van den commissaris Jeremias van Vliet (Journal notes of Commissioner Jeremias van Vliet), 1 Nov. 1641, fo. 776v; VOC 1362, Missive Faa to Batavia, 26 Dec. 1680, fo. 956v.
71. Dhiravat, "VOC Employees and their Relationships with Mon and Siamese Women", pp. 206–7.
72. Dhiravat, "Daniel Brochebourde and his Descendants", p. 35.
73. Dhiravat, "VOC participation in Siamese Society", pp. 54–6.
74. Ibid., 29 Jan. 1741, fo. 227; 10 Feb. 1741, fos. 251-3; 11 Feb. 1741, fo. 258.
75. Ibid., 11 Feb. 1741, fos. 253–7.
76. Ibid., fo. 55.
77. Smith, *The Dutch in Seventeenth-Century Thailand*, p. 102.
78. Remco Raben, "Batavia and Colombo: the Ethnic and Spatial Order of Two Colonial Cities" (Dissertation, Leiden University, 1996), p. 197.

CHAPTER 8

Cultural Interaction between the British Diaspora in Madras and the Host Community, 1650–1790

Søren Mentz

The portrait of the British officer William Palmer in the India Office Library is a remarkable painting. Palmer is situated in the centre of the canvas, together with his household, including his Muslim wife, their children, sister-in-law and three servants, apparently the children's nannies. He gazes devotedly towards his wife and children, while holding hands with his sister-in-law.[1]

The painting displays the easy domesticity of a late eighteenth century Englishman, comfortable in an Indian setting, although carefully maintaining the fact that he has not gone native. It asserts his English identity, even though the scenario lacks any illusion to European culture.

The impression which strikes the spectator is one of harmony — cultural interaction without racial undertones. However, the motive and the composition are remarkable. Indeed, the painting was executed during an extraordinary period in Indian history, during which the Subcontinent was being transformed from various independent states ruled by Indian princes into a colony under British hegemony.

Few scholars have described the social and cultural aspects of the British society in Madras or studied the interaction between the British merchants and the Indian population. The focus has been directed towards Bengal and Calcutta rather than towards the Coromandel Coast.[2] Exceptions are H. Dodwell's *The Nabobs of Madras* and Percival Spear's book *The Nabobs. A Study of the Social Life of the English in Eighteenth Century India*, in which the author describes cultural interaction as a difficult process:

Fig. 1 "William Palmer and his family," by Johan Zoffany. ©British Library Board. All Rights Reserved.

> The contact of two races so dissimilar in character, in culture and in institutions as the English and the Indian raises the problem of the contacts of cultures in its most acute form. Mutual influence is easiest when two cultures are basically the same; radical difference tends either to mutual repulsion or to absorption of one by the other.[3]

Although the global age of the twenty-first century has proven Spear's assumption to be incorrect, his view was generally accepted in the heyday of imperialism during the 1930s.

When describing social life in Madras, Spear divided the period from 1650 to 1790 into two chronological periods:

(1) 1650–*c.*1740: a period with limited social relations between the English merchants and Indians. The English kept to themselves, creating a diaspora of the mother country in order to avoid assimilation with the host society.

(2) 1740–*c.*1790: a period during which the position of the East India Company changed. Merchants became soldiers, diplomats and administrators. It was the golden age of the adventurer and diplomatist and Englishmen became more familiar with Indian society. However, relationships developed primarily with Indian princes and members of the military aristocracy.

> The military success had given Europeans an entry into aristocratic Indian society during a period when the Indians still maintained positions of authority.

Spear's argument has been challenged by scholars like Holden Furber and Peter Marshall. In their view, the period from 1600–1750 was an age of partnership, during which Englishman and Indians lived in mutual respect and dependence. British commerce was carried out in partnership with indigenous merchant groups who invested capital in English vessels, while English traders bought merchandize on credit while drinking tea in the bazaars.[4] As the English did not speak the Indian languages, they preferred to use commercial middlemen, who could act on their behalf in the Indian market; as such, "a complex pattern of relations arose through which British and Indian traders rendered one another services".[5]

The logic of these arguments is that one cannot undertake commercial activity without personal contact. Naturally, the British merchants bought and sold goods from their Indian counterparts. For instance, during the 1670s, the diamond merchant, Nathaniel Chomley, frequently travelled from Masulipatnam and Madras to the mines in Golconda. He purchased precious stones in person.[6] Chomley spoke several local dialects and was on friendly terms with many Indian merchants. However, the extent to which he actually interacted with Indian society is a relevant question, and, in the following, I will argue that Spear's chronology is worth studying.

The Period 1650–1740

I have elsewhere argued that the development of an English society in Madras was, to a large extent, inspired by the mother country.[7] Social interaction with Indians was kept to an absolute minimum. Aspects of English daily life in Madras resembled those of a British provincial town, although newly appointed company servants would be overwhelmed by their confrontation by Indian culture and finding their colleagues under the influence of several Indian habits.

Going native was considered the worst possible behaviour for an Englishman; far from home, the private merchants protected their cultural identity. They considered themselves loyal British subjects, even though circumstances had forced them to leave their own country for a while. Spear describes the relationship between the English community and the Indians as follows: "In thought and opinion there was separation and disapproval without contempt."[8]

When going to Madras, the British merchants anticipated that their stay would be temporary; five to ten years at most would be sufficient to earn a small fortune, which would enable them to return home again. They had no ambition to make India their permanent home. Thus, it was of the utmost importance to maintain contact with the mother country, not only financially but also socially and culturally.

The circulation of persons between India and the mother country was essential for the preservation of a distinct British identity. Newly appointed merchants arrived each year in order to succeed those who had returned home after a successful period and the less fortunate who had found their last resting place in Madras. In England, former company servants kept in touch with friends and former colleagues, acting as their commissioners and informing them of developments in London. New members of staff acted as intermediaries, conveying the latest fashions in social and cultural behaviour to the English outposts. These changes within the group of Englishmen living in Madras secured continuity. It prevented a process of "creolization", whereby company servants might marry into the local community or turn against their homeland. According to Robin Cohen, the core of a diaspora construction is precisely "a continuing connection with the homeland, a deference to and imitation of its social and political institutions".[9]

Compared with the societies that the English created in America and the West Indies, the social element in India was almost non-existent. However, in spite of the limited number of English residents, Madras developed a distinct form of social life that was firmly rooted in metropolitan behaviour. A limited number of English families chose to settle permanently in Madras, thereby creating an English society in miniature, where the implementation of social behaviour and cultural habits supplied this far-flung outpost of the British Empire with stability and continuity. Social ties with the mother country also provided company servants with a competitive edge. On the one hand, Madras served as a regional South Indian port city in the Asian trading world while, on the other hand, becoming an important component in the first British Empire long before it served as a bridgehead for territorial expansion.

The families residing permanently in Madras formed the spinal cord in the social life of Madras. Although they had given up hope of returning home, they kept in touch with relatives and friends in England and exchanged letters on a regular basis. The children were often sent to school in the mother country, living under the care of relatives or friends. After finishing their education, the young persons were expected to return to Madras to assist in commercial activities or, in the case of females, to be married to a suitable company servant. Education in England was an important cultural aspect. Such young persons were also trained in correct social behaviour and transferred the latest cultural developments in the English metropolis to India, thereby ensuring that social life in Madras did not lag too far behind, which served to reduce the risk of stigmatization.

The number of Englishmen living in India was not large. Approximately 250 soldiers resided in Madras at the beginning of the eighteenth century; of these, only the officers would have had sufficient status to take part in the social activities of the town. In addition, there were about 150 English persons, half of whom were free merchants and ships' crew, and a quarter were company servants. The last quarter consisted of women, who comprised an important group in the population.

Madras accommodated a relatively large number of English women, compared with the male population, whose presence secured a growing social awareness by developing a lifestyle that was in accordance with English values and restricting social contact with the surrounding Indian society. Among the social activities preformed in Madras were dinners parties, balls, and afternoon functions; "the Company keeps a handsome table and for my own part I keep a very good court of music and purpose now and then to treat the Lady's with a ball" wrote Governor Collet to his mother, when explaining the social obligations that his position implied. These social events were important. Although company servants were commercial rivals and aspired to the same promotions, they could still meet each other in the evenings under more relaxed circumstances. Social functions also served as meeting places for unmarried Englishmen and everybody in the community took an interest in such events.

Although sexual relationships between Englishmen and Indian women occurred, as they were frowned upon and not considered acceptable behaviour, such liaisons were normally kept secret. Unlike the Portuguese, the English never encouraged mixed marriages and Anglo-Indians found it very difficult to gain social status in Madras. Source material dealing with the decedents of mixed marriages is hard to find. A letter written by the British surgeon of Trichinopoly, Richard Wilson, constitutes an exception. As a doctor, he knew the private soldiers well and was familiar with their living conditions in the garrisons of several towns on the Coromandel Coast. His report contains concrete evidence that sexual relations between low ranking British soldiers and Indian women resulted in children of mixed blood. In his letter dated 1778, written to the company, he claimed that the British community did not take proper care of these children:

> It has long been a severe and unanswerable reproach from the natives of this country that Britons, above all other Nations, have neglected and despised this their progeny and perhaps we never appeared with more disadvantage in the eyes of foreigners than when considered in this light.[10]

In Madras, Indian concubines are seldom described as living with company servants, although Indian women of Portuguese descent occasionally married English merchants. As it was socially unacceptable to have a relationship with an Indian woman, such relations were either kept secret or handled with the utmost discretion. According to Durba Ghosh, "the practice of concubinage enabled societies like British India to pretend that they were uncontaminated by racial or cultural mixing while sustaining multiple hierarchies of racial and social inequality".[11]

Her study is based on more than 600 testaments from Calcutta and Bengal in the late eighteenth century, in which she has found references to the sexual relations between British men and Indian women. Unfortunately, no information regarding Madras is provided.

Regular soldiers in the army were not included in the social activities of the English elite and so must have found their pleasure in the Indian punch houses. According to the British officer, Corneille, who arrived in Madras in 1754, sexual intercourse with Indian women was one of most frequent causes of death among the soldiers. Out of 79 deaths among private soldiers, 60 were related "to drunkenness and women", 11 died due to the climate and 8 deaths were recorded as accidental.[12]

It is relevant to ask if the British community in Madras was unique in its wish to preserve its cultural identity. Compared with the social behaviour of the Indian merchants, it appears that cultural segregation was the norm. A map of Fort St. George, created in the first decade of the eighteenth century, reveals that the English population was residing in the so-called "White town", that was protected by the bastions of Fort St. George. Besides a number of administrative buildings, "White Town" consisted of six streets and St. Mary's Church. A British officer visiting Madras for the first time described 'White Town' as being well built and consisting of lofty houses with flat roofs, although the streets were very narrow except for those immediately adjacent to the governor's residence, which was the first building erected by the English after landing.[13]

During the seventeenth century, company servants stayed within the walls of "White Town" but, as the area became too cramped in the following century, Englishmen began to buy property in the surrounding "Black Town", predominantly inhabited by Indians. The Indian population dominated the town and comprised some 100,000 persons in the eighteenth century.[14] Different merchant groups, such as the Chettys, the Chulias and the Armenians, lived in separate parts of the town, enjoying a large degree of autonomy. These merchants formed networks which linked the communities in the Indian Ocean together. Even though the Muslim Chulias married local Malay women in places such as Aceh, they still preserved their own Tamil identity in order to stay in touch with their place of origin. Ethnic identity was an important factor in long-distance trade.

In spite of the British wish to isolate themselves from the surrounding Indian environment, social habits gradually changed as several Indian practices became part of British behaviour. The social standards of the company servants were much higher in Madras than at home and played an important part when some families chose to make South India their permanent home. After many years abroad, they were fully adapted to the climate, and life under such special conditions had its advantages — numerous personal servants, comfortable houses, cheap food prices and a sense of solidarity among the English population, who were mutually dependent and used their cultural and ethnic identity to hinder assimilation with the local population. They might be commercial rivals, they might charge each other with misconduct and corruption but they would also attend the same social functions in the town and converse amicably at dinner parties held at the governor's house.

Descriptions of the aspects of daily life, living conditions and other social matters are very rare. Fortunately, Lady Gwillim and her sister, Mary Simonds, described life in Madras in a letter to their mother in England. The women were always surrounded by a number of servants, all wearing white muslins, white turbans and large golden earrings. At dinner parties, each guest would bring one or two servants, so there might well be at least 30 of them waiting at the table. The guests would arrive in palanquins, each requiring 9 to 13 bearers, besides two lantern men. The house would be lit up, there would be dining or dancing on the verandas, particularly at a ball, and the guests would stroll in the leafy gardens. It was customary to invite 150–200 guests to a ball and there would be around 500 white-clad servants in attendance. A young woman who had just arrived noticed how the English in Madras had as many servants as a duchess, making them intolerably lazy. She continued:

> It would make you smile, mummy, to see your child carried along in a palanquin which is a coach carried by five blacks and a soldier marching before with a sword in his hand and a boy running by my side to keep my petticoats down.[15]

The number of personal servants was one of the pleasanter aspects of life in Madras and some British merchants preferred to remain in India.

One of the main problems for Englishmen living in India was their insistence on dining according to English traditions. They ate too much meat and too few vegetables; too much protein combined with large quantities of wine and alcohol left its mark. In the late 1720s — a few years after his arrival in Madras — William Monson discovered that the clothes he had ordered from a tailor in England no longer fitted him, due to his increased weight. The clothes worn by the English were unsuitable for the Indian climate, as they stubbornly clung to their wigs, woollen coats, black hats and everything else belonging to an English gentleman's wardrobe. The high mortality rate was one of the negative consequences of the refusal to adapt to the social behaviour associated with life in the tropics. Diarrhoea, dehydration and fever killed many Englishmen and no doubt a more healthy diet would have prolonged their lives. However, clothes and eating habits characterized an Englishman in Asia and distinguished him from the local population. They provided was a cultural shield, protecting the English from losing their cultural identity, and making life tolerable by focusing on aspects they knew from home. However, inventories after the decease of British merchants refer to Banyan coats, pallaqueens and other Indian items, suggesting that, behind the "stiff upper lip", the British quietly adjusted their social behaviour to suit their surroundings.

The company servants in Madras were able to live a much better life in India than they could in England, and, although they took pride in the preservation of their English habits, their lives were gradually transformed under the influence of Indian culture. The general picture of the British in Madras during the years from 1650 to 1740 is that they avoided social interaction with the Indian population in order to preserve the social and cultural ties with the mother country. However, the Anglo-Indian population in Madras has not been studied in detail, although this group deserves greater attention.

The Period 1740–90

The period from 1740 to 1790 marked a dramatic change in the relationship between the British in Madras and the Indian population. Two elements were central in the process. During the 1720s, the East India Company introduced new regulations in order to curtail the commercial activities of its servants, especially the flow of private money to London. A reduction in public expenditure in Madras was also implemented. The directors were more concerned with domestic stability than the situation in Asia. The fortification of Madras was neglected, giving rise to great concern among the inhabitants about the political instability in South Asia. After Nadir Shah's invasion in 1738, Maratha soldiers plundered the region close to Madras, culminating in the plunder of Arcot. The directors were unmoved by the pleas of their servants and the negligence culminated with the French occupation of Madras in 1746. In a period characterized by political instability, company servants did not feel obliged to follow the orders that they received from London and began to play a more active role in the political conditions in India in order to compensate for the loss of commercial opportunities. As company servants discovered that private fortunes could be made much faster from war than from trade, Britons became more deeply involved in Indian affairs.[16]

The second element that was central in the changing circumstances was the Anglo-French wars. Whereas the British in Madras previously had isolated themselves with regard to the Indian population, the wars forced them to seek allies and establish relationships in order to survive. An increase in the number of British soldiers in India was one consequence of the wars. Low ranking soldiers were not afraid of involving themselves with the Indian population. "Going native" would not terminate their careers and they did not aspire to participate in the social life of their superiors. They found entertainment in the Indian punch houses and one consequence of their sexual activities was an increase in the number of Anglo-Indian children born, who were brought up on the fringes of society.

Due to the lack of source material, our knowledge about this is scarce. However, one interesting source regarding the Eurasian problem in the late eighteenth century was written by the British surgeon of Trichinopoly, Richard Wilson.[17] He was among the first to describe publicly the poor living conditions of children of mixed blood: "The distressed and forlorn condition of the numerous male issue of European soldiery in India has long attracted my attention, employed my thoughts, and powerfully moved my compassion."

The surgeon regretted that Anglo-Indians were not regarded as a good protestant colony of useful subjects and industrious members of society. He wanted to present a fair description of their living conditions and state of education, suggesting that "an active, bold and useful body of people, could strengthen the hands of dominion with a colony of subjects attracted to the British nation".

Wilson estimated that the number of Eurasian children baptized in the presiding decade was about 2000 and, had the company taken better care of them and treated them well, "we might at this day have been enabled to draw an army equal to the large body of troops now in our pay". Instead of loyal subjects, the Anglo-Indians inhabited towns such as Pondicherry, where approximately 700 children of Englishmen lived.

The mothers are described as belonging to the lowest class of Indians, neither knowing nor practising the rules of morality and honesty. These women took good care of their children, however, and gave them a decent upbringing: "At fourteen years of age, speaking English and understanding most of the languages of India, fully acquainted with the manners of the people and customs of the country." This mixture of culture made them ideal cultural brokers between the British and Indian society, but, due to the neglect of the company, the Eurasians offered their services to other Europeans. As Durba Ghosh observes: "Sexual relationships with native women were a type of public secret in which the community at large was aware of these relationships, but native companions and their children were rarely seen, acknowledged or entertained at public events."[18]

It is essential to study the social relationship which developed outside the higher circles of the Indian princes, and describe the Anglo-Indian population that lived in Madras.

In Madras, high-ranking British merchants and officers became familiar with the Indian rulers and the aristocracy. The centre of cultural and social exchange was the court of the Nawab of Arcot Mohammad Ali in Chepauk Palace. During the Anglo-French wars, the Nawab became a close ally and borrowed extensively from British merchants in order to pay for the military services that he needed in order to remain in power. This financial dependency created social relationships whereby the British became more familiar with Indian customs and ways of life.

The British merchants and soldiers had, in previous years, developed a taste for nautches or dances, hookah smoking, and elephant fights; now, they also developed an interest in ancient Indian literature, art and language. On the personal level, alliances or friendships were established primarily among the elite groups, such as high ranking soldiers or company servants and Indian rulers.

Mohammad Ali began constructing Chepauk Palace in 1767 on land near the company's garden house, a mile south of Fort St. George. When visiting the site in the 1770s, George Paterson found a mixture of two cultures, an amalgamation of European and Moorish styles. The Nawab had a taste for Western furniture and had chairs, lamps and tables, together with portraits of family members by English artists. His British creditors were often invited to breakfast and treated with great hospitality.

George Paterson was a doctor by profession, who arrived in Madras as secretary to Sir John Lindsay in the early 1770s. Paterson became a close associate of the Nawab of Arcot and won his confidence. Due to his position, he learnt much about Indian society and experienced the bridging of cultures which the Nawab introduced in Madras. However, Paterson, along with the crowd of British creditors who frequented Chepauk Palace, did not generally change their social and cultural outlook or behaviour, although their knowledge of Indian society was far greater than that of their predecessors.

Social ties occurred in the top level of Indian society. Mohammad Ali's family were newcomers to the Carnatic and his grandfather was the first among them to hold a high office, which had been granted by the Mughal Emperor Aurangzeb. Without British support, he would have disappeared in 1749. He knew that maintaining a good relationship with influential groups within British society was essential for his future. The British, on the other hand, were financially dependent on the Nawab. Many had invested heavily in what was known as "the debt of the Nawab of Arcot". If he failed to honour his financial obligations, they would go bankrupt and lose the prospect of returning to England with a fortune.

Men like Paul Benfield were disinterested in Indian culture, although they were familiar with Indian customs and enjoyed the more luxurious aspects of life. They regarded India as a temporary residence and looked forward to the day when they could return home to England. If these men maintained informal households with native women, it was a way of maximizing their domestic comfort without damaging their public reputation.

However, considering the fact that the East India Company was becoming a territorial power in South India, the level of social relationship which historians have recorded is not overwhelming. While Sinnappah Arasaratnam's book, *Maritime Commerce and English Power*, describes the rising dominance of the British in South India, there are few indications of social interaction besides the ties established between powerful zamindars, like the Raja of Vijayanagaram, and EIC officials, like governor Rumboldt in Madras, who cooperated in order to seize control over estates.[19] The Danish scholar, Niels Brimnes, who has examined caste disputes in Madras, argues that such cases were resolved by the British judicial system. The institutions of the colonial capital had assumed a bureaucratic aspect and, as the British operated from a position of strength, they could intervene in Indian society with authority.[20] A real blend of cultures did not occur on any great scale. British men who cohabitated with native women did not change their cultural identity and were constantly aware of the need to maintain certain codes of masculinity, by which they dominated the household.[21]

British subjects who went native are often found outside the large British settlements. William Dalrymple's, *White Mughals*, is a fascinating study of those who adapted themselves completely to the Indian way of life. One example is Major James Achilles Kirkpatrick (1764–1805). He was the British resident at the court of Hyderabad in the Deccan in the final years of the eighteenth century. His fellow British companions treated him often with contempt due to his Indian habits. Mountstuart Elphinstone confessed, during a visit to the Nizam of Hyderabad, that "Major Kirkpatrick behaved like a native and with great impropriety", but, after Elphinstone got to know Kirkpatrick better, he discovered that the resident also "behaved like an Englishman" and got along well with him.

Kirkpatrick enjoyed Indian cooking, hunted in the Indian fashion and took several Indian courtesans, even marrying a Muslim woman of noble family. He was a regular guest at the house of the Nizam's court painter, Tajalli Ali Shah, and attended the Tuesday cockfights at the chief minister's house. As Dalrymple observed: "If James Kirkpatrick's participation in the social and cultural life of Hyderabad led to much cross-fertilisation of ideas and the growth of a number of deep friendships between the Residency and the *omrahs* (nobles) of the court, it also led to some very real political benefits."[22] His knowledge of culture and behaviour thus helped to create diplomatic relationships based on trust.

If Kirkpatrick appeared suspect to his compatriots, his behaviour was not always regarded positively by Indians. Kirkpatrick's admiration for Indian costume made him socially suspicious. According to Arthur Wellesley, several Indians complained about the British resident:

> [T]he Mir launched into abuse of Kirkpatrick saying that he had long respected the English for their steadiness and their adherence to their own manners and customs in private life, and their respect upon all occasions for the manners and customs of Hindustan, particularly those relating to women ... but that Kirkpatrick, by dressing himself in the garb of a native and by the adoption of their manners, had made himself ridiculous, and was detested for his interference with their women.[23]

Men like James Kirkpatrick and William Parmer differed from the likes of Paul Benfield and George Paterson. The former two had families in India and were doubtful about whether to return to England, whereas the latter two regarded Asia as a temporary residence. As Kirkpatrick wrote to Palmer, "Recollect my dear friend that you were long ago yourself doubtful how far you could stand the rigour of an English summer, how then can you think of braving an English winter?" Perhaps it was the fact that they had no ambition to return home made that made them special in comparison with their compatriots.

Notes

1. The painting is kept in the India Office library in London and has been attributed to either Francesco Renaldi or Johan Zoffany. See B. Toibin, *Picturing Imperial Power: Colonial Subjects in Eighteenth Century British Painting* (Duke, 1999); W. Dalrymple, *White Mughals. Love and betrayal in Eighteenth-century India* (London, 2002), pp. 209, 248.
2. See, for instance, D. Ghosh, *Sex and the Family in Colonial India. The Making of Empire* (Cambridge, 2006).
3. P. Spear, *The Nabobs. A Study of the Social Life of the English in Eighteenth Century India* (Oxford, 1933), p. 126.
4. H. Furber, "Asia and the West as Partners before 'Empire' and after", *The Journal of Asian Studies* XXVIII, no. 4 (1969): 711–22.
5. P.J. Marshall, "Masters and Banians in Eighteenth-Century Calcutta", in *The Age of Partnership. Europeans in Asia before Dominion*, ed. B.B. Kling and M.N. Pearson (Honolulu, 1979), pp. 191–215.
6. S. Mentz, "English private trade on the Coromandel Coast 1660–1690: Diamonds and country trade", *The Indian Economic and Social History Review* 33, no. 2 (1996): 155–73.
7. S. Mentz, *The English Gentleman Merchant at Work. Madras and the City of London 1660–1740* (Copenhagen, 2005).
8. Spear, *The Nabobs*, p. 129.
9. R. Cohen, *Global Diasporas: an introduction* (London, 1997), p. 104.

10. The letter is published in H.D. Love, *Vestiges of Old Madras vol. III* (London, 1913), pp. 179–82.
11. D. Ghosh, *Sex and the Family in Colonial India*, p. 30.
12. Oriental and India Office Collection OIOC MSS EUR b215, Corneille Papers, Memories of an expedition to the East Indies undertaken in the year 1754, p. 145.
13. OIOC, MSS. EUR b215, Memories of an expedition to the East Indies undertaken in the year 1754 fol. 64–5.
14. O. Prakash, "European Commercial Enterprise in Pre-Colonial India", in *The New Cambridge History of India*, vol. II.5 (Cambridge, 1998), p. 148.
15. OIOC MSS EUR. d546/1-2. Fowke Papers, Fort St. George, August 25, 1749, E. Fowke to her mother.
16. P. Lawson, *The East India Company* (London, 1993), p. 81.
17. The letter is dated 1778 and published in H.D. Love, *Vestiges of Old Madras*, vol. III (London, 1913), pp. 179–82.
18. D. Ghosh, *Sex and the Family in Colonial India*, p. 70.
19. S. Arasaratnam, *Maritime Commerce & English Power (Southeast India 1750–1800)* (London, 1996).
20. N. Brinmes, *Constructing the Colonial Encounter. Right and Left Hand Castes in early Colonial South India* (Curzon, 1999).
21. D. Ghosh, *Sex and the Family in Colonial India*, p. 108.
22. W. Dalrymple, *White Mughals*, p. 98.
23. Ibid., p. 167.

References

Arasaratnam, S. *Maritime Commerce & English Power (Southeast India 1750–1800)* (London, 1996).

Brinmes, N. *Constructing the Colonial Encounter. Right and Left Hand Castes in Early Colonial South India* (Curzon, 1999).

Dalrymple, W. *White Mughals. Love and Betrayal in Eighteenth-century India* (London, 2002).

Dodwell, H. *The Nabobs of Madras* (London, 1926).

Ghosh, D. *Sex and the Family in Colonial India. The Making of Empire* (Cambridge, 2006).

Mentz, S. *The English Gentleman Merchant at Work. Madras and the City of London 1660–1740* (Copenhagen, 2005).

Nightingale, P. *Fortune and Integrity. A Study of Moral Attitudes in the Indian Diary of George Paterson, 1769–1774* (Oxford, 1985).

Spear, P. *The Nabobs. A Study of the Social Life of the English in Eighteenth Century India* (Oxford, 1933).

CHAPTER 9

The Hindu Courtier and the French Governor: Pondicherry, 1744–60

Philippe Haudrère

The diary that Ananda Ranga Pillai, a Hindu courtier from Pondicherry, kept daily from 1736 to 1760, is an invaluable document for the study of the relationship between the French and the native inhabitants of the trading post.[1] The author asserts: "I proceed to chronicle what I hear with my ears; what I see with my eyes; [...] and whatsoever wonderful or novel takes place" (I, 1). Ranga Pillai's intention was to keep a record of important events, as we can see from two passages written in 1755: "About noon a peon came and said that M. Barthélémy [the second of the trading post] wanted me. [...] He also asked if I had translated into French Venkâji Pandit's cadjan letter [...]. I replied that I had given him the original, and the French translation soon after M. Godeheu's departure. M. Barthélémy said that he did not remember it. I observed that I must have recorded it in that day's diary. 'Would you really?' he asked. 'Certainly,' I replied. 'Then, bring me a copy,' he said. I agreeing took leave, and came home. I examined my diary for February 16 [...] and found there a note that I had given it. I wrote accordingly, made copies of Venkâji Pandit's letter and its French translation as written in the diary, and put them ready in the admirah" (IX, 204). "Monday, June 16 – The Governor then said that a letter must be written to the Râjâ of Cochin-China. I replied that I thought no letters had been written before, but that I would make sure by looking at the Persian list. [...] I [...] took leave in order to come home and examine the Persian list to see if any letters had been written to the Râjâ of Cochin-China. Finding that none had been, I sent word immediately about it [...]" (IX, 315).

Who, then, was Ananda Ranga Pillai? Born in 1709, in a family of Tamil merchants originally from Madras, who had settled in Pondicherry at the start of the eighteenth century, he succeeded his father, upon the latter's death in 1726, as the head of an important business company.

A Business Relationship

The most striking aspect of the diary is the relationship of reciprocal trust between Ranga Pillai and Governor Joseph-François Dupleix. Two years after he arrived, Dupleix had the merchant appointed courtier in second for the business of the French East India Company: "Friday, 3rd January: The leading caste men of Pondicherry paid a visit this afternoon at four, to the Governor. He had sent me orders to accompany them, and consequently I did so — not knowing the object he had in summoning me. He then, in the presence of the whole assembly, presented me with torches, and caused a salute of seven guns to be fired. He also accorded permission to me to move about within the fort, in my palanquin. […] His treatment of me was particularly considerate. This is due to the special regard which the Governor, M. Dupleix, entertains for me." (I, 245–246).

A few months later, when the first courtier died, Dupleix petitioned the head office of the East India Company for the appointment of Ranga Pillai, who was informed by one of the councilors: "Sunday, 12th June 1746: M. de Bausset having sent for me this morning, I waited on him. […] M. de Bausset chatted with me in this manner of various topics connected with Kârikâl, and then he remarked: "How is it that the post of chief dubâsh has not yet been conferred on you". In response to this I said: "Why should I desire the appointment? As I am, what honours do I fail to receive? I am granted torches, I am allowed a palanquin, I enjoy, far and wide, the good will of the European gentry, and indeed all marks of distinction that I could wish for are accorded to me, even when not holding office. Why then should I covet it? As long as I am in the enjoyment of favour of you all, what is there that I lack? […] He then observed: "[…] There is at present no one so competent as yourself. […] M. Dupleix, too, has expressed himself in like terms as to your merits. The members of the Council, one and all – are praying to God that the appointment may be given to you, for your conduct has so commended itself to them that they have entire confidence that in the event of your securing it all their business will be most skillfully managed. […] But what the Governor wrote confidentially to the Company is not known. […] In my opinion, the place cannot but fall to you" (II, 63). A month and a half later, the rumour became even more insistent: Saturday, 30th July 1746. As M. de la Villebague and I were walking out of the room where we had been conversing, we met […] M. Dubois […]. M. Dubois looking towards me said: "Now that you have been appointed as courtier of the Company, we fully believe that all our concerns will be successfully managed by you." Congratulating me, he approached, according to the custom of his people, to embrace and kiss me. I thanked him, half accepting his congratulations; but eluded his salute, making as if I did not understand his purpose. I replied to him: "How will this appointment benefit me? […] The Governor has entrusted to me all his private affairs, and half of the Company's concerns pass through my hands. […] The only advantage which the situation gives the holder of it are the oversight of the contract of the Company, and the Company's merchants. […] His annual profit on account of his concern in the contracts is 2000 pagodas and no sooner does he receive this amount than he has to pay it away in very many directions. On the other hand, if as a private merchant, I take a little trouble, I may realize instead of this 2000, 4000 or even 6000. […]" He rejoined: "True. But from Cape Comorin — in this part of the country — as well as in Bengal, in Golconda and to the westward, in Mysore, there is not one who is not your friend and there is none who will not honour your drafts and bonds. Nobody possesses so much credit here as you do in the way of being able to procure at any time every kind of merchandise. The acquaintances and friends of other men are to be found only within the boundary hedge of Pondicherry, and they have none in the interior. If therefore you agree to take up the appointment, the business of the Company will be carried on successfully, and it will, from the pecuniary point of view, be much benefited" (II,155–156). Ranga Pillai's official appointment finally took place in November 1747.

The courtier repeatedly stated his trust in Dupleix, as in the entry for July 16, 1746: "In the course of conversation with me this morning at 9, the Governor said […] many […] disparaging things of M. de la Bourdonnais [squadron leader]". Not only did I throughout express myself in harmony with his views, but I dwelt at length, and in highly eulogistic terms, on the address with which he administered the affairs of this city at so critical a time as the present […]. I remarked that the ability and success of the administration of his predecessors could not bear comparison with those of his, and that it was problematical whether any of his successors would reach the standard of his qualifications" (II, 128). Pillai's answer could seem somewhat sycophantic, but he was more outspoken in a brief conversation which took place two years later: "Saturday, August 31 — He then asked me if I would really stand by him. I answered, 'Whether you believe me or not, I have always stood by you, and am resolved that my life is yours.' – 'I know,' he answered, and, without saying more, he went and sat with the others […]" (V, 283).

Pillai's relationship with Dupleix' successors, though not quite as close, was still one of reciprocal trust. On January 2, 1755, Godeheu publicly declared to the Tamil notables who had come to present their wishes: "'Henceforth you need not report news to me, but go to Ranga Pillai and do as he orders.

Whoever does not, will be fined or otherwise punished'" (IX, 134). Governor Leyrit, although he had entrusted his own business to another Hindu merchant, repeatedly paid public homage to the ability of the courtier, notably after the death of his wife: "Thursday, April 22 [1756] – Two chobdars […] and other officials of the company came to me at nine o'clock this morning to say that the Governor, M. Leyrit, wanted me […]. So I took them to the Governor who was in the central hall of the *Gouvernement* with the councilors and officers. He received me with the same respect as he shows to gentlemen his equals. Wearing his hat and sword, and with his cane in his hand, he advanced to the door to receive me, brought me in, condoled with me on my wife's death […]. Then he himself sprinkled rosewater, put round my neck a six-stringed necklace with a pendant set with diamonds round a ruby centre […]." (X, 63). Two years later, Lally, a general officer of the French army who had been sent to Pondicherry to repress embezzlement by Company employees, relied on the courtier. He met him discreetly at a third party's house: "Wednesday, August 30 [1758] – In the evening at half past six I went to M. Boyelleau's house. On my arrival, he told me to wait upstairs […]. At half past seven, all three — M. Boyelleau, M. Lally and M. le Comte de Montmorency — entered under cover of the darkness. I could not clearly see M. Lally, who wore a black coat and held a walking stick; but recognized him by his bright Cross worn high on the right breast, and by his voice. […] I then went aside, but M. Boyelleau called me. When I approached, M. Lally said to me: 'Sit down, Monsieur Ranga Pillai.' I sat down beside him. […] He then rose and took me aside, and, patting me on the back, said, 'Give me an account, and I will beat them like dogs that they are, and make them tremble at the sight of you'" (XI, 262–263). The friendly relationship between the courtier and the notoriously bad-tempered general surprised everyone in Pondicherry: "Wednesday, May 31 [1758] – I […] met Kandappa Mudali, who said, 'What sir! M. Lally says, 'Call Leyrit.' He calls the Second and others by their mere names and never says Monsieur So and so. […] When he was at table, he said, 'Monsieur Ranga Pillai, Monsieur Ranga Pillai' a dozen times'" (XI, 184–185).

The good relationship between the courtier and the Europeans was largely based on business. We must distinguish between Ranga Pillai's private business, and the one he effected on behalf of the Company. Ranga Pillai prepared the contract passed between the Governor, acting on behalf of the Company, and local merchants, for the supply of cotton-cloth cargo. He acted as a go-between for the different parties, for instance on September 19, 1747: "While I was with the Governor to-day, M. Cornet [his advisor] came. As he was about to go, he asked whether I and the other merchants would not sign the contract. The Governor answered that cotton and thread were said to be very dear in the country, and that we were demanding an increase of nine per cent, as we had heard many ships were coming which would raise prices; and that we also said the English disturbances in the country made it difficult to send money out and get cloth back" (IV, 141). Then, Pillai organized the collecting of cotton-cloth around the trading post: "Wednesday, June 10 – He [the Governor] then told me to make the merchants send at once for goods, to be dispatched by the ship, from Salem or Udaiyâpâlaiyam, if none could be had here. I agreed, sent for the merchants, told them to write letters for cloth to Salem [...] and elsewhere to the north" (VII, 245). He got advance payment to start the manufacture: "16th May 1743 – This morning at 10, the merchants [...] executed the usual annual contract, and were paid 5000 pagodas" (I, 224).

He also prepared cargoes for local business carried out on behalf of the Company: "Thursday, 3rd November 1746 – [...] He [the Governor] also directed me to make ready 300 scores of coarse blue cloth, valued at 10 000 pagodas, for shipment to Mocha in the Dutch ship leaving Tai [January] next, and gave me 5000 Pondichery crescent pagodas, in part payment of the order" (III, 71).

On the other hand, the Governor kept an eye on the courtier's activities: "16th March 1746 – I was at home this morning at 8, when a Company's peon came, and stated that the Governor desired to see me. In obedience to the summons, I at once repaired to his house. He took me to his office-room, where no one else was present, and said: "You owe a good deal to the Company; you are in arrears. What do you do with all your money? What interest do you charge, when you lend it?" I replied: "Your money has not been embezzled. I have not squandered it in gambling. I have not expended it in vain. I have invested my funds in trade —in commercial enterprises beyond sea and in the manufacture of goods locally, as well as at places in the interior [...]. This is how my money has been laid out. My assets are double of my liabilities. The goods which I have on board ships, and the arrears which I have to recover locally, will be a sufficient security for what I owe the Company." He rejoined: "I do not say that you are not worth the amount, or that you cannot meet your liabilities, but if you pay the Company the 10 000 pagodas which you have received from the Brahman of Trichinopoly who has come here, it will be wise on your part." I answered: "Sir, please summon the person who gave you this information, and also the individual said to have paid the money to me, as he is here; and hold a judicial inquiry. If it comes to light that I have received even a single cash, I will submit without demur to any penalty that the Company may choose to impose upon me. On the other hand, if it be proved that the allegation is false and unfounded, your informant must be held liable to the same punishment." [...] I however continued: "I beg to be pardoned for making another observation. [...] The whole town speaks ill of me, saying that I interest myself too much in your service. Some even watch for opportunity to attack and kill me. In spite of calumnious language such as this, and of attempts on my life, I have, with singleness of purpose, ever aimed at meriting your favour. This I have considered a sufficient reward, and have never cared to benefit myself pecuniarily.' To record my whole speech on this occasion would occupy about five or six pages. But in all essential points, it was as I have already mentioned. The Governor then, to turn the conversation, asked me how the accounts of Sunguvâr and those of the elephant dealer stood. I again said, 'Is it not necessary for you to ascertain whether I am honest or dishonest? It is only after you have done this that you will be relieved of any suspicion against me'" (I, 326–328).

Beside his work for the Company, Ranga Pillai also conducted business not only in his own name, but also on behalf of other Europeans who would entrust him with their funds. First and foremost among them was Dupleix: "Monday, 8th October 1742 – The French ship *Marie Joseph*, bound for Queda, set sail this evening […]. The goods shipped were: […] Cloths belonging to the Governor, procured through my agency: 59" (I, 201). "August 1st, 1746: The Governor sent for me this morning and said: "I have now in my possession a sum of Rs 10 892 which belongs to you. This amount was realized by the sale at Mocha of the merchandise shipped on two occasions in the *Neptune* […]. I have also received from M. Lhostis, to whom you lent them on a premium contract, 500 pagodas, exclusive of the premium of 18, and another sum of 10 pagodas, being interest and special charge for monsoon risks [risk of delay]. You have thus to your credit an aggregate sum of Rs 13 031, which please note in your account as having been received, and then debit against me" (II, 160–161). "6th August 1746: This forenoon, about half past 11, M. Dupleix, sent for me, furnished me with a list of goods to be manufactured for him, and desired that they should be supplied by the end of October next" (II, 171). This collaboration went on until Dupleix left for France: "Monday, October 14 [1754] – I visited the old Governor at the Fort, and asked him to sign some accounts regarding our transactions. I said, 'You have shown me great kindness for the last thirteen years. Be pleased to remember me and continue your kindness.' – 'I will do so,' he answered" (IX, 51) and the courtier concludes his account of the interview thus: "Twelve years and nine months ago yesterday on the morning of Sunday, January 14, 1742, he landed here from Bengal to become our Governor. In all this time, he has gained lakhs upon lakhs by my efforts, but has never troubled about me. […] I dwelt in truth and justice under his government; but from first to last, he regarded neither justice nor truth" (IX, 54–58). We will come back to this judgment later.

Dupleix was not Ranga Pillai's only customer. Among the Europeans, one could mention Mrs Albert, Mrs Dupleix's mother: "26th August 1746: Madame Albert sent for me and said: "The year before the last, when the Neptune sailed for Mocha, you let me have the sum of Rs 1000 on condition of my paying a premium on it, and I made it over to M. d'Auteuil. He has to pay 18 per cent premium, and another 10 per cent, being special charge for monsoon risks … you therefore have to receive, over and above the principal of Rs 1000, a profit of Rs 337, being the interest, etc. due on it. Of this sum he gave me Rs 837 now. For the balance I will give you a promissory note stipulating to pay the interest usually leviable in case of land traffic" (II, 240–241). There was also Mahé de la Villebague, La Bourdonnais' brother: "M. de la Villebague received from me the indent and receipt for 10 000 rupees, which he gave me on the 25th August, gave me another sum of 10 000 rupees, , and obtained for me a receipt for the whole 20 000" (II, 290). And also : "Tuesday, July 9 – […] He [the Governor] then asked me whether I had not been a partner with M. de la Villebague in the Manila trade. I said, 'I was not the only partner; there were also M. Guillard, M. Pilavoine, M. Robert, M. La Beaume, Pedro, Sunguraman and M. Cornet, as well.' He then asked what my share had been. I said 4065 pagodas" (V, 111–112).

Ranga Pillai also had business connections with the other Tamil merchants, among whom his position was prominent.

The Head of Hindus

As a courtier, Ranga Pillai was, beside his activity as a businessman, the representative of the native community in their dealings with the Europeans.

This function required the mastery of several languages, as is explicit from its Tamil appellation — *dobash* — i.e. "a man who can speak two languages". Ranga Pillai could speak and write six: Tamil, Telugu (III, 31), Hindustani (VIII, 189), Persian (II, 93; III, 344; IV, 448; V, 229; IX, 413), French (II, 93; III, 183; IV, 448; V, 4–11; VI, 192), and when he met the Governor or the councilors, he spoke basic Portuguese, which was the *lingua franca* of trading posts (XII, 126–127).

He had to be available at any time to work as an interpreter. Thus, on August 22, 1748, as a fight between British and French forces was raging under the walls of Pondicherry: "When I was about to go to the nut-godown, the Governor said, 'Where are you going to? Stay here and let people come here for their orders. […] I am going to stay in the Fort; you must be with me there day and night.' I said I would do so" (V, 229).

He was an invaluable go-between: "I said, 'All the townspeople know that if even a cooly comes to me, I always give him a proper reply, and send him away after hearing what he has to say" (V, 403–404). He then petitioned the Governor, thus: "I next entreated him, most earnestly, to give a favourable reply in Kârikâl Tiruvengâdam's case. […] He spoke of him in very angry terms indeed […]. To all his objections, I returned suitable explanations, and by the promise of a present I succeeded in appeasing his wrath, and in inducing him to consent to allow the man to resume his appointment" (II, 35). Or again: "Saturday, June 22 [1748] – […] I went to the nut-godown and called Sûrappa Mudali […] and said, 'I have spoken to the Governor about the affair which you and M. Miran [council secretary] told me of. Go and present your petition now.' He thanked me and took leave" (V, 57).

Yet the governor did not always follow Pillai's advice: "Friday, April 28 [1747] – Arumpâtai Pillai's son, Muttayan, who was imprisoned last Monday week, was released today, because Appu Mudali gave the Governor 2000 rupees. But what can I say of the Governor's wisdom? He told me to get Arumpâtai Pillai into a difficulty and make him pay 10 000 rupees. I had nearly succeeded in doing so, but now he releases Muttayan for […] 2000 rupees […] Appu got for this 500 rupees and ear-rings set with square emeralds" (IV, 69–70).

And Pillai sometimes put friendly pressure on the Governor: "Wednesday, November 8 [1747] – […] '[…] If you refuse, I myself will give them [two sepoys who spread the Governor's fame] a present and send them away.' I spoke about this for twenty minutes or so. At last, the Governor asked, 'What did they lose?' – 'More than 200 pagodas,' I said, 'and their two horses. But they will be quite content with only 200 pagodas. Mahfuz Khân, the paymaster and the news-writer will be pleased with your liberality and extol your merits.' He then called his writer, Ranga Pillai, and told him to bring 640 rupees" (IV, 198–199).

The courtier sometimes presented collective requests, in particular concerning the organisation of Hindu religious festivals: "11th August 1746: I then said to him: 'The people of Kâlâpêttai say that a festival should be held in the village, and beg permission to conduct it in the usual way.' He replied: 'Let them celebrate it according to custom.' I communicated the order to them […]" (II, 188).

When the request was unusual, he waited for a favourable moment before presenting it, as he did after the French victory at Madras: "Thursday, 22nd September 1746 – The Governor then turned to me and said: 'Ask any thing that you desire, and I will, with pleasure, grant your request.' […] I now called to mind how the poor in every street, and every corner of the town, and even the little children, hooted and execrated Vâsudêva Pandit [tax collector for betel and tobacco] calling him a villain and a perfidious wretch, for having reduced the selling price of betel-leaves from nine to seven leaves per cash, and finally to five, and that of tobacco from twelve to ten palams, per fanam. As I had repeatedly heard the people complain that this formed the only serious blot in the administration of this justly governed town, and as I desired now to put an end to this reproach, I asked the Governor to direct that tobacco and betel-leaves be sold at their former prices. He immediately summoned Vâsudêva Pandit, and directed him to sell, as before, nine betel-leaves for one cash, and twelve and-a-half palams of tobacco for one fanam" (II, 321). Pillai acted in a similar way when the Governor noticed the price of rice on the market had soared: "Sunday, 25th December 1746 – I said 'Sir, you may be sure that I will exert myself; […] In former days, M. Lenoir, when similarly circumstanced, acquired repute by a generous act; for he cancelled the tax, imported provisions at his own cost, and gained the credit of having saved the people from famine. […]' He remarked: 'All that you say is true. […] Let the cost be what it may, paddy must be sold at 3½ measures. Any loss that may arise from this, can be entered in my account; […]'" (III, 208).

The courtier kept the Governor continually informed of changes in public opinion. We shall limit ourselves here to a single testimony, after the French victory at Madras: "He [the Governor] asked me then what news there were about Madras? […] I said: "All your great deeds have been rendered into lays, and are being sung." […] He then asked what the import of the songs was. I replied: "They set forth, among other matters, how undauntedly and courageously you faced the days when no ships appeared here, and when enemies were overwhelming you; how the very mention of your name so terrified the English as to cause their bowels to fall out, how, within six months, you erected earth-works and fortifications on the beach which would have taken another person not less than three years, how you, having procured men-of-war from France, defeated and dispersed the English ships — sinking one and seriously damaging the rest, and how your heroic achievements have won the admiration of the Emperor of Delhi, and indeed of all European countries. […] He then retired into the room where his wife lay, and in consultation with her, sent word […] to the minstrels to attend and sing before them. […] I then went home, ate my dinner, and was about to lie down for a rest, when the singers told me they were summoned by the Governor […]. I then instructed them, at some length, how they should conduct themselves in the presence of Europeans, and bade them go.

The musicians were taken into the house of the Governor where he, his consort, his sister-in-law, and the wife of Pedro Mousse, were assembled. A carpet was spread for them to sit upon, and they were asked to proceed. As the songs were poured forth by the minstrels in all their melodious grandeur, two or three European ladies translated them into Tamil to Madame Dupleix, who in turn rendered them into French to her husband. They all enjoyed the performance very much" (II, 275–318).

The courtier sometimes informed the Governor of local customs which could, at first sight, shock Europeans, as he did in September 1750: "He said angrily, 'As I was driving, Chandhâ Sâhib [the subab of Trichinopoly]'s son and five or six horsemen who had gone to see the image being carried in procession, turned their backs on me. Should they behave so disrespectfully?' […] I said: 'Among Muhammadans, when one meets his father or master or one older than himself, it is not proper to meet him face to face but to stand aside. That is also the practice of the Tamils. As Razâ Sahib regards you as his father, he stood aside. That is all.' – 'In that case it is all right,' he said […]" (VII, 382).

Ananda Ranga Pillai was the go-between between the French and Indian princes. To fulfill this diplomatic role, he had at his disposal a network of informers, which is mentioned several times in his diary: "Thursday, 17th November 1746 – This evening, I interpreted to the Governor the contents of the letter sent from Arcot by Vakîl Subbaiyan. […] the Governor said to me: '[…] Send some more suitable men – say five or six – to Arcot to obtain further intelligence.'" (III, 113). "Sunday, August 13 [1747] – The Governor took me in, after dismissing the merchants, and when we were alone he said to me, 'I have good news for you also. As there are matters which should be spoken of only in private, it would be well if you were to come tomorrow afternoon.' The Governor also gave me news which I cannot write down now […]' (IV, 138). "Sunday, January 4 [1750] – I went to the Governor when he returned from church this morning, and told him that according to his order of yesterday, I had sent four spies to Nâsîr Jang's camp [subab of the Deccan] […] to bring back a report" (VI, 351).

Ranga Pillai was in charge of the correspondence in Persian addressed by the Governor to Indian lords: "Wednesday, September 24 [1749] – After talking about these affairs, he told me to write to Chandâ Sâhib, saying that he was surprised not to have received the usual daily letters for the last six or seven days" (VI, 179). The letters were written by the courtier himself: "Thursday, 24th November 1746 — The Governor said to me today: 'Muhammad Alî Khân, son of Anwar ud-dîn Khân, has, as you know, returned from a campaign on the banks of the Krishna, beyond the Pass. Now write a letter to him.' I replied: 'I will, if you so desire, but give me instructions how to draft it.' 'For the last forty days,' exclaimed he, 'you have, at my bidding – which has been to use your discretion – written letters to various persons, and even to the Nizâm, without once asking for any hints from me. How is it that, in this instance, you seek for directions to guide you in drafting one?' 'Hitherto,' I replied, 'I had no occasion to ask for express instructions, as your custom has been to hold a conversation with me on the subject of a letter, before requiring me to write it, and, from, that, I gathered your views on the matter, and framed my communications accordingly.' 'Well, well,' said the Governor, 'write now without having obtained any such clue to my ideas. Use your own judgment in drafting the letter. This will be a test of your ability.' I did so, and read it out to him. He approved highly of it, and ordered me to dispatch it […]" (III, 129–130).

Ranga Pillai sometimes disagreed with Dupleix: "Wednesday, August 21 – […] He [the Governor] came and asked if I could not tell Chandâ Sahib's wife [who was then in Pondicherry] to write to the English. I said that it could be done, and asked what I should write. He told me to ask her to write as follows: 'How can you attack this town when I am here? […] If you attack this town, consider what my husband will do when he comes; […] He thought that such a letter would alarm them. But I reflected that though such a clever man could not but succeed, yet, no matter how clever a man might be, there was still that greater thing, the nectar of help, which is also called 'good fortune' or 'the favour of God'. So I answered, 'This is not the best time to write such a letter, and we should wait for another occasion.' He listened to what I said, but remained silent. I think I ought not to write much in comment upon what he says, however surprising it may be' (V, 221).

The courtier also took part, in his capacity as an expert, in the negotiations between the French and local lords, and writes with a certain smugness: "Sunday, 26th February 1747 – It having, by the grace of God, fallen to my lot to conduct the affairs of the Company, I have spent my days and nights in thought, and have counseled the Governor on all manners of subjects, with the result that he has acted on my advice. By the decree of the Ruler of all sentient beings, the actual head of this kingdom attacked us, and was defeated. He voluntarily sued for peace, and coming to the Governor, begged him to arrange it. This was to the glory of the French. […] I was with the Governor when the Muhammadan envoy made his request; but he was obliged to agree to receive even less than one-tenth of the amount for which he asked. […] When the delegate treated with the Governor for terms, my exertions in the matter, my conduct of the business, and the skill and dexterity which I displayed in the negotiations, all became known to the Governor, and the public. He received presents which added to his glory. No one has acquired the reputation that I have; and my fame is in the mouths of ambassadors at courts, Governors of provinces, men of rank, and all people living within 300 leagues of this; from Delhi in the North to Malayalam in the south; and from the eastern to the western sea. They all say: 'We have never seen, or heard of, a man equal to Ânanda Rangappan in diplomatic skill, in keenness of intellect, or in boldness of conception; or in fact, in any qualification whatsoever'" (III, 366).

Which lessons did Ranga Pillai draw from this long intercourse with Europeans? First and foremost, he admired their technical achievements: "I myself […] saw the mortar being fired. […] The shell weighed 136 pounds, and when it was fired from the mortar, it rose up into the skies […]. Its roar and its beauty as it fell, spitting fire, reminded me of the burning star in the Râmâyana. I have seen and heard God's thunder. I think this is man's thunder

— no less. […] This can be handled by none but Europeans; for they only can handle it with skill' (V, 313). Apart from that, he did not find them superior in any way: "Tuesday, March 26 [1748] — […] I thought the Tamils were very stupid people, who believed whatever was said to them, but that Europeans were different. […] But now I have learnt that there are many Europeans […] as stupid as asses and more foolish than the Tamils.' The Governor laughed and said that the Europeans knew nothing of the customs of the country. I replied that even those who had lived here for fifteen, twenty or thirty years, still appeared to be very stupid" (IV, 462).

Ranga Pillai's relationship with Dupleix also had its moments of tension. Some were mere trifles, like the Governor's abrupt judgement on the dietary customs of the Tamil: "The Governor then asked what I took in the mornings. I said, cold rice, buttermilk and pickles. The Governor continued, 'Tamil food is not worth eating. They eat animals' food. What else is their vegetables and curry stuffs? It is not food fit for men. Now a Muhammadan *pilaû* is something; but there is nothing like our food in the world, either for cooking or ingredients; and it is served at a well-laid table, where wives, husbands, relations and friends all sit round and eat at their leisure in social enjoyment. The Muhammadans and Tamils always want our food but we don't want theirs. We don't like their vegetable food.' He thus depreciated our food, dwelling on its defects, and added, 'You eat at a table like a European, don't you? But you have long lived with Europeans and are intelligent, so you do not think it a breach of custom to do so. I am glad of that. Though the Tamils have long lived with us, still they say it is against their custom, and speak ill of us, comparing us, in their brutal ignorance, to Pariahs.' He spoke like this at some length" (VIII, 296–297).

Then there was Madame Dupleix. Born in India, she was the daughter of a clerk in the French East India Company, and of an Indo-Portuguese mother. She therefore spoke the country's languages, and could keep her husband informed. The courtier loudly lamented her influence, which often rivalled his own, as we can gather from several examples: "Friday, March 24 [1747] – […] His [Dupleix'] wife wants to share in the government. […] Speak of money to her and she will stick at nothing. She exercises all authority. […] As he listens to his wife, he tells me not to interfere, and says, 'Let us see what Madame advises.'" (IV, 31–33). "Tuesday, December 12 [1747] – I do not think this state of things can continue; God must have devised a way of delivering us from this evil, as we shall understand in the fullness of time" (IV, 263). "Sunday, June 30 [1748] – But as she is obstinate, I expect she will get the management of affairs again. […] she is a *Nîli* [the evil she-monkey of the Râmâyana]" (V, 89). "Saturday, September 7 – […] he [the Governor] gave Madame the whole management as if this were a village which lived by selling cucumbers […]"

(V, 296). "Madame alone has caused all M. Dupleix' troubles; but he did not understand this till matters were irretrievable" (IX, 53).

Why was the relationship so hostile? It might have been due to Madame Dupleix's temper, and the fact that the courtier resented any form of criticism. Madame Dupleix's "political" activity was in sharp contradiction with the place attributed to women in Hindu society. Another bone of contention with the courtier was her eagerness to see as many inhabitants of the trading post as possible converted to Catholicism.

Religious Tensions

Ranga Pillai was deeply religious. He closely scrutinised unexpected natural phenomena, which he took as signs: "Friday, March 24 [1747] – A burning star, as long as a Palmyra tree, fell from the north-east towards the south-west. I cannot describe its brightness. [...] M. Changeac [a lieutenant], who was with me, said, 'This forebodes a rebellion in which many will die or the death of Nawâb Anwar-ud-dîn Khân.' – 'Do Europeans believe such things?' I asked. He replied, 'Such predictions are always fulfilled.'" (IV, 35). He consulted astrologers and sometimes reported their predictions to the governor: "Tuesday, March 14 [1747] – After April, your affairs will prosper, day by day, and you will receive from the King a title of nobility [...]. He asked how I knew this. I replied that a Brâhman astrologer had foretold that this would happen after April, and before the expiry of May. On hearing this the Governor laughed [...]" (III, 441). Three weeks later, Dupleix heard that he had been made a knight of the Order of St-Michel, which carried nobility rights! (IV, 47).

Most of all, Ranga Pillai was a devout Hindu. For that reason, he had to face the hostility of Jesuit missionaries, who wished the head of the local population to be a Christian. Thus, when Europeans pressed Ranga Pillai to accept the position of courtier, he answered: "30th July 1746 – "This is what is under consideration. [...] But those of the church of St Paul [i.e. the Jesuits] will be much troubled. M. de Villebague upon this observed: "The idea of the priests of the church of St Paul is that if a Christian was appointed, they would be cognizant of every matter occurring in the town, and could bring under their influence any person that they wished. [...] Upon this, the ministers of France left it to the discretion of the Council [i.e. of the Company] to do as they considered fit, observing that the authorities of the church of St Paul were liars, and that it was owing to the mischief done by them that Pondicherry had not attained any name, and was in a moribund condition. In consequence of this, the words of the priests of the church of St Paul will carry no weight; and promotion of the Company's trade will be the main consideration in the selection from the candidates for office. Nevertheless, the priests will not remain aloof; they will strive their utmost to obtain the appointment of a Christian, and will even try to move the authorities at home to support them. Their character is too well known. Where, however, is the man in that community competent for the situation?" (II, 157–158).

After Ranga Pillai's nomination, Dupleix did his best to humour the Jesuits: "Tuesday, September 19 [1747] – He [the Governor] [...] asked me what terms I was on with the padres of St. Paul's Church. I answered, '[...] Now I seldom go there. They used to flatter me publicly for doing good to the Christians. They even said they had sometimes prayed for me so that I might not be separated from them in Heaven. When I went to see them at the New Year, they would call me from out of the crowd and flatter me for an hour and a half together. But as soon as I became Chief Dubâsh [...] they began to say they would be better off if a Christian were appointed, and that they could not expect help from a Hindu [...]; that they had written to the King and would write again unless they soon received a favourable reply. So they have persuaded the Christians that their claims are just. Till now I have said nothing about this, lest you should think I spoke out of self-interest, but as you ask me I cannot avoid saying a little [...].' – They are deceitful people,' the Governor said, 'and can be overcome by nothing but deceit. You must pretend outward respect for them and win their confidence.' As I remained silent, he went on, 'You must take occasion to visit the Superior, and tell him how you have till now always experienced kind treatment from them, and how you have been surprised to hear from some Christians that they now speak differently about you. Say all this with a smiling face, and tell him that although you have always been ready to serve him, your feelings will change if he believes what common people say about you and if he too speaks ill of you'" (IV, 143–145).

The following day, September 20th, Ranga Pillai seized an opportunity to visit the superior: "[...] I went in and paid my respects. 'What! Is this the gate of Heaven?' he asked; 'What has brought you here? Are you better now?' I answered that so long as I had his blessing there was no doubt of my getting better. 'What is our blessing to you?' he exclaimed; 'It was the Brâhman's blessings that cured you.' – 'I have always acted,' I rejoined, 'impartially between Hindus and Christians. You must have heard from your catechists that I always give immediate attention to their complaints. Till recently you have always been very gracious to me, but for the last few days you have been speaking of me unkindly. I can only ascribe it to my bad fortune.' – If we had a Christian as Chief Dubâsh,' he said, 'we could trust him; and before you became Dubâsh, you were favourable to us; but as soon as you were appointed, you began patronizing Hindu temples, giving them privileges, but quite neglecting the Christians. [...]' – 'It is true,' I answered, 'that there has been much distress these last three years[...] but no one is to blame for that. [...] – 'We all know that you belong to a respectable family,' he answered, 'that has been held in esteem for two generations. You have held important places and won the good will of Europeans. But if you had been a Christian, many others would have become so too.' – 'Your words astonish me,' I said. 'The Christians form only a sixteenth of all the people here, and all are poor [...]. You know this well, and that it is not so for the Hindus. [...]' – 'Say what you will,' said the Superior, 'I am sure that all would become Christians if only you would set the example. We should be quite satisfied with you as Chief Dûbash if you were a Christian. As you are not, we have had several times to urge M. Dupleix to appoint one. We have written to Europe, and we will write again. [...]' – I never asked for the appointment,' I answered. [...] – 'Quite true,' he said; 'and you are more capable than any one else; but I think that if a Christian were Dûbash, even though he were a fool, many Christians would prosper. If you were a Christian, you would make many converts. [...] May God bless you and take you to Himself.' – 'If it be so decreed,' I said, 'it will surely come to pass.' (IV, 148–150).

The hostility between the courtier and the Jesuits is a leitmotiv throughout the rest of the diary. Let us quote only two examples. On August 12, 1748, Dupleix asked Ranga Pillai about the evolution of public opinion, and the courtier confirmed that many resented the missionaries: "The Brâhmans of the town are no use to anybody; and besides their worrying people, they cause disturbances in the town.' – He said, 'You are right. If you can somehow drive the Brâhmans out of the town, I shall be extremely pleased'" (V, 190). Another example: "Tuesday, May 8 [1753] – The Kârikâl priest at the St Paul' Church said, 'I hear that you have permitted the celebration of the *Kinni-thêr* festival by the blacksmiths in honour of Kâli. This has not been celebrated for five or six years. A festival which has long ceased ought not to be revived. I shall tell the Governor.' I replied, 'Owing to the English troubles, no festivals were celebrated in the several temples; but, when I spoke to the Governor, he ordered the celebration of festivals as before. Therefore this also is being celebrated.' He went away, saying that it ought not to be allowed" (VIII, 334). Four days later, the courtier noted: "To-night Kâli was drawn in the *kinni-thêr*" (VIII, 338).

The hostility between the Jesuits and the Hindus was particularly glaring about the temple of Isawaran, dedicated to Siva, and close to St-Paul church, as we can see from the entry for Thursday, March 17, 1746: "On Wednesday night at 11, two unknown persons entered the Iswaran temple carrying in a vessel liquid filth, which they poured on the heads of the gods around the altar, and into the temple, [...] having broken the pot of dirt on the image of the god Nandi, they went away through a part of the building which had been demolished." (I, 332). This caused considerable emotion, and the faithful gathered in front of the temple, menacing to go on hunger strike. Dupleix scattered the crowd in front of the temple, summoned the leaders and threatened them with death should they go on with the movement, before putting the courtier in charge of an inquiry, which, strangely enough, led nowhere.

During the siege of Pondicherry by the British, the temple was destroyed. Ranga Pillai relates these events with distress: "This morning tents were pitched round St Paul's Church, and two hundred soldiers [...] were quartered there. The Governor, M. Paradis [the Commander in Chief] and others went thither and desired that a mortar might be mounted there. But they [the Jesuits] asked that the Îswaran temple should be pulled down. I think the Governor may have arranged (through Madame) for their help in certain Europe matters; so, as this is a time of war, there was much talk, a council was held, and the priests were told that the Îswaran temple would be demolished. The Governor then went home" (V, 295). Destruction began the following day, without a single attempt from the courtier to make the Governor change his mind: "Lastly, the priests of St Paul's Church have been trying for the last fifty years to pull down the Vêdapuri Îswaran temple; former Governors said that this was the country of the Tamils, that they would earn dishonor if they interfered with the temple [...] But the Governor listens to his wife, and has ordered the temple to be destroyed, thereby adding shame to his dishonor" (V, 297).

This incident irretrievably upset the fragile balance which Ranga Pillai had tried to preserve. In April 1746, after the attack against the temple of Iswaran, he told the Governor: " 'Sir, if you do not take the necessary action to punish the evil done, the good name which you have acquired will be tarnished. Besides, you have invited all the merchants from Madras to Pondichery, and have a mind to make it a rich city, like Madras. If you take steps such as those you mention, you will obtain help in the direction at which you aim, and the merchants will have confidence in you. [...]'" (III, 224–225). Later, in April 1747, when Dupleix asked him why the merchants still refused to leave Madras, he answered: "'The French,' they have been saying among themselves, 'will make us Christians by force. They [...] will allow us no liberty. Their punishments are too severe. They will hang us and cut our ears off; nor will they listen to our complaints'" (IV, 65–66). And again in March 1748: "In order to produce an impression on the Governor's mind, I answered, 'As the English treat their people kindly, they let him spend whatever he pleases and accept whatever he can obtain for them. That is why Madras and Fort St David are so full of Tamils.' He moved away as though he had not heard what I said" (IV, 448).

In October 1754, Ranga Pillai pleaded with Godeheu to allow the temple to be rebuilt: " 'Your predecessor unjustly destroyed the temple, and grieved the towns-people. [...] If you give such orders, the town will decline yet more. [...] Among us Tamils, worship comes first. [...] The English Company at Madras and the Dutch Company at Negapatam not only make a monthly allowance, but send officers with a dozen soldiers, sepoys, or peons at festival times to prevent disorder. I myself have seen this. Our Company's merchants are always saying that the town will not flourish unless the same is done here; otherwise it must decay" (IX, 61). But Godeheu refused to make such a decision.

The worst happened in July 1760, a few months before the death of Ranga Pillai, followed by the storming and destruction of Pondicherry by the British. A profanation brought matters to a head: "M. Lally ordered this evening that the Brâhman's ears should be cut off close as well as his nose and that he should then be hanged. [...] All these 60 years since the town was founded, no Brâhman had been slain here till to-day this one was hanged. In former times when a Brâhman was about to be hanged, I would explain to the Governor that it was a great sin to kill a Brâhman, so he would be let off, because the town was then destined to prosperity, but now a Brâhman has been hanged for the town is destined to ruin" (XII, 290–291).

Thus, the relationships between the courtier and the Governor were good as long as commercial prosperity was maintained. Ranga Pillai and his co-religionists made money through the exchanges between India and France, and they appreciated the order and security which prevailed in the trading post. The commercial and military rivalry between the French and the British exacerbated these tensions, which resulted in religious conflicts detrimental to the trading post.

Notes

1. *The Private diary of Ananda Ranga Pillai, dubash to Joseph François Dupleix ... translated from the Tamil and edited by ... Fr. Price, K. Rangachari and H. Dodwell*, Madras, 1904–1928, 12 vol. (references in the present text correspond to this edition). French translations: *Les grandes pages du journal d'Ananda Ranga Pillai, courtier de la Compagnie des Indes auprès des gouverneurs de Pondichéry, 1736–1760, présentées par Pierre Bourdat* (Paris, 2003); *Les Français dans l'Inde, Dupleix et Labourdonnais. Extraits du journal d'Anandarangapoullé courtier de la Compagnie Française des Indes (1736–1748), traduit du tamoul par Julien Vinson ...* (Paris : E. Leroux, 1894). Index of the diary: *The colonial world of Ananda Ranga Pillai, 1736–1761: a classified compendium of his diary ... by R. Alasubdaram* (Pondicherry, 1988). Biography of Ananda Ranga Pillai: SRINIVASACHARI, Chidambaram S., *Ananda Ranga Pillai: the "Pepys" of French India* (Madras, 1991).

   About the different currencies: a pagoda of 3,39 g of gold is the equivalent of 3,5 rupees or 24 fanam; a rupee of 1,13 g of silver represents 7,5 fanam; the silver fanam is worth 64 cashes; the cash is a copper coin. A lakh corresponds to 10 000 rupees.

CHAPTER 10

The Factories and Facilities of the East India Companies in Surat: Locations, Building Characteristics and Ownership

Nagashima Hiromu

The aim of this chapter is to trace the locations, building characteristics and ownership of some of the factories of certain East India Companies in Surat under the Mughal Empire. The Dutch of the Dutch East India Company were confined to Deshima, a small artificial island in Nagasaki under the Seclusion Order in Japan. The houses at Deshima were built by leading Japanese merchants of Nagasaki by the Japanese government's order and rented out to the company. They were constructed in the Japanese style at first, although the Dutch were allowed to reconstruct two of the houses in the European style shortly after they moved to Deshima. Therefore, compared with conditions in Nagasaki, under what conditions were the factories of the European companies located in Surat? Could they live in any corner of Surat freely? Could they construct their buildings in the European style or in any other style? Could they have ownership of their buildings?

First, I will trace the locations of the factories and their facilities, such as wharfs, warehouses and cemeteries. Contrary to the case in Nagasaki, their 'locations in Surat are relatively unclear at present. For the purpose of the present study, which is to compare the locations of the factories and facilities of the European companies in Surat with those in Nagasaki, it may be unnecessary to explore the details of their locations. However, I wish to do so in order to show how difficult it is to trace their locations in Surat. In order to establish

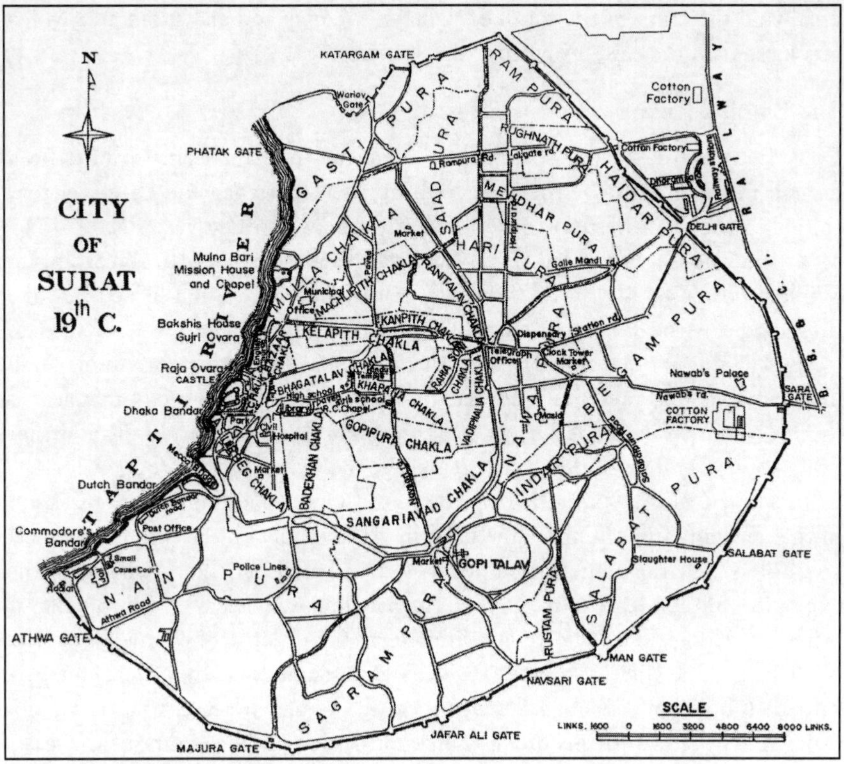

Fig. 1 Map of Surat in 1877

Source: V.A. Janaki, *Some Aspects of the Historical Geography of Surat*, University of Baroda, 1974, p. 88.

the location of the factories, I will also consider the locations of some of the important buildings of Surat, such as Mughuli Saray (an inn) and Mulla Muhammad Ali's residence and mosque.

The Locations of the Factories

Surat has a fort. It was constructed in the middle of the sixteenth century and survives today. It is located on the western side of the city, facing the Tapti River (see Fig. 1). Surat had two city walls. The inner wall was constructed during the period from 1664 to 1679 after the sack of the city by the Maratha army led by Shivaji in 1664 and 1670. The outer wall was constructed in the late 1710s in order to defend the city against the attacks of the Marathas. The area inside the inner wall can be divided broadly into two areas: the merchant area (*Saudagar-pura*) and the office area (*Sultan-pura*). The former was located to the north and the latter to the south of the fort. We may add an artisan area which was located to the east, away from the riverside.

The English Factories

Every European factory (also called a "lodge" or "house") seems to have been located in the area inside the inner wall up to 1762, when the Dutch factory shifted to the southwestern corner of the area between the two walls.

The English factory at Surat was first established in 1612. According to William Foster's study on the locations of the successive English factories, the first abode of the English factory is unclear. The inhabitants were forced to leave it in the middle of 1616 and rented a house belonging to Khwaja Arab Turbati[1] that had previously housed the city's mint. Foster infers that it was located to the southeast of the fort, near the *darbar*, i.e. the court of the governor (*mutasaddi*) of Surat, and was later rented by the Dutch as their lodge.[2] It came to be known as the *Walandani kothi*, i.e. the Dutch building. The possession of this substantial dwelling by the English was strongly objected to by the local authorities, but the English retained possession of it for three years until the expiration of their lease in mid-1619. At that time, they were forced to look for a fresh dwelling. Their choice was limited by the order of the Mughal prince, Shah Jahan, the then governor (*subadar*) of Gujarat, that they were not permitted to buy, build or rent a factory near the waterside [Roe: 510n1; Habib: 93]. We will return to this order again later. Following the expiry of the lease, they were obliged to occupy "sundrie pettie habitations" [EFI 1618–21: 135–36]. In November 1621, the English factors wrote that they had been allowed by the Mughal authorities to build a house for their best convenience and that it was already half finished, although the rent had not yet been agreed upon [EFI 1618–21: 325]. It is unknown whether the English were able to move into the new house or not, but, even if they did, their sojourn there appears to have been very short because, shortly afterwards, they were then permitted to rent, on a seven year lease, the house and grounds of one Khwaja Hasan Ali, near the end of 1623 [EFI 1622–23: 309–310, 321; EFI 1624–29: 28; cf. Commissariat III: 215, 216].[3] It is also unknown to where they moved after this lease expired. Thus it is clear that the location of the English factory changed several times at the beginning of their activities.

Their factory was located to the north of the fort, next to Haji Zahid Beg's house and warehouses in 1664, when Shivaji of the Maratha plundered Surat. Haji Zahid Beg was one of the two greatest merchants in Surat at that time, and resided in the merchant area (*Saudagar-pura*) of the city. It is unknown when and from where the English moved into this house. This factory was sometimes called the "old lodge", as opposed to the "new lodge", which was located on the riverside to the west of the old lodge. Foster infers that the old lodge was that described by J. Ovington in 1689 as a commodious building in the north-western quarter of the city. According to Ovington, the lodge belonged to the Mughal emperor, Aurangzeb, and he permitted the rent to be spent mostly on repairs or augmentations to the building [Ovington: 227]. According to Hamilton, the French owned a small Church near the old English Factory, which maintained a few Capuchins [Hamilton I: 96]. In England, the new East India Company was established in 1698, which sent their factors to Surat. Although the history and location of the new English Company at Surat has not yet been fully traced, it is clear that its factors, represented by Sir Nicholas Waite, had begun to stay in Surat by October 1700 [SFR. 6:1ff.]. Both the old and new companies were united in July 1702, and a letter outlining this union reached the English at Surat on 11 June 1703 [SFR. Vol. 5A: 14 June 1703], although the union could only be completed in 1709 and both the old and new factories continued separately, exhibiting a strong rivalry towards each other in Surat, until 1709 [cf. SFR, Vols. 5A & 6]. The old factory must have been the same lodge which Ovington mentioned, as the cost of reparations to the lodge was "deducted out of the Kings (Mughal emperor's) rent", as in Ovington's day [SFR 5A: 23 May and 29 June, 1704]. The location of the new factory is not very clear, although it is probably the same one that was called 'the new factory' later. Ashin Das Gupta also mentions that 'the new factory' was "occupied at the turn of the 18th century" [Das Gupta: 30n2]. It was located close to the Tapti River in the northwestern part of the city. As Das Gupta mentions, this "English factory is still standing, although it is doubtful how much longer it will last" [Das Gupta: 30n2].

The Dutch Factories and the Factories of Certain Other Companies

According to Balkrishna Govind Gokhale, an Indian scholar, the first Dutch house in Surat in 1616 was rented from Khwaja Hasan Ali, one of the leading merchants in Surat, at an annual rent of 600 *mahmudis* [Gokhale: 164; cf. Broecke, I: 112].[4] The English had feared for some time that the Dutch would attempt to be allocated the new English house, although this fear ultimately proved groundless [SC: 77, 78]. The Dutch rented a large house from the same Khwaja Hasan Ali for 1,200 *mahmudis* per year in November 1622, although we do not know whether it was the same house as the previous one [Broecke: II: 278n3]. However, soon afterwards, in January 1623, the Dutch moved to a new house belonging to Pelowan Saffedts Beg, on a four year lease of 1,250 *mahmudis* per year [Broecke II: 280; Gokhale: 164].

Foster states that the Dutch appear to have moved to the house of Khwaja Arab some time later and that this house must have come to be known as *Walandani kothi* subsequently, as we have seen. Foster, at first, inferred that the *Walandani kothi* had been Khwaja Arab's house, although he changed his view later and inferred that the *Walandani kothi* had been the first factory of the Dutch. He fails to offer any reason for his change of opinion [compare Roe: 510 and Foster 1922:1]. In any case, Foster's initial view, which equates Khwaja Arab's house with the *Walandani kothi*, is still only an inference. As we have seen, in January 1623, the Dutch moved into a new house belonging to Pelowan Saffedts Beg on a four year lease. Khwaja Arab's house had nothing to do with the Dutch up to that time. Further investigation will, therefore, be necessary. According to the *Bombay Gazetteer*, at the beginning of the eighteenth century, the Dutch factory was located in the same place [cf. *Bombay Gazetteer*, Vol. II: 307], but this inference also, therefore, needs further scrutiny.

According to L'Escaliot, when Sivaji sacked Surat in 1664, the Dutch house was on the other side of the town, "almost an English mile asunder" from the English house [Foster 1921: 316]. This suggests that the Dutch house had shifted to the so-called *Walandani kothi* by that time.

At the end of the seventeenth century, the Dutch Company were the tenants of Mirza Mosem and, after his death, of his sons, Mamet Sahed and Mirza Mamet Aref [VOC 1620: 248a]. In 1692, the Dutch signed a contract with the two sons to construct a new lodge on the site of their old lodge. The new lodge consisted of two parts. One part was attached to the old lodge and the other part was two stories high, separated from the old lodge (see Fig. 12) [VOC 1620: 236a–51]. Although it is not very clear, this complex of the old and new lodges may be the *Walandani kothi*.

The Dutch attempted to obtain a more commodious house. In 1712, they procured an order (*farman*) from the Mughal emperor which permitted them to rent the house of the late Itibar Khan, the former governor of Surat. It was situated close to the north of the fort on the riverside [HR: 855: 118; Stavorinus, III: 95; VEL: 873]. It is unclear whether they actually rented it or not. According to Das Gupta, the Dutch failed to buy it and it was eventually sold to the Sindhi merchant, Suleimanji, for 40,000 rupees [Das Gupta: 33n1; VOC 1913: 26]. Das Gupta states that, throughout the first half of the eighteenth century, the Dutch Company made ceaseless efforts to build a "new lodge" at Surat and that, by 1719, they had found there was no room in the inner town for this purpose and that they must seek suitable ground outside the inner wall. The Dutch also tried to purchase the aforementioned "old lodge" from their landlords without success, as the latter demanded too much for the building [Das Gupta: 33n1; VOC 1897: 36].

In 1762, the Dutch shifted their factory to the so-called Dutch Bandar, which lay to the southwestern corner of the area between the inner wall and the outer wall, close to the river [*Gujarat State Gazetteers*, Surat District (Revised Edition) 1962: 969]. It is said that the Dutch experienced difficulties in obtaining the consent of the governor of the Surat fort to transfer their effects

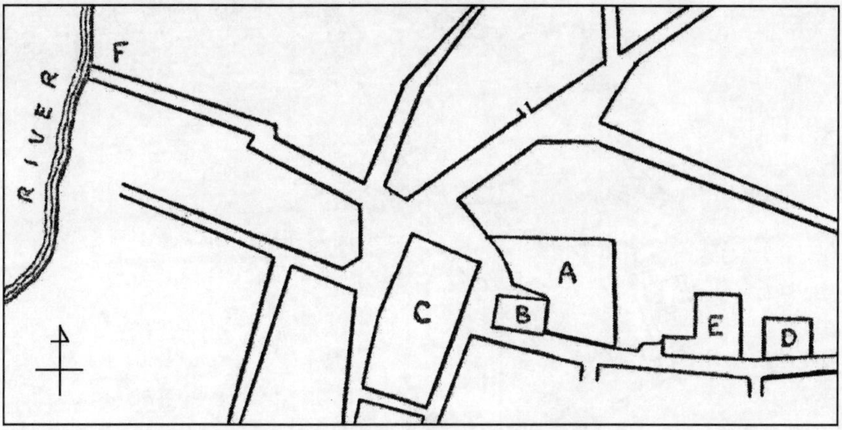

Fig. 2 Map of Northwestern Corner of Surat in the 1660s (Foster's Inference) Cited from *The English Factories in India, 1661–64*, p. 297

A: English factory B: Saray and mosque of Mirza Zahid (Zahid Beg) C: Dadimar or Racket Court (18c.), originally a saray D: Armenian church (18c.) E: French factory (established a little later) F: The subsequent English factory

to the *bandar* (wharf) and that the governor was instigated to do so by the English, who had occupied the fort and controlled the governor since 1759 [Stavorinus III: 126–27].

According to Foster's study, the Portuguese lodge was located near the old lodge of the English in 1664. He infers that a French factory was also established near the English and Portuguese lodges slightly later [EFI 1661–64: 297. cf. Foster's note there], but, as his view is mainly based on some eighteenth and nineteenth century maps, it is unclear when the factories were first established there. The factory of the Swedish Company can also be seen in the northwestern corner of the inner part of the city on a map of 1750, which was recorded by Christopher Henrik Braad [Franks: 158–59].

Although our foregoing investigation is a tentative one, it may be said that the locations of the factories of each company at Surat were relocated several times and so it is very difficult to trace their exact locations for each period. In the next chapter, I will explore other problems connected with identifying their locations on some earlier maps of Surat.

The Locations of the Factories as Depicted on Earlier Maps

As for the locations of the English and Portuguese factories in 1664 and the French factory in later years, Foster provides a map showing the result of his study based on certain descriptions, maps and his inferences (see Fig. 2). The

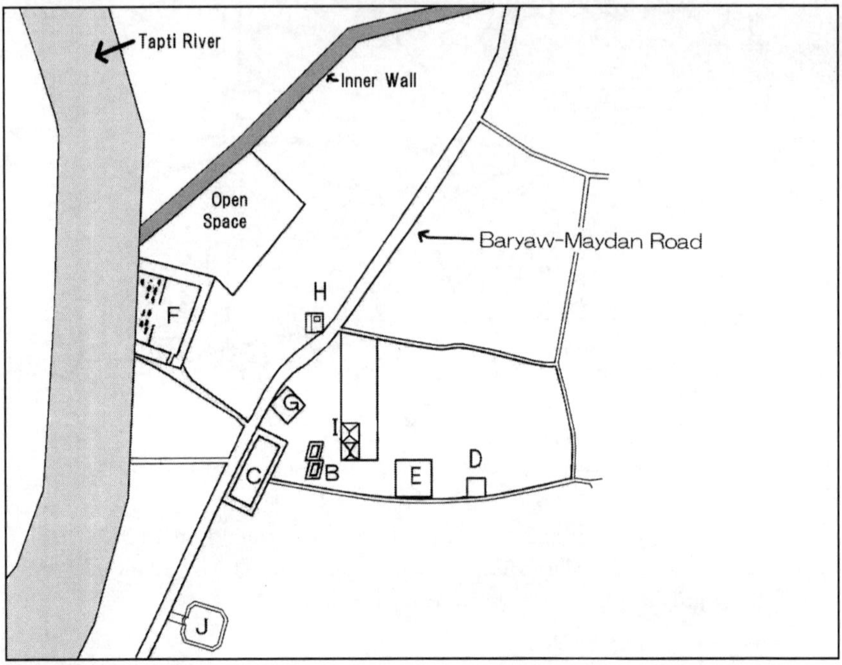

Fig. 3 Remains of the Factories, etc. (based on the 1817 Map of Surat)

B: Mirza Zahid's Masjid C: Racket Court D: Armenian Church E: French Factory; F: English Factory G: Portuguese Church H: Mulla Abdul Fath's Masjid I: Portuguese Factory J: An Old Saray (now considered Mughuli Saray = Municipal Corporation)

descriptions concern Shivaji's plunder of Surat in 1664, and show that the English factory lay next to Haji Zahid Beg's house and warehouses. The maps consulted by him were as follows: (1) A French map in the British Museum, based upon one compiled by Captain De Gloss in 1753; (2) *The Plan of the City of Surat*; and (3) a large-scale map of that portion of Surat, furnished by Mr. F.G.H. Anderson, I.C.S., a contemporary of Foster. Map (2) is a modern map based on a scientific survey conducted by Lieutenants Adams and Newport in 1817 (hereafter called "the 1817 map"; see Figs. 3, 4 and 5).[5]

His inferences seem to be, on the whole, correct, although, as he himself admits, "the boundaries shown for 'A' [i.e. the English factory] are partly conjectural". The location of the English factory in 1664 was not included on the 1817 map and the Portuguese factory and a smaller square building are shown instead (see Figs. 3 and 4).

There is another earlier, excellent map of Surat which shows the distribution of the localities (such as *wara*, *pur*, *pura*, *pol*, *muhalla*, *chakla*) within Surat.

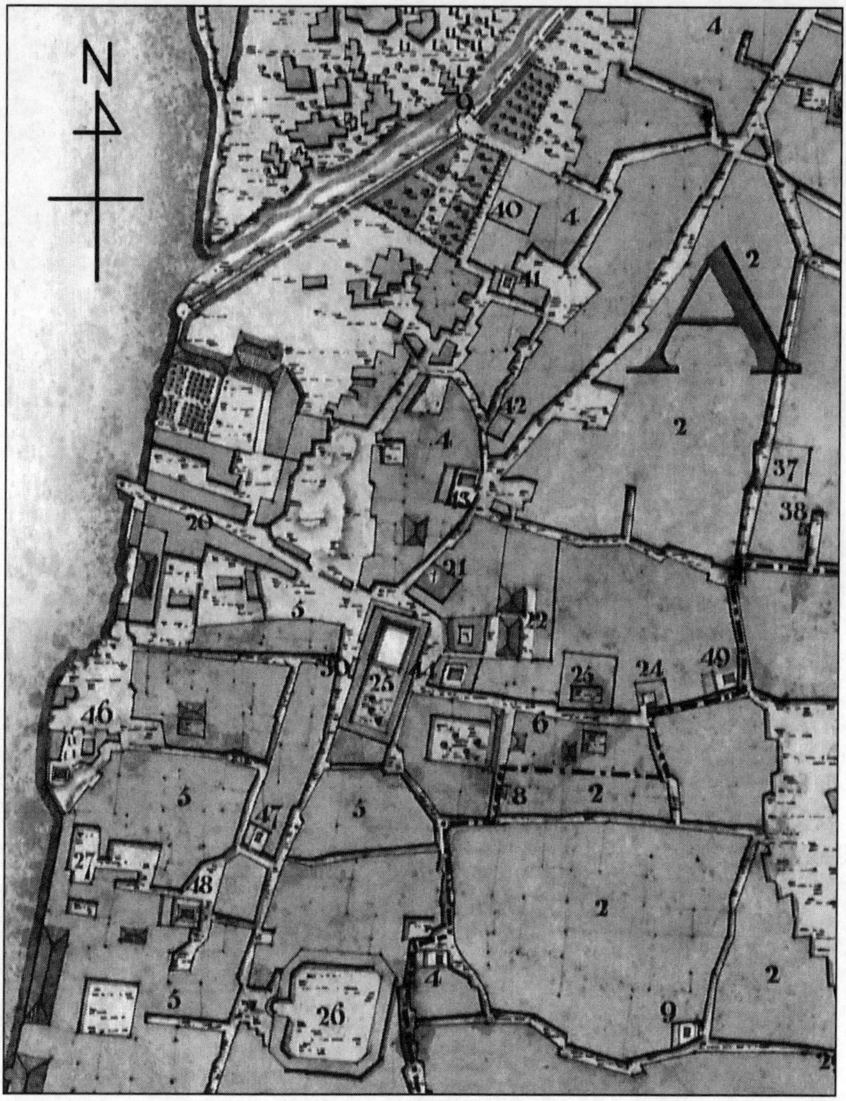

Fig. 4 Northwestern Corner of the Inner Wall Area of the 1817 Map of Surat
A part of the *Plan of the City of Surat*, Surveyed in 1817, IOR: X/2737, ©British Library Board. All Rights Reserved.

A: Moolna Chukla (i.e. Mulla Chakla) 5: Moghul Suraee (being not the name of a building but that of an area) 6: Ungrez Chukla (English Chakla) 44: Meerza Zaeeds Musjid (Mirza Zahid's Masjid) 25: The Racket Court in an old suraee 24: Armenian Church 23: French Factory 21: Portuguese Church 43: Moolla Abdoolfut's (Mulla Abdul Fath's) Musjid 22: Portuguese Factory 26: An old Suraee (filled up as an Invalid Barrack, from unhealthiness of the place the men do not reside in them. i.e. No. J of the Fig. 3)

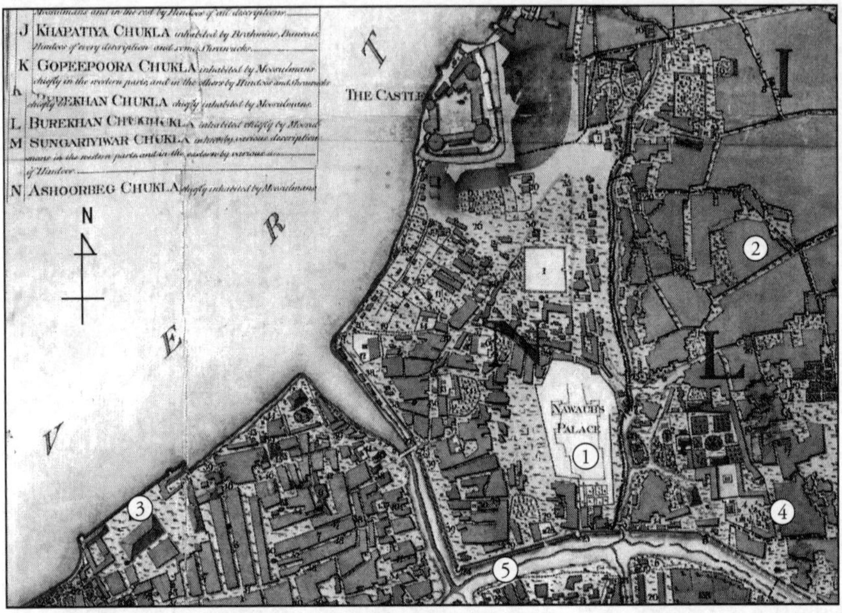

Fig. 5 Southwestern Corner of the Inner Wall Area of the 1817 Map of Surat
A part of the *Plan of the City of Surat*, Surveyed in 1817, IOR: X/2737, ©British Library Board. All Rights Reserved.

① Nawab's Darbar (Court) ② Buildings called Velinde ka Kote (i.e. Walandani kothi) ③ Velende Baree or Dutch Bunder ④ Kazee's Musjid and Burial Ground (i.e. Khwaja Diwani Masjid) ⑤ Southern part of Inner Wall

It is preserved in the Maharaja Sawai Man Singh II Museum in Jaipur, India. The map was probably created around 1730 (hereafter called "the 1730 map"; see Figs. 6, 7a, 7b and 7c). It does not appear to be a European type map but an Indian type map, since, for example, the place names are written in both Persian and Hindi. [cf. Nagashima 2006; Gole: 164–65; Singh, Ch.: 185–92]. Neither Foster nor Das Gupta mentions it at all.

The English and French factories are depicted on the map in different locations from those which Foster infers. According to him, the locations of both the old English lodge and the French lodge are to the east of the main road which runs from the Baryaw Gate to the Maydan in front of the castle (hereafter the Baryaw-Maydan road; see Figs. 3 and 4). His inference of the location of the French lodge is also supported by the French map of 1758 drawn under the inspection of S. Anquetil de Briancourt, chief of the French factory at Surat. The French factory is depicted as lying to the east of the Baryaw-Maydan road on the French map (see Fig. 8). The locations of both the English and

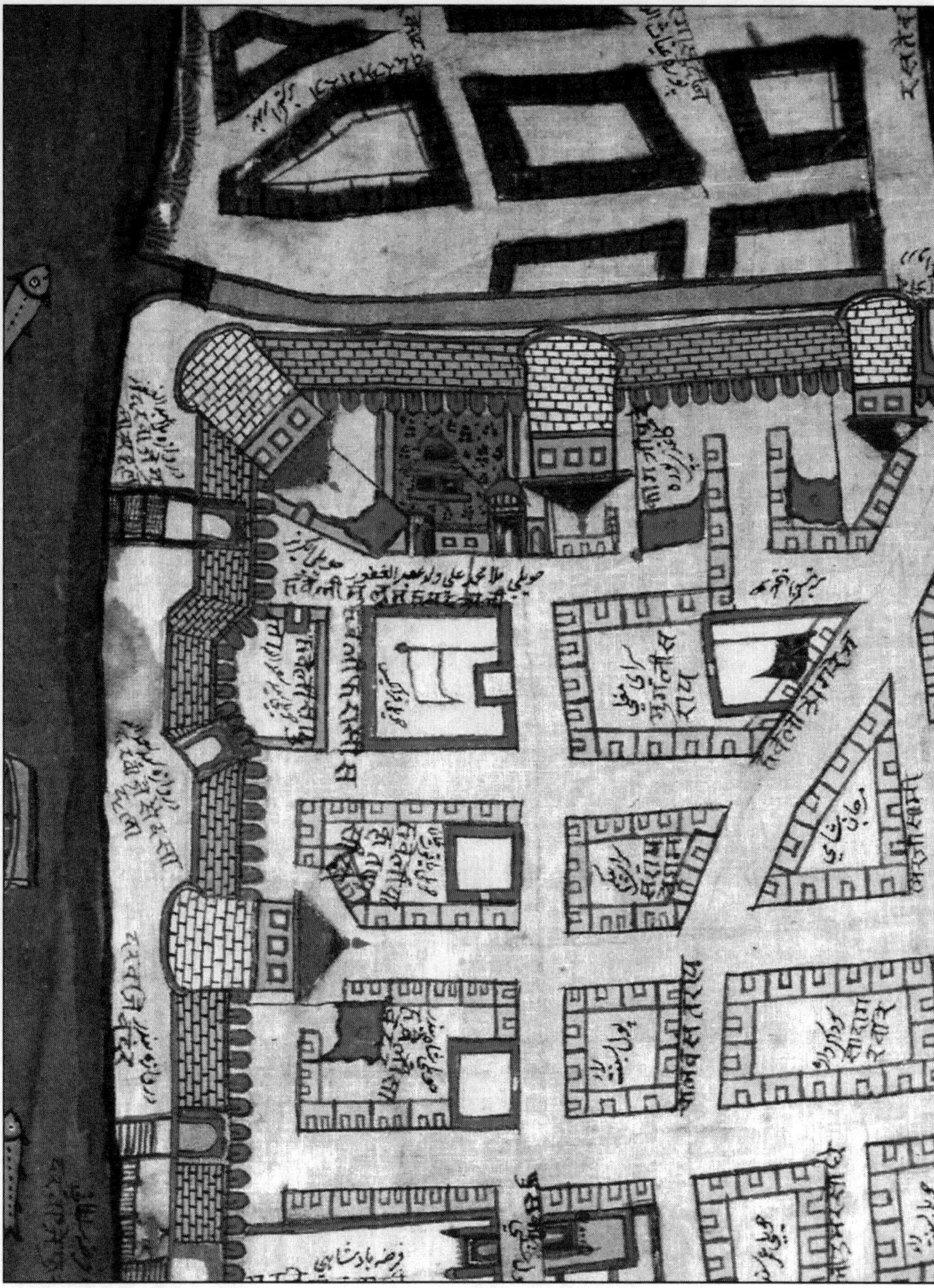

Fig. 6 The Northwestern Corner within the Inner Wall on the 1730 Map of Surat
Courtesy of the Maharaja Sawai Man Singh II Museum, Jaipur, India

French factories are, however, indicated as lying to the west of the main road on the 1730 map (see Fig. 7b).

The location of Mughuli Saray (Saray-i Mughuli CP.); Mugali Saray (H.)) on the 1730 map is also different from the location of the so-called Mughuli Saray, i.e. the building of the present Surat Municipal Corporation. The former is depicted to the west of the Baryaw-Maydan road on the map, while the present Mughuli Saray is located to the east of the road. Mughuli Saray and the English factory are depicted in the same ward on the 1730 map and the French factory is shown as lying to the west of Mughuli Saray (see Figs. 6 and 7b). The building of the so-called Mughuli Saray itself is depicted on the 1817 map, but it is simply described in the *References* attached to the map as "an old Saraee, filled up as an Invalid Barrack, from the unhealthiness of the place the men do not reside in them" [References 1820: A-26]. Lieuts Adams and Newport depicted "Moghul Saraee" as a large area lying to the south of "Ungrez Chukla", i.e. English Chakla (i.e. ward). It is clear, therefore, that although the building of the so-called Mughuli Salay is located within the Moghul Saraee area, Adams and Newport were unaware that the building was the Mughuli Saray. It was later discovered that it had been constructed by Haqiqat Khan, the governor (*qaladar*) of the Surat fort, in 1644 [cf. Commissariat 1980: 233–36]. However, it is not yet evident whether it was called Mughuli Saray. It remains, therefore, open to question whether the building of the present municipal corporation is actually the former Mughuli Saray. In any case, the 1730 map raises many questions about the topography of Surat in those days.

According to Das Gupta's study, the new English factory was located next to the house of Mulla Muhammad Ali at the beginning of the eighteenth century [Das Gupta: 30]. The latter was the richest merchant in Surat at that time. The 1730 map also depicts the new English factory next to Muhammad Ali's residence, which lay in the northwestern corner of the area within the inner wall (see Figs. 6 and 7b). On the 1817 map, however, next to the new English factory, lies an open space (see Fig. 4). At some time after Ali's death, his descendants must have moved elsewhere. According to Das Gupta, Muhammad Ali built a mosque that survives today, within a stone's throw of the remains of the new English factory [Das Gupta: 30n2]. There is no mosque next to the new English factory on the 1817 map, however; instead, there is a mosque called "Moolla Abdoolfut's Musjid" on the western side of the Baryaw-Maydan road, to the east of the new English factory (see Figs. 3 and 4). Mulla Abdul Fath was one of the grandsons of Muhammad Ali [Nadri: 202]. This might be the mosque of Muhammad Ali mentioned by Das Gupta. The English president and Muhammad Ali consulted each other very often and both played leading roles in the merchants' uprising against the governor of Surat in 1732. The Dutch, on the other hand, were reluctant to join the uprising initially, because their lodge was very close to the *darbar*, i.e. the court and official residence of the governor (*mutasaddi*) of Surat (see Fig. 5). The English in Surat, therefore, could enjoy a great deal of freedom of action at that time, compared with the Dutch in Japan. The French also participated in the uprising. According to Das Gupta's study, the owner of the French factory was Muhammad Ali at that time [Das Gupta: 30n3]. The French factory was actually depicted as lying close to Muhammad Ali's residence on the 1730 map (see Figs. 6 and 7b). This may be correct, considering that it was rented from Muhammad Ali.

Other Company Facilities

We find references to other kinds of facilities of the companies, that were separated from the main lodges, in the descriptions and maps of that time, including the houses inhabited by the lower ranking members of the factories; wharfs, gardens, cemeteries, warehouses, churches, monasteries and chapels.

Houses Situated Outside the Main Lodges of Respective Companies

When the main lodge was too small to contain the whole company, the lower ranking members had to live in rented houses which were situated outside the lodges. Della Valle commented that, in 1623–24, for example, many inferior members of the Dutch Company lived outside the great inclosure (i.e. the main lodge), dispersed elsewhere in the city, and, when occasion required, they all repaired to the palace of the commendator [Della Valle I: 26].

Wharfs and Gardens at Swally Marine, i.e. the Anchorage of the European Ships

J. Fryer describes the facilities of the European nations around 1672–81 as follows:

> The several colours of the three nations, English, French, and Dutch were flying on the flag-staffs erected for that purpose, who here land and ship off all goods, without molestation. Before President Matthew Andrew's time (1659–62) the Europeans at Swally always lodged in tents; but since then, wooden houses tiled with pan-tiles have been raised in an enclosure allotted by the governor of Surat. In the compound are included warehouses, stables, and other out-houses, with as good a garden as this sandy soil will allow [Fryer I: 210–11].

Fryer does not mention the Portuguese, but, on the 1730 map, their wharf and garden are also depicted along with the wharfs and gardens of the other three nations (see Fig. 7a).

Fig. 7a The Western Part of the Inner Wall Area of the Fort of Surat on the 1730 Map (copy and English tr. by Nagashima)

Ch: Chakla Gd: Garden (or Orchard) Gt: Gate Gy: Graveyard M: Market Mh: Muhalla Pr: Pur, Pura St: Storehouse

R: Residence T: Tomb V: Village Wf: Wharf Wr: Wara

The terms Wara, Pur, Pura, Pol, Muhalla and Chakla mean ward

Fig. 7b The Northwestern Part of the Inner Wall Area of the Fort of Surat on the 1730 Map (copy and English tr. by Nagashima)

Ch: Chakla Gd: Garden (or Orchard) Gt: Gate Gy: Graveyard M: Market Mh: Muhalla Pr: Pur, Pura St: Storehouse R: Residence T: Tomb V: Village Wf: Wharf Wr: Wara

The terms Wara, Pur, Pura, Pol, Muhalla and Chakla mean ward.

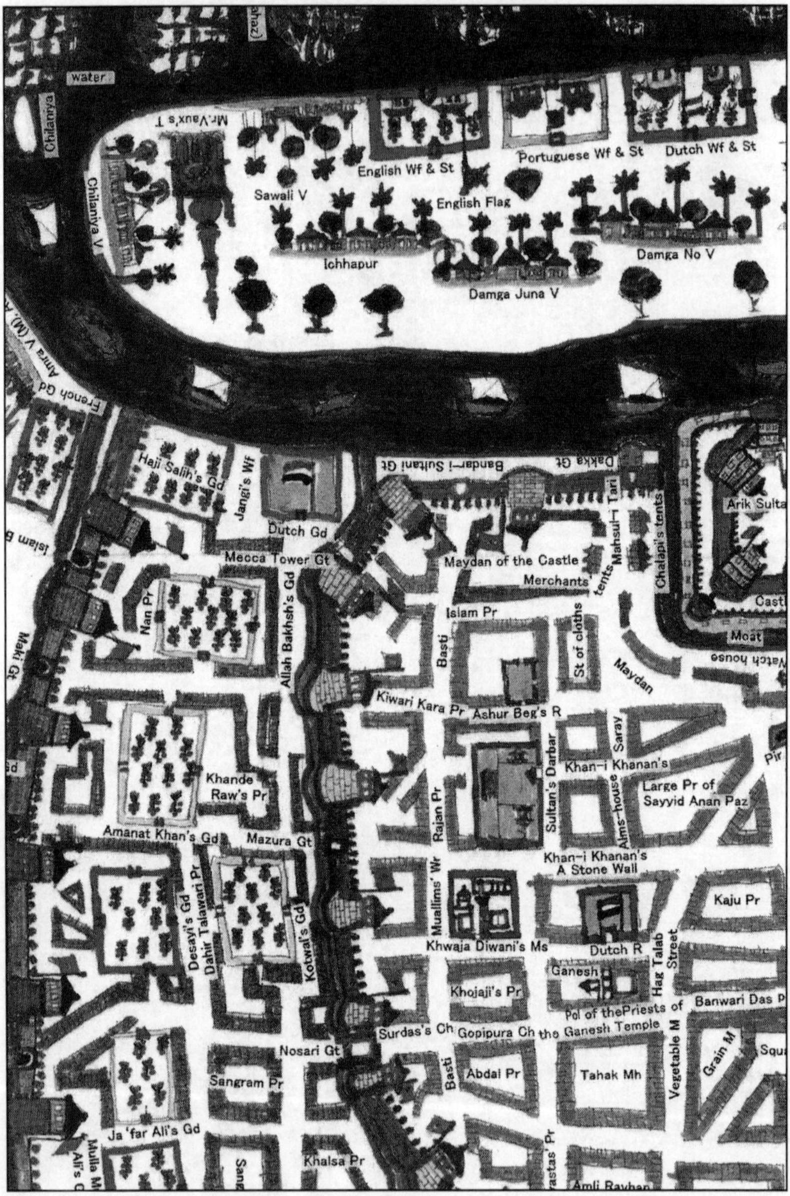

Fig. 7c The Southwestern Part of the Inner Wall Area of the Fort of Surat on the 1730 Map (copy and English tr. by Nagashima)

Ch: Chakla Gd: Garden (or Orchard) Gt: Gate Gy: Graveyard M: Market
Mh: Muhalla Pr: Pur, Pura St: Storehouse R: Residence T: Tomb V: Village
Wf: Wharf Wr: Wara
The terms Wara, Pur, Pura, Pol, Muhalla and Chakla mean ward.

According to M. Godinho, at Swally, around 1663, the English and Dutch had their own custom-houses, through which they sent their goods [Godinho: 46].

Wharfs and Gardens Outside the Inner Wall, Separated from the Factories Inside the Inner Wall

The wharfs and gardens of the English, Dutch and French are depicted along the Tapti River on the 1730 map: the English wharf to the north of the northern part of the inner wall, the Dutch wharf to the south, in between the two walls, and the French one further south, outside the outer wall (see Figs. 7a, 7b and 7c). It is relatively unclear, however, when they were established respectively. These riverside wharfs do not seem to have been mentioned in any traveler's accounts by the end of the seventeenth century. It is true that Fryer describes the European wharfs around 1675 as follows: "We [European companies] fortify our Houses, have Bunders or Docks for our Vessels, to which belong Yards for Seamen, Soldiers, and Stores: To that which belongs to the Dutch is a sweet Garden, shor'd up with timber from the incroaching River, with Arbors and Beds after the Europe Mode" [Fryer I: 289; cf. Gokhale: 164], but these facilities were probably established in the Swally region. Manucci, an Italian traveler, in fact, comments that, "Upon the sea-shore, on the other side of the river, the Europeans have their gardens, to which they can retire should at any time the Mahomedans attempt to attack them" [Manucci I: 62]. He fails to make any mention of the existence of the gardens and wharfs on the fort side of the river.

As to the Dutch wharf in the south-western suburb of the city, called *Jenghi-bandar*, Stavorinus states that it was ceded to the company, partly as a purchase, and partly as a donation, at the time of the embassy of Mr. Ketelaar, in 1712 [Stavorinus I: 158–59]. The Dutch garden, however, must have originated earlier than 1712. There is a VOC document which was sent from Surat to Batavia in 1699. The document contains the ground plan of a garden and is entitled "The description of the company's garden ..." The rest of the title is indiscernible, as the document is badly stained, but the title of the ground plan, although it was written by a modern archivist later, is as follows: "Plan of the buildings that could be built in the yards and the surrounding grounds, bought by the VOC" [VEL 872; VOC 1620: 253–57]. The fact that the garden had been established by the turn of the eighteenth century is also confirmed by a document which was received in Amsterdam in 1735. According to this document, the block contains, among other things: (1) ground which was bought from a widow in 1707; (2) a house which was brought from the Dutch lodge at Swally (in 1707); and (3) ground which was bought in 1710 [VEL 874]. According to Stavorinus, this wharf and garden of the VOC on the riverside was about seven or eight acres (i.e. about 28,000 or 32,000 square meters) in extent [Stavorinus I: 159].

The Dutch also had a warehouse at Rander, a town on the opposite side of the Tapti from Surat. According to Mandelslo, the Dutch had a warehouse at Rander in 1638 [Mandelslo: 7]. Thévenot adds that the Dutch had "a very good Magazin" at Rander in around 1666 [Thevenot: 32].

As for the English, the then English president, Fremlen, described how, in 1638–39, fire seized on the timbers placed to support the vines of the English garden. It seems to have been to the east of the city [Fremlen: 310]. Fryer states that it had a neat garden (probably in the city), but Shivaji Maratha came to destroy it. The English, during his time, therefore, had "no gardens in the city, or a very few", although, outside the city, they had many gardens, like a wilderness, with many trees [Fryer I: 214–15].

The English seem to have established a garden in the area between the two walls of the city by the middle of the eighteenth century. It was located to the south of the Dutch wharf and to the north of the garden and wharf of the French company. It is depicted on the French map of 1758 but not on that of 1730 (see Figs. 7c and 8).

Warehouses Inside the Inner Wall, Separated from the Factories

The warehouses were usually established in the yards of the main lodges of the respective companies, but were sometimes located outside the main lodges. The Swedish map of Surat of 1750 shows, inside the inner wall of the city, such warehouses lying outside the main lodges: the Dutch storage building in 1670, the new Dutch storage building and the Swedish storage building [Franks 1998: 158–59].

As to the English company, there was a magazine to the south of the new English factory near to the riverside (see "J" of Fig. 8). We also meet, in the Factory Records of the English company, three English warehouses situated, probably, very near to the old factory. They were rented from Hodji Zaid Beeg (Haji Zahid Beg), at an annual rent of 168 rupees in total [SFR 5A: 13 June 1702].

Itibar Khan, the Governor of Surat, granted the English company permission to build a place (a kind of warehouse) in the mint for coining and keeping the silver of the company, although the mint's shroffs (money changers and testers) were opposed to this. Finally, when the English had almost completed the digging, they accidentally hit upon a hollow place in the ground, which the shroffs, etc. laid hold of and said it went as far as the castle: upon which, all was stopped again and the governor was forced to order the ground to be filled in again, promising the English land in another location [SFR 5A: 24 August and 21 September, 1702]. This appears to reflect the governor's special favour towards the English.

Cemeteries

The Dutch, English, French and Portuguese had their respective cemeteries in the northeast of the city. The English cemetery still lies just beyond the Katargam gate of the outer wall, and the Dutch cemetery is situated adjacent to the Armenian cemetery inside the same Katargam Gate. Dilip K. Chakrabarti has studied the cemeteries in considerable depth [Chakrabarti: 133–39]. It is, therefore, sufficient for us to confirm their approximate locations around the Katargam region, relying on some documents that are useful for that purpose.

Godinho mentioned three European burial grounds in 1663 as follows: Outside the city, towards the east, one can see two vast fields containing innumerable Muslim graves. Further ahead there are two enclosures, one for the burial of the Dutch and another for the English. It is worth seeing the mausoleums of some of the Dutch *commandeurs* and the English presidents, who died in Surat, from the point of view both of their design and of their fine finish. There is also a separate burial ground for Catholic Christians which can be easily recognized by the crosses placed on the graves [Godinho: 50].

Around the 1670s, Fryer described a Portuguese burial-place between the Dutch cemetery and the English cemetery [Fryer I: 254; cf. Chakrabarti: 133], which must have been the aforementioned burial ground for Catholic Christians.

Fryer adds that, "The French have a separate place to deposit their dead over against the English, with only one single tomb, and that a small one" [Fryer I: 254].

The relative positions of these cemeteries are clearly depicted on the French map of Surat in 1758: The Catholic cemetery, the Dutch cemetery are drawn near the Katargam gate within the outer wall, while the famous English cemetery and an old French cemetery lie outside the Katargam gate (see Figs. 8 and 9). Although another English cemetery is depicted next to the Dutch cemetery within the Katargam gate on the French map, it must not be the English one but the Armenian one which still exists at present (see Figs. 8 and 9).

The English had tombs on the coast at Swally, besides Mr. Vaux's tomb, a famous land mark at the mouth of River Tapti [Fryer I: 212; cf. Das Gupta: 22]. The French cemetery is depicted close to the French wharf and garden in the Swally region on the 1730 map.

Churches, Monasteries and a Christian College

There were a French Capuchin monastery and a Jesuit college (the latter only in an earlier period). The French map of 1758 depicts a Convent of the French

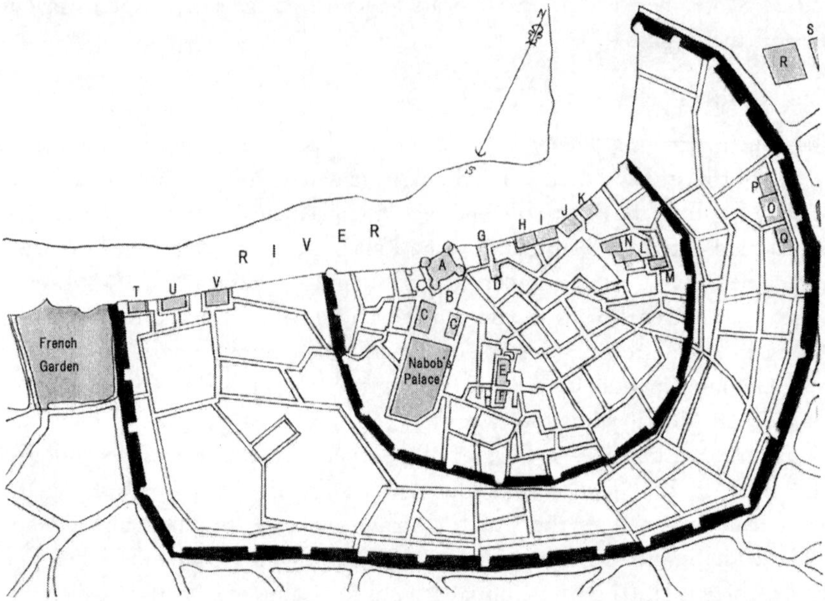

Fig. 8 The 1758 French Map of Surat (Based on the map cited after p. 96 of Anirudda Ray, *The Merchant and the State: the French in India, 1666–1739*, 2 vols. New Delhi, 2004, Vol. I)

A: Fort; B: Maydan (Open Place); C: Saray; D: Mint; E: Dutch Lodge; F: Stable; G: Customs House; H: Sidi's House; I: Mosque; J: English Magazine; K: New Lodge of the English; L: Portuguese Lodge; M: French Lodge; N: Convent of the English; O: Dutch Cemetery; P: Remain of the Catholic Cemetery; Q: Armenian Cemetery (wrongly written "Anglais (English Cemetery")); R: English Cemetery; S: Old French Cemetery; T: English Garden; U: Sidi's Wharf; V: Dutch Wharf

mission between the Portuguese lodge and the new English lodge. The Swedish map of 1750 also depicts the French church, although the 1817 map does not, but, rather, a Portuguese church instead (see "G" of Fig. 3 and No. 21 of Fig. 4).

Godinho states that there was once a Jesuit college in Surat and its priests had ample work to do in that mission city, but John Correia-Afonso, the translator of his diary, notes that there are no records of a Jesuit college, although the Jesuits visited Surat at various times from 1580, and had a small chapel and residence there. Godinho adds that the Jesuits abandoned that mission because, whenever the Mughals wanted something from the Portuguese, they would seize the priests, thereby compelling the viceroys (of Portugal) to accede to their demands, in order to avoid endangering the lives and freedom of the prisoners. They were replaced by two bearded French Recollects, "sent to India

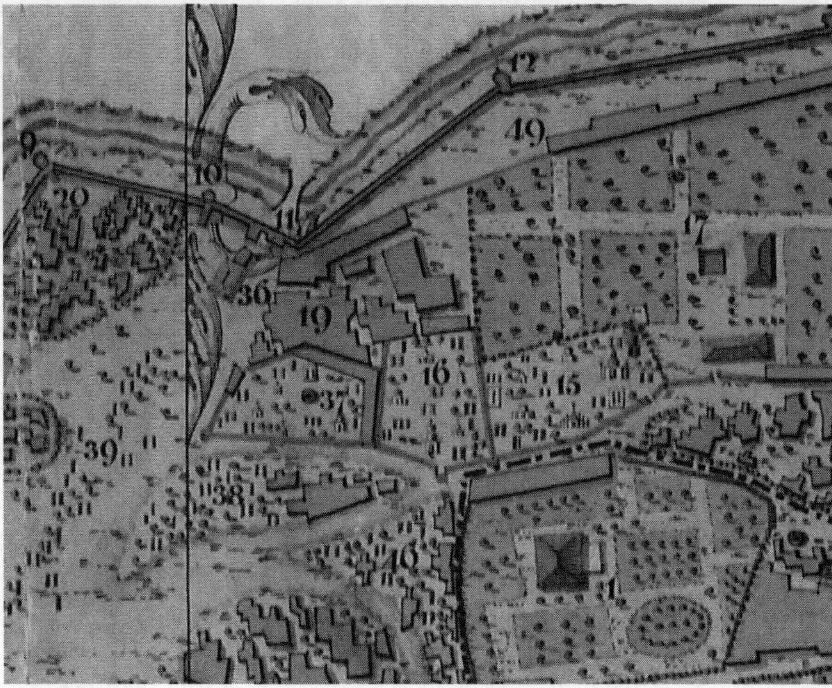

Fig. 9 Northern Corner inside the Outer Wall of the 1817 Map of Surat

A part of the *Plan of the City of Surat*, Surveyed in 1817, IOR: X/2737, ©British Library Board. All Rights Reserved.

11: Katargam Gate; 15: Armenian Burial Ground; 16: Dutch Burial Ground; 17: Armenian Garden; 37: Portuguese Burial Ground and Small Chapel

by the Congregation for the Propagation of the Faith, and who now render signal service to God. They have their little church inside their house where the Catholics attend Mass on Sundays and days of obligation".

On the other hand, the French Capuchin fathers were active in their missionary work and already held in high esteem by 1664. According to Manucci, on his first visit to Surat (in 1655), there was "a little church belonging to the French Capuchin fathers, whose superior was the famous priest Brother Ambrozio (Ambroise, Ambrose). Afterwards the French came and built a handsome factory" [Manucci I: 61]. Tavernier adds that the reverend Capuchin fathers built a very commodious one [house] upon the model of the houses of Europe, with a beautiful church [Tavernier I: 7; also cf. Hamilton I: 96]. Bernier writes, albeit based on hearsay, that Shivaji Maratha respected Ambroise, and the Maratha armies spared the Capuchin church when they attacked Surat in 1664 [Bernier: 188; cf. also EFI 1661–64: 310].

The bearded recollects mentioned by Godinho must have been the same missionaries who accompanied the French Capuchin fathers as mentioned by Manucci and others. It is true that the French recollects belonged to a different sect from that of the Capuchin fathers. However, they must have been closely related, as both belonged to the order of St. Francis. Godinho visited Surat in 1663 and the Capuchin fathers were already well known by 1664. Neither Godinho nor Tavernier mentioned the activities of the two Catholic orders. Thus, we can judge that both were one and the same at Surat. The Capuchin fathers, especially Ambroise, acted as an intermediary between the European companies and the governor of Surat. For example, when the English, Dutch and French companies decided, together, to call away all of the factory employees from Surat to Swally in 1671, the governor, alarmed at the new development, sent Padre Ambroise to Swally to mediate for peace [EFI 1670–77: 211]. Ambroise even seems to have tried to help the French company. A letter from Aleppo, dated June 1667, states that he had kept out boats all through September 1666 to pilot in the expected ships from France [EFI 1665–67: 268n]. According to Thévenot, "there may be very well a hundred Catholick Families in Surat" [Thevenot I: 22].

The Dutch and English neither had churches nor undertook missionary activities outside their respective factories in those days, as was the case in Japan for the same period.

Although not European, the Armenians also observed the Christian religion in Surat. According to M.S. Commissariat's study, the Armenians in Surat seem to have had a church or chapel as early as the last quarter of the sixteenth century, but this was said to have been destroyed by the Mughal governor of the city at a date unknown. After this, the community held religious services in a house set apart for the purpose until a beautiful new church , dedicated to the Virgin Mary, was erected in 1778 [Commissariat III: 512–13]. An Armenian church is depicted on the 1817 map to the east of the French factory (see "D" of Fig. 3), although it does not appear on the earlier maps. Streynsham Master writes, in 1672, that "the Armenians have a house, chappell and priest maintained at their common charge" [Hedges, Vol. II: cccv]. This shows that there was no Armenian church, besides a chapel, in his time.

Chapels

As for the chapels in the European factories, Streynsham Master described them as follows in 1672:

> The English perform all of their Public Devotions in the Company's Factory house, where there is a Room set apart on Purpose in the manner of a chappell for Divine Worship. The Dutch have the like in their Company's

> house. The French and all of the Romish Persuasion Perform their Devotions at a Convent of the French Capicheins (Capuchins) lately built, where they have also a Chappell, and the Armenians have a house, chappell and Priest maintained at their Common charge … [Hedges, Vol. II: cccv].

The Dutch had another chapel in their garden on the riverside at the south of the inner wall later [VEL: 874].

It can be concluded from the above investigation that, contrary to the situation of the Dutch company in Nagasaki, many different kinds of company facilities were established throughout the city; that is, both on the inside and outside of the inner wall and on the outside of the outer wall. It also can be said that, contrary to the English Company at Madras, the Dutch Company at Pulicat, the French Company at Pondicherry and the Dutch Company at Batavia, for example, the European factories at Surat were not settlements which possessed strong forts and most of the other necessary facilities. Although Fryer stated in the 1670s that they had fortified their lodges in Surat, his statement must be mainly related to their facilities in the Swally region as we have mentioned earlier. The European factories of Surat were not separated from the Indian houses but mingled with them.

Building Characteristics of the Factories and other Facilities

Compared with the large, strong factories with forts, the factories at Surat were small but housed many facilities, and were sometimes called buildings of the caravan-saray type. The caravan-saray had a yard at the centre, which was surrounded by many rooms or apartments, the entrances of which faced the yard, although this does not necessarily mean that they were previously caravan-sarays. The European companies usually rented houses owned by the wealthier Muslim merchants of Surat, although the names of the Mughal emperor and a Bania merchant (i.e. a Hindu and/or Jain merchant) also feature on the list of the owners of the European factories.

The English lodge that was rented from Khwaja Arab in 1616 had a couple of fair warehouses and was reasonably commodious. It had an orchard and pleasant walks upon the roof (after the Spanish and Moorish building style); having chambers, a diet, servants, coaches and horses, with the attendance of Indians called peons for the way [Roe: 510n1; Downton: 134]. This house was said to have been a former mint.[6]

The English lodge around 1629–30 had, as Peter Mundy describes it, the following characteristics: The English house is of the best sort in town, very fair and strongly built, the roof in general flat and terraced aloft to walk on, very substantially done with lime, etc., so that no rain can pierce it, and below a fair hall, chambers and rooms for the president and council, etc. merchants, with complete warehouses, walks, etc. below; also a garden which for its bigness is the neatest and costliest in all the country hereabouts; being near 4 square, having 4 very fair long walks round about it … [Mundy II: 25–26].

This flat-roofed building had two stories and a roof terrace on which one could walk. Upstairs was a fair hall, cambers and rooms for the president, council members and merchants. Downstairs, there were warehouses, walks, etc. There was also a very neat, costly garden of nearly 4 square yards. It is, however, unclear whether this factory was of the caravan-saray type or not.

Mandelslo also describes the scale of the settlements of the European companies in 1638 as follows: None of the foreigners resident in Surat had such large, wealthy settlements as had the Dutch and the English settled at Surat [Mandelslo: 10].

The Dutch factory of 1623 had the following characteristics:

> He (*the Commendator*) lives in a goodly palace, which has many distinct apartments, with several entrances into a court, like so many different houses, only included within the same wall, which is entered into by one great gate: Here, the *Commendator* holds the best, and largest, apartment, to himself; in the rest lodge some of their gravest merchants, which are of the council for management of affairs, in order to their better conveniency, and union, besides many others of inferior condition, which live out of this great inclosure, dispersed elsewhere in the city, and when occasion requires, they all repair to the palace of the *Commendator* [Della Valle I: 25].

This building is of the caravan-saray type. The English lodge next to Haji Zahid Beg's house was also commodious. Fryer described it in the 1670s:

> The house the English live in at Surat, is partly the King's gift, partly hired; built of stone and excellent timber, with good carving, without representations; very strong, for that each floor is half a yard thick at least, of the best plastered cement, which is very weighty. It is contrived after the Moor's buildings, with upper and lower galleries, or terras-walks; a neat oratory, a convenient open place for meals. The president has spacious lodgings, noble rooms for counsel and entertainment, pleasant tanks, yards, and a hummum (Turkish bath) to wash in [Fryer I: 214].

Ovington depicts the house in a similar way [Ovington: 227]. At some point, the English factory had a small bell-turret with a small vane. When, in November 1616, the English factors set up a small bell-turret with a small vane (weathercock) on the outside of the common hall of their factory, the people of

Surat made outcry to the governor of Surat that the infidels (i.e. the English) had taken possession of Surat, alleging that the sign of the cross (i.e. the vane) was an especial token of victory and of winning the town. The governor understood the intention of the English and was rather sympathetic towards them, but the *shahbandar* (head of the foreign merchants of the town) and the other officials of Surat were of a more violent disposition. Behind the ill feeling of the ship owning merchants of Surat towards the English lay their fear at the English's new venture, i.e. their investments in cloth for the Red Sea besides their investments in cloth for Southeast Asia [Letters Received IV: 346–48].

The governor was rather sympathetic towards the English in the above case. On the contrary, in the case of the Dutch factory at Hirado in Japan, the Japanese government exploited the fact that the year of the construction of the warehouse was depicted using the Christian calendar on the upper portion of its wall in order to force the Dutch to move to Deshima in Nagasaki. The sympathetic attitude of the governor of Surat towards the English contrasted strikingly with the harsh attitude of the Japanese government in the above case.

In order to imagine the various characteristics of the factories, pictures of them are useful. An engraving of "the English factory at Surat" is said to have been cited in the first English translation of Mandelslo's *Travels* by J. Davies in 1662, although I have not consulted this book. It also appears as a frontispiece to *English Factories in India*, 1634–36, as well as in J. Ovington's *A Voyage to Surat* (see Fig. 10). The English factory depicted in it is a lodge of the caravan-saray type. A photograph of the remains of the new English factory to the north-western corner of the area inside the inner wall also shows that the factory was of a caravan-saray type, in which many rooms surrounded a courtyard [Janaki 1974: Photographs Nos. 23 and 24].

Another engraving very similar to the above one appears in the *Pieter van den Broecke in Azië* (Vol. II: Fig. facing p. 349) and in some later works, such as M.N. Pearson's *Port Cities and Intruders* (p. 33), as 'the Dutch lodge of Surat' (see Fig. 11). Pearson states that he reprinted it from Isaak Commelin's work published in 1646.[7] If so, the engraving might have been that of the Dutch lodge, as the latter antedated Davies' translation of Mandelslo's *Travels*. Although it has to be confirmed further, such pictures do not seem to be actual reproductions but imaginary ones. We should, therefore, be careful about using these engravings.

The image of the engraving became very different from the ground plan of the old Dutch lodge at the end of the seventeenth century (see Fig. 12) [VEL 869: Plan of factories or rented houses of the VOC in the city of Surat, the seventeenth century, received from Surat 1699; cf. also the Atlas of Mutual Heritage (website)]. As we noted earlier, in 1692, the Dutch Company contracted with the owners of their lodge to construct a new lodge on the site of

Fig. 10 The So-called "English Factory at Surat in 1638"

Source: *Frontispiece*, EFI 1634–36.

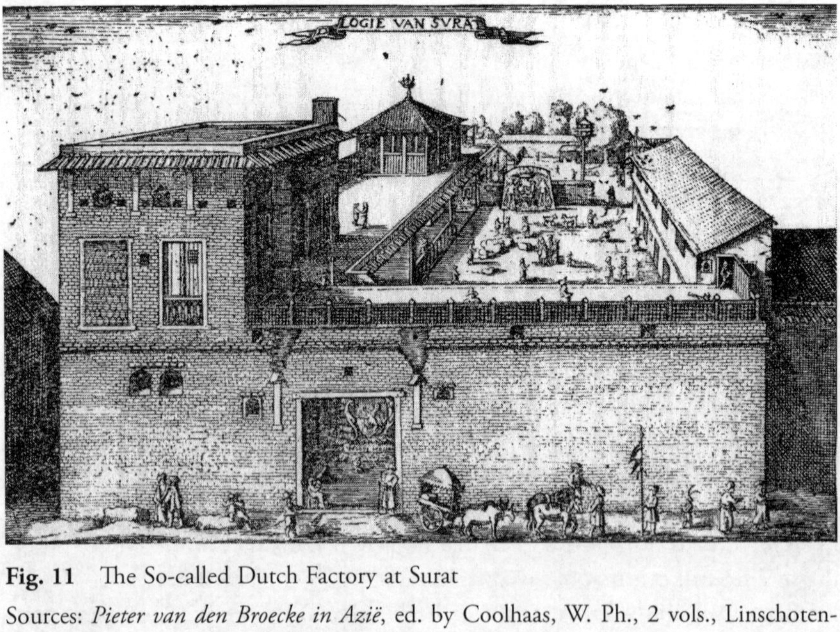

Fig. 11 The So-called Dutch Factory at Surat

Sources: *Pieter van den Broecke in Azië*, ed. by Coolhaas, W. Ph., 2 vols., Linschoten-Vereeniging, 's-Gravenhage, 1962–63, Vol. II, p. 349.

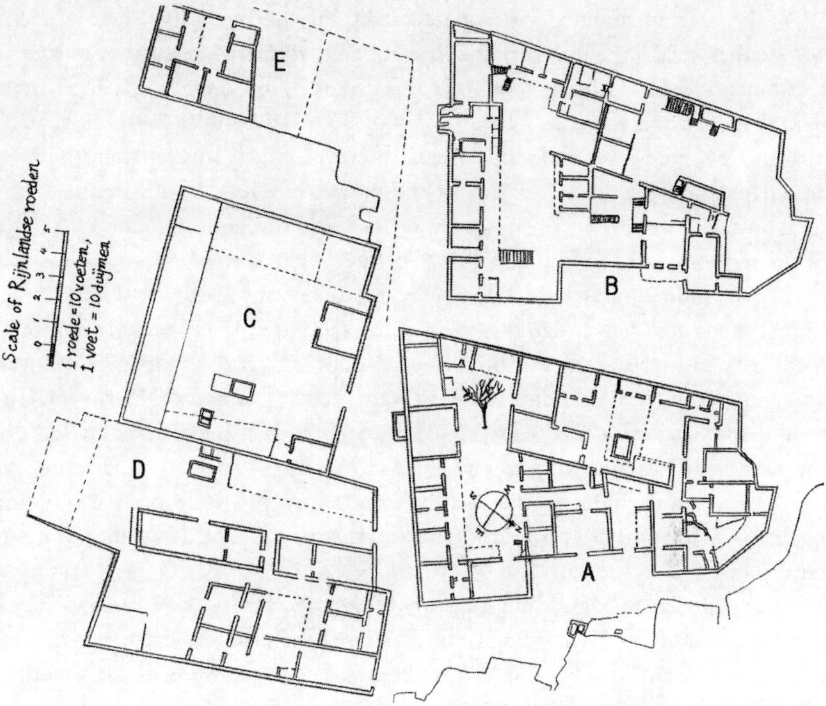

Fig. 12 The Ground Plan of the Dutch Factory at Surat around 1699

Source: VEL 869, Nationaal Archief, Den Haag; See also VOC: 1620, 236a–239b.

A: Downstairs of the New Lodge; B: Upstairs of the New Lodge; C: The Ground Plan of the Old Lodge; D: The Newly Rented and Built House; E: The House Belonging to Pieter Vosburugh, Assistant

their old lodge. The new lodge consisted of two parts. One part was attached to the old lodge and the other was two stories high and separated from the old lodge (see Fig. 12) [VOC 1620: 236a–251b].

According to the ground plan, the old lodge was more or less square, the length of a side being about 40 meters, and covering an area of about 1,550 square meters.[8] It was a one-storey building and used as an auxiliary building after 1692. It consisted of a horse stable, a cow stable, dispensaries, a blacksmith's forge, the stableman's house, a dovecote, a water tank, warehouses and a toilet. It also had a large courtyard.

The ground plans of both parts of the new lodge were not square but triangular-shaped. The two storied part had a courtyard. The total floor area of the old and new lodges, including the upstairs area, was about four times that of the old lodge (see Fig. 12) [VEL 869].

The area of about 1550 square meters of the old lodge, before 1692, was neither very large nor very small, compared with the area of the houses in Deshima. The total area of Deshima was about 3,969 *tsubo*, i.e. a little more than 13,000 square meters [Toyama 1990: 26–27; Morioka 2001/2005: 91]. The area of the houses in Deshima was, however, much smaller than the total area. If we consider that the area of the houses covered about a tenth of the total area, this would be 1,300 square meters, and was almost equal to the area of the old lodge of the Dutch in Surat before 1692.

The amount spent on the timber, carpenters' wages, etc. for the construction of the Dutch new lodge cost the company about 2,033 rupees. The amount for bricks and mortar (lime), bricklayers' wages, etc. cost about 1,731 rupees, and the amount for iron and workers' wages, etc. cost about 235 rupees. The total cost was about 4,010 rupees [VOC 1620: 249a]. The ratio of the cost of the timber, bricks and mortar, and iron and workers' wages for the respective construction may indicate the relative importance of the respective building materials, with timber and bricks (and mortar) being considered more important than iron.

The aforementioned buildings of the Dutch factory were made of brick and timber, although, according to Fryer, as we have seen, the English lodge was built of stone and timber and Ovington added that the walls of the wealthier houses were made of brick or stone [Ovington: 130]. Houses built of stone must have been very rare in Surat, however. Thévenot commented, around 1666: "Because there is no stone in the country, the houses cost dear; seeing they (houses) are forced to make use of brick and lime, a great deal of timber is employed. Timber must be brought from Daman by sea. Brick and lime are very dear also. One cannot, therefore, build an ordinary house at less charge than five or six hundred *livres* (about 400 rupees) for brick, and twice as much for lime" [Thevenot I: 22]. M. Escaliot describes the houses at Surat as follows:

> And for buildings consisting partly of brick (so the houses of the richer sort), partly of wood; the main posts of which sort only are timber, the rest is built of bamboo. In the greater part of the town, scarcely two or three brick houses are to be seen in a street, and, in some parts of the town, not one for many streets together. Those houses which are built of brick are usually built strongly, with walls 2 or 2½ feet thick and flat roofs covered in plaster, like plaster of Paris, which makes most commodious places to take the evening air in the hotter seasons [Foster 1922: 313–14].

As for the characteristics of the cemeteries in Surat, both the English and the Dutch cemeteries contained very lofty mausoleums, with domes and arches. Ovington describes these cemeteries as follows, at the end of the seventeenth century:

Fig. 13 The Mausoleum of Baron van Reede tot Drakesteijn (d. 1691)

Fig. 14 The Mausoleum of George Oxenden (d. 1669)

> The English and all the Europeans are previledg'd with convenient Repositories for their Dead, within half a mile of the City. There they endeavour to outvie each other in magnificent Structures and stately Monuments, whose large Extent, beautiful Architecture, and aspiring Heads, make them visible at a remote distance, lovely Objects of the sight, and give them the Title of the Principal Ornaments and Magnificencies about the City. [Ovington: 235–36]

The two highest tombs among them, those of George Oxenden of England and Baron van Reede of the Netherlands, are 10 meters tall (see Figs. 13 and 14). H.G. Rawlinson, editor of the revised edition of Ovington's journal, commented: "These curious and, to modern taste, ugly structures may still be seen by the visitor to Surat. They were evidently built in rivalry to the great tombs of the Mahommedans at Sarkej near Ahmedabad and other places" [Ovington: 235n2]. As Rawlinson notes, they must have been influenced by the lofty mausoleums built by the Mughal emperors and nobles and the followers of the Muslim religious saints. As Ovington states, these mausoleums also seem to indicate a rivalry between the English and the Dutch. Such huge European mausoleums with arches and domes appear mainly in Gujarat. We can also see the remains of relatively tall mausoleums in Pulicat in southern India, although the shape of their upper portion in Pulicat is very different from

Fig. 15 The Dutch Cemetery at Pulicat

those in Surat (see Fig. 15). Although some tombs in Pulicat also have domes and arches, their domes are not as tall as those in Surat. It is unclear where this shape originated. Such huge, tall remains of the European mausoleums as those in Gujarat seem to occur neither in Southeast Asia (Batavia, Bantam, Ayutthaya) nor in Japan (Nagasaki).

Ownership of the Lands and Houses of the Factories

The European companies do not seem to have been allowed to buy houses for their factories up to the end of the seventeenth century. At the beginning of their commercial activities, they do not seem to have been permitted to rent houses on the riverside, either.

We have already seen that the English were forbidden by Prince Shah Jahan to buy or build a factory, or to hire one near the waterside. Tomas Roe explains the reasons behind the stiff attitude of the Mughal authorities towards them as follows:

> First, because our (the English) eagerness for continuing to lease Khwaja Arab's house gave them suspicion; next, because it was the ancient mint;

> thirdly, because it stood against their great mesquite (*masjid*, mosque), and offended the moores (Muslims), especially our people (the English) pissing rudely and doing other filthiness against the walls, to the dislike of the mahometans (Muslims), who with reverence regard their holy places; lastly, because there was a rumor that we meant to surprise the said mesquite and being of stone and flat at the top it was supposed that we intended to make it our fort and to annoy the castle from there [Roe: 509–10].

The Mughal authorities were, therefore, deeply afraid of the European Companies' military might. Roe's description also highlights the difference in the cultural habits of the Muslims and the English or the Christians.

In the middle of the seventeenth century, Tavernier made the following statement:

> The dwellings of the English and Dutch only hired houses, the King (Mughal emperor) not permitting any Frank (European) to possess a house of his own, fearing that he would have that of which he might make a fortress. The Reverend Capuchin Fathers have built a very commodious one upon the model of the house of Europe, with a beautiful church, and I (Tavernier) myself furnished a large portion of the money which it cost; but the purchase had to be made under the name of a Maronite (a sect of Syrian Christians) merchant of Aleppo named Chelebi [Tavernier I: 7].

Ovington also confirmed in 1689 that the English house at Surat was a rented one. He emphasized that the landlord of the house was the Mughal emperor, Aurangzeb, and that he was "extreme kind and liberal in permitting us (the English) to expend the rent, which was 60 pounds (about 533 rupees) yearly, either in beautifying, repairing or in adding additional rooms to the house, so that he seldom received much rent from us" [Ovington: 227].

According to Das Gupta, the French Company was the tenant of the Mulla Abdul Ghafur's family in the 1720s [Das Gupta: 30n3].

Ovington's remark that the Mughal emperor Aurangzeb was the owner of the English lodge can be confirmed by other English documents. The governor of Surat, for example, sent to the English to demand rent for that part of the factory which belonged to the Mughal emperor, Aurangzeb, and the English company paid 500 rupees towards the rent of the said part of the house in 1702 [SFR. 5A: 14 May 1702]. Thus Aurangzeb was the owner of a part of the old English lodge.

The other remark of Ovington on the method of payment for the repair of the lodge can also be confirmed. When the tenant repaired his rented house or constructed an additional room, the amount spent was to be deducted from the rent. Thus, 300 rupees for house reparations were deducted from the emperor's rent in 1704 [SFR. 5A: 21 May 1704; 29 June 1704].

The Dutch also had the same kind of experience. As we have seen earlier, when the Dutch contracted with Mamet Sahed and Miersia Mamet Aref, the owners of their old lodge, to construct two houses in the yard of the old lodge in 1692, the Dutch factory was allowed to deduct the amount of 4,010 rupees from the rent for the old lodge. In this case, however, at first, the house rent was increased from 20 rupees to 26 rupees per month, but, considering the above payment for the additional houses by the Dutch Company, the rent was in fact lowered to the former amount of 20 rupees [VOC 1620: 247a–47b; 248a–49a].

The English and Dutch were allowed to purchase land and houses at Surat probably at the turn of the eighteenth century. As we have seen, the Dutch Company could buy land for a garden on the riverbank to the south-west between the inner wall and the outer wall before 1699 [VEL 872; VOC 1620: 253–57], and land was bought in 1707 and 1710 as well [VEL 874].

As we have seen, when the Dutch wished to purchase their old lodge from their landlords, the latter wanted 25,000 rupees for the old, decayed building. As the amount was too high, they abandoned the purchase. This shows that the Dutch could buy land and buildings both inside and outside the inner wall, if they wished, although they failed to make the purchase in this case [Das Gupta: 33n1].

In 1733, when the English wished to buy "that part of the decayed factory (i.e. the old lodge) facing the gateway",[9] the owner, Kishandas Bhagwandas, said "he can't let it go under 13 rupees the square *covitt* (*covid*), it being the value of ground hereabouts, and this was rejected by the English as being very unreasonable". His ground measures 1,654 square covitts and will amount to 21,502 rupees [SFR 17: 101; Das Gupta 33n1]. As one covit was about 24 inches [Ovington: 269], 1,654 square covitts were about 615 square meters. Compared to the ground of the Dutch old lodge (either 1550 square metres or about four times that), the ground of that part of the old English lodge (615 square meters) was too small. It appears correct, therefore, that Das Gupta's estimate of the price of 25,000 rupees for the building of the old Dutch lodge almost certainly did not include the ground on which it stood [Das Gupta: 33n1].

Thus, by the turn of the eighteenth century, the European companies were allowed to buy land and buildings for their factories and gardens, and, as we have seen, there are in fact several examples of buying the land and buildings for their gardens. However, it is unclear whether there is any example of buying the land and buildings for the factory itself before 1759 when the English company occupied the fort. It is unclear whether the English bought the new English lodge or not. In any case, the English company could obtain *zamindari* rights, i.e. a kind of feudal lordship, in the region of the future

Calcutta in Bengal under the Mughal Empire by the end of the seventeenth century. It may, therefore, be rather late for the English company in Surat to buy the land and buildings for their factory. In fact, some consideration must have been necessary for a European company before deciding whether they should buy or rent the grounds and buildings for a factory. It depends on the purchase price of and rent for the factory, and the security of the area for the company. If the purchase price is too expensive or if the area is too unsafe, any company will choose to rent rather than to buy, thus avoiding excessive risk.

Finally, it may be of some use to list the amount of the rent of the English and Dutch lodges for comparison with each other and with the companies in other regions (see Table 1).

At the beginning of their activity, the annual rent of the English was 240 rupees. This was increased to 560 rupees, i.e. about twice the previous amount, in the 1620s, which probably indicates that a more commodious house was rented. The Dutch factory also shows a similar tendency, i.e. their rent was doubled in the 1620s. The figures for the rents at the turn of the eighteenth century cannot be compared with the figures in the 1620s, because they are either for a part of the house only or an amount proposed by the English themselves for a decayed house. The rents for the warehouses are naturally lower than those for the lodges. The nature of the English payment for the wharf is relatively unclear. It may not be the rent for the wharf, and it is also unclear whether the Europeans rented or bought the land which they used for their cemeteries.

Conclusion

The European companies transferred the locations of their factories within the inner wall of Surat several times. It is difficult for us to trace these locations exactly. This shows that they were not confined to any fixed region of the city, as was the case of the Dutch in Japan. The Mughal authorities, however, took precautions against the European companies, forbidding them to establish strong lodges near the riverside, at least in the initial stage following their arrival. The English were able to establish their new lodge on the riverside by the beginning of the eighteenth century. The European companies were allowed to own land and houses from around the same period. The English and Dutch succeeded in renting commodious lodges respectively after the initial trial and error period. Their lodges usually followed the design of the "Spanish and the Moorish building" or rather the Muslim buildings of Gujarat and northwestern India.

In the latter half of the seventeenth century, the Europeans constructed huge mausoleums with arches and domes in their cemeteries. These mausoleums were intended to dignify not only the persons buried there but also their

Table 1.

Year	*Characteristic of the factory*	*Annual rent in respective units*	*Annual rent in rupees*	*Sources*
A: The rent for the English Factory in Surat				
1616	Khwaja Arab's house	600 mahmudis	240	Supplementary Calendar: 66
1623	Khwaja Hasan Ali's house on a 7 year lease	1400 mahmudis	560	EFI 1622-23: 321
1674	A Mughal government building	£60	534	Anderson: 126, cited in O.P. Singh: 43
1702	That part of the factory which belongs to the Mughal emperor		500	SFR 5A: 14 May 1702
1733	The rent proposed by the English for that part of the old and decayed English factory which belongs to Kishandas Bhagwandas		50	SFR 17: 101
B: The rent for the Dutch Factory in Surat				
1616	Khwaja Hasan Ali's house	600 mahmudis	240	Broecke I: 112
1622	Khwaja Hasan Ali's house (a new contract)	1200 mahmudis	480	Broecke II: 278n3
1623	Pelowan Saffedts Beg's house	1250 mahmudis	500	Broecke II: 280
1692	The house which belongs to Mirza Mosem and later his sons	20 rupees per month	240	VOC 1620: 247
C: The rent for the warehouse				
1702	Three English warehouses rented from Hodgee Said in the Tank-yard		168 in all	SFR 5A: 13 June, 1702
1703	"		168	SFR 5A: 8 July, 1703
1704	The English warehouse at Rander		100	SFR 5A: 22 May, 1704
D: The rent for the wharf				
1702	Payment for the use of the English wharf at the south of the fort		475	SFR 5A: 10 Dec. 1702
1735	The Dutch wharf at the south of the fort		20	VEL 874

respective companies and nations. Such huge mausoleums were not built in Japan, probably due to the Japanese government's restrictions. Even in India, the characters of the Dutch mausoleums at Pulicat on the Coromandel Coast, for example, seem to have differed from those in Surat in terms of their shape and height, probably influenced by local mausoleums or some other kinds of buildings.

Notes

1. He was one of the prominent merchants who were friendly towards the English in 1614 [SC: 47].
2. Hereafter I will write the Persian, Arabic and Hindi terms without diacritical marks. In English quotations, I will not always follow the original spellings literally.
3. Khwaja Hasan Ali was the *shahbandar* of Surat from 1611 to 1615. He and his father-in-law, Mirza Jafar, were among the prominent merchants of Surat at that time [cf. Nagashima 1996: 8–10].
4. According to the English Factory Record, the Dutch were allocated the 'late dwelling house' of the English, as the latter had shifted to a house belonging to Khwaja Arab [SC: 76]; this house of the English must have been a house rented from Khwaja Hasan Ali.
5. The map of Surat called *The Plan of the City of Surat*, together with *The References*, is preserved in the map section of the British Library. Das Gupta also mentions that this is the earliest and best map which shows the distribution of the localities within the city. Das Gupta uses it effectively in his *Indian Merchants and the Decline of Surat c. 1700–1750* [Das Gupta: 31n3].
6. Downton says that he had seen the Moors before in Spain and Barbarie. 'The Moorish building' in the above passage must mean the houses in Barbarie (or north western Africa near Spain) [Downton: 133; see also Ovington: 130].
7. Isaak Commelin, *Beginn ende Voortgangh van de Vereenigde Nederlandtsche Geoctreerde Oost- Indische Compagnie* (Amsterdam, 1646). In his Dutch editon of *De geschiedenis van de VOC*, Femme S. Gaastra cited the engraving of the so-called English factory at Surat as "the Dutch factory at Agra" (p. 50), but rightly omitted it in the English version of the book; See also the website entitled "The Atlas of Mutual Heritage".
8. The longer side is about 11 roeden and the shorter side is about 10 roeden. One roede (i.e. Rijnlandse roed) is 3.7674 meters.
9. Although Das Gupta seems to equate Kishandas Bhagwandas' ground with the old English lodge, the former was a part of the latter. The owner of the other part was probably the Mughal emperor or someone else who inherited his property [SFR. 17: 101].

Bibliography

1. The Unpublished Sources with their Abbreviations

HR: Hooge Regeering te Batavia, Nationaal Alchief, The Netherlands. No. 855 contains the translation of the *farmāns* from the Mughal emperor.

SFR: India Office Records, G. Factory Records: Surat, Vol. 5A (1702–04, Consultations of London Company's President and Council); Vol. 6 (1700–02, Consultations of English Company's President and Council); Vol. 17, The British Library.

VEL: Maps collections in the Nationaal Archief, The Netherlands, Nos. 869, 872, 874.

VOC: Documents of the Dutch East India Company with serial numbers preserved in the Nationaal Archief, The Netherlands, Nos. 1620 and 1913.

2. The Published Sources and the Secondary Works with their Abbreviations

Anderson, P. 1854. *The English in Western India*, Bombay (Cited in O.P. Singh 1977: 43).

Bernier, François. 1968. *Travels in the Mogul Empire 1656–68*, Tr. on the basis of Irving Brock's translation by A. Constable with notes. First Edition, London, 1891; Indian Edition, New Delhi.

Bombay Gazetteer. 1877. *Gazetteer of the Bombay Presidency*, Vol. II: Gujarat, Surat and Broach, Bombay.

Broecke, Pieter van den. 1962–63. *Pieter van den Broecke in Azië*, ed. by W. Ph. Coolhaas, 2 vols., Linschoten-Vereeniging, 's-Gravenhage.

Chakrabarti, Dilip K. 2003. *The Archaeology of European Expansion in India: Gujarat, c. 16th–18th centuries*, New Delhi.

Commissariat, M.S. 1980. *History of Gujarat*, Vol. III, Ahmedabad.

Das Gupta, A. 1979. *Indian Merchants and the Decline of Surat c. 1700–1750*, Wiesbaden.

Della Valle, Pietro. 1892. *The Travels of Pietro della Valle in India*, tr. by Edward Grey, Hakluyt Society, 2 vols., London.

Downton, N. 1939. *The Voyage of Nicholas Downton to the East Indies 1614–15*, ed. by W. Foster, Hakluyt Society, 2nd Series, London.

EFI. 1907–27. *The English Factories in India*, ed. by W. Foster, 13 vols., Oxford.

Foster, W. 1921–22. "Shivaji's Raid upon Surat in 1664", *Indian Antiquary* 50: 312–21 and 51: 1–6.

Franks, Jeremy. 1998. "The Observant Braad: a Sweedish enquirer in Gujarat in the 1750s", *Moyen Orient & Océan Indien XVI*[e]*–XIX*[e], 10, Paris.

Fremlen, William. 1922/23. "President Fremlen's Journal, 1638–39", by W. Foster, *Journal of Indian History*, Vol. 2.

Fryer, John. 1909, 1912 and 1915. *A New Account of East India and Persia being Nine Years' Travels, 1672–81*, 3 vols., ed. by W. Crooke, WHS, 2nd Series, London.

Godinho, Manuel. 1990. *Intrepid Itinerant: Manuel Godinho and his Journal from India to Portugal in 1663*, ed. with an introduction and notes by John Correia-Afonso, tr. by Vitalio Lobo and John Correia-Afonso, Delhi, Calcutta and Madras.

Gokhale, B.G. 1979. *Surat in the Seventeenth Century, A Study in Urban History of pre-modern India*, London and Malmö.

Gole, Susan. 1989. *Indian Maps and Plans: From earliest times to the advent of European surveys*, Delhi.

Haastra, S.F. 2002. *De Gesciedenis van de VOC*, Vijfde druk, Zutphen.

Do. 2003. *The Dutch East India Company: Expansion and Decline*, Zutphen.

Do. 2006. "On a Map of Surat (a Mughal Port Town) Drawn in the Former Half of the 18th Century", *Nagasaki Prefectural University Journal*, Vol. 40, No. 2.

Habib, Irfan. 1969. "The Family of Nur Jahan during Jahangir's Reign", *Medieval India: a miscellany*, Vol. 1, Department of History, Aligarh Muslim University, Bombay.

Hamilton, A. 1930. *A New Account of the East Indies*, 2 vols., ed. by W. Foster, London.

Hedges, William. 1887–89. *The Diary of William Hedges, Esq., during his Agency in Bengal & c.*, 3 vols., ed. by R. Barlow and H. Yule, WHS, 1st Series, London.

Janaki, V.A. 1974. *Some Aspects of Historical Geography of Surat*, Baroda.

Letters Received. 1900. *Letters Received by the East India Company from Servants in the East*, 6 vols., ed. by W. Foster, London.

Mandelslo, J. Albert de. 1931. *Mandelslo's Travels in Western India (A.D. 1638–39)*, extracted tr. by M.S. Commissariat, London.

Manucci, N. 1907 and 1908. *Storia do Mogor or Mogul India 1653–1708*, 4 vols., ed. by W. Irvine, London.

Morioka, Yoshiko. 2001/2005. *Sekai no naka no Dejima (Dejima in the World), Nagasaki* (in Japanese).

Mundy, Peter. 1914. *The Travels of Peter Mundy, in Europe and Asia, 1608–1667, Vol. II: Travels in Asia, 1628–34*, ed. by Sir R. C. Temple, Hakluyt Society, 2nd Series, London.

Nadri, Ghulam Ahmad. 2009. *Eighteenth-Century Gujarat: The Dynamics of Its Political Economy, 1750–1800*, Leiden and Boston.

Nagashima, Hiromu. 1996. "The Shahbandar at Surat in the Mughal Empire", *Nagasaki Prefectural University Review*, Vol. 29, No. 4.

Ovington, J. 1929. *A Voyage to Surat in the Year 1689*, ed. by H.G. Rawlinson, London.

Pearson, M.N. 1998. *Port Cities and Intruders: The Swahili Coast, India, and Portugal in the Early Modern Era*, Baltimore.

Ray, Aniruddha. 2004. *The Merchant and the State: The French in India, 1666–1739*, 2 vols., New Delhi.

References. 1820. *References to the Plan of the City of Surat Executed by Officers of the Revenue Survey Department*, ed. by Survey Office, Goojerat. This is preserved at the British Library, Shelfmark: X/2738.

Roe, T. 1926. *The Embassy of Sir Thomas Roe, 1615–19*, 2 vols., ed. by W. Foster, London.

SC. 1928. *A Supplementary Calendar of Documents in India Office Relating to India or to the Home Affairs of the East India Company, 1600–1640*, ed. by W. Foster, London.

Singh, Chandramani. 1986. "Early 18th-century painted city maps on cloth", *Facets of Indian Art: a symposium held at the Victoria and Albert Museum*, ed. by Robert Skelton *et al.*, London.

Singh, O.P. 1977. *Surat and its Trade in the Second Half of the 17th Century*, Delhi.

Stavorinus, J.S. 1969. *Voyages to the East Indies by J.S. Stavorinus*, 3 vols., tr. by S.H. Wilcocke. First published in London 1798; Reprint ed. London.

Tavernier, J.B. 1925. *Travels in India, 1640–67*, 2 vols., tr. by Ball, V., Second edition revised by W. Crooke, London.

Thevenot and Careri. 1949. *The Indian Travels of Thevenot and Careri*, ed. by S.N. Sen, New Delhi.

Toyama, Mikio. 1990. *Nagasaki Rekishi no Tabi*, Tokyo (in Japanese).

3. Maps

The map of Northwestern corner of Surat in the 1660s, EFI, 1661–64, p. 297 (Map depicted by W. Foster).

The Map of Surat (c. 1730): Preserved in the Maharaja Sawai Man Singh II Museum, Jaipur, India (abbreviated as "the 1730 map").

The 1758 French Map of Surat: Plan de la Ville de Surate et du Jardin Française. Dressé en 1758. sous l'inspection du S. Anquetil de Briancourt; alors Chef de la Nation Française à Surate, cited in Aniruddha Ray, *The Merchant and the State: the French in India, 1666–1739*, 2 vols., New Delhi, 2004, Vol. I, inserted between pp. 96 and 97.

Survey Office. 1820. *The Plan of the City of Surat*, Surveyed by Lieutenant Adams and Newport, 1817, IOR: X/2737, The British Library (abbreviated as "the 1817 map").

The 1877 Map: Map published by the Govt. Photozincographic Office, Poona, 1877, Cited in V.A. Janaki, *Some Aspects of the Historical Geography of Surat*, Baroda, p. 88.

Contributors

Bhawan Ruangsilp, Lecturer, Department of History, Faculty of Arts, Chulalongkorn University, Thailand.

Leonard Blussé, Professor, Research Institute for History, Leiden University, The Netherlands.

Haneda Masashi, Professor, Institute of Oriental Culture, University of Tokyo, Japan.

Philippe Haudrère, Professor of Modern History, University of Angers, Member of Académie de Marine, France.

Ito Shiori, Curator, Chiba City Museum of Art, Japan.

Liu Yong, Associate Professor, Research School for Southeast Asian Studies, Xiamen University, China.

Liu Zhaohui, Associate Professor, Department of Museology and Cultural Relics, Fudan University, China.

Matsui Yoko, Professor, Historiographical Institute, University of Tokyo, Japan.

Søren Menz, Curator and Senior Researcher, The Museum of National History at Frederiksborg Castle, Denmark.

Nagashima Hiromu, Professor, Department of Regional Policy, Faculty of Economics, University of Nagasaki, Japan.

Index

Africa, 12, 145, 225
Amakusa-Shimabara Rebellion, 25, 27
Anglo-French wars, 169, 171
Anglo-Indian, 166, 169–70
Arabian
    Peninsula, 4
    Sea, 2, 8, 126
Arita porcelain, 88, 94, 111
Asian
    maritime world, 2–3, 6–7
    port cities, 1, 4–10, 12, 14, 129
Aurangzeb, 171, 195, 221
Ayutthaya, 9, 126, 133, 139–40, 142–8, 150, 152–7, 220

Bakufu, 24, 27, 29–30, 34–6, 38–9, 90
Bandar Abbas, 8, 13, 18–21
Batavia, 8–10, 12, 18, 28–9, 32, 34, 119–36, 141, 143, 147–8, 151, 154–6, 158, 207, 213, 220
    Castle, 121, 124–5, 128–9
Battle of Plassey, 123
Bengal, 123, 132–3, 162, 167, 177, 180, 223
    Bay of, 126, 134–5
British
    East India Company, 4
    Empire, 165
    merchants, 162, 164, 168–9, 171

Calcutta, 162, 167, 223
Canton, 12–3, 16–21, 43–62, 124, 126, 145
    system, 16, 43
    trade, 43, 51–2, 55
Cape of Good Hope, 131, 134
Ceylon, 132–4
Chao Phraya River, 143, 145–7
China, 10, 28, 43, 45, 47–8, 51–2, 55, 58–60, 63–6, 75, 80, 83–5, 89–91, 99, 102, 109, 116, 120, 124, 131, 133, 135, 143
    Sea, 30
    trade, 45, 48, 53, 56
Chinese merchants, 46, 49–50, 53–4, 57, 59, 62, 91
Christianity, 10, 18, 24, 27–8, 65
Ciliwong River, 121, 124
Co-hong, 49, 55, 62
Cochin China, 29, 132, 175
Coen, J.P. (Governor-General), 119–20
Colombo, 147–8
Coromandel Coast, 132, 134, 162, 166, 225
Cross-cultural exchanges, 1, 3–7, 10, 44, 156

Deshima, 8, 14–5, 28, 32–3, 37, 126, 145, 192, 215, 218
Dutch
    East India Company (VOC), 6, 12–3, 15, 19, 44–5, 47–50, 52–60, 63, 90–1, 109–11, 119, 120, 123–6, 129–31, 133–5, 140–8, 150–9, 192, 207, 215, *see also* European East India Company

East Indiamen, 120–1, 126, 146
factory, 194, 196, 214–8, 222–5
Republic, 48, 55, 119, 121–3, 130, 140
Dutch-Siamese Treaty of 1664, 141, 143–4, 148, 151, 154, 156

East Asian
maritime world, 8, 13, 22
port cities, 21
East China Sea, 2, 126
Edo, 15, 25, 27–8, 34, 37, 64, 67–8, 70, 73, 83
bakufu, 90
period, 7, 18, 24, 33, 35, 63–4, 83–4, 86
Ekathotsarot, King, 145
England, 165, 168–9, 171–3, 195, 219
English
East India Company (EIC), 4, 6, 19–20, 23, 53–4, 56, 58, 123, 172, *see also* British East India Company
factory, 194–5, 197–8, 202, 208, 214–6, 224–5
Eurocentric, 1–2
European East India Companies, 4–6, 10, 43, *see also* British East India Company, Dutch East India Company, English East India Company
European
market, 89, 109, 113–4, 116
Union, 2

Fort St. George, 167, 171
French
East India Company (CFI), 53, 143, 176, 186, *see also* European East India Companies
factory, 197–200, 202–3, 212
Fourth Anglo-Dutch War (1780–84), 55

Gentlemen Seventeen, 55, 120, 134
Goa, 124, 143
Golconda, 164, 177
Guangzhou, 8–9, 124, 126
Gujarat, 194, 219–20, 223

Hirado, 22, 27–9, 31–2, 90, 215
Holland, 63, 84, 120, 122, 124, 128
Hong merchants, 9, 43–4, 48–51, 54–5, 58
Hoppo, 16, 43, 48, 51–2, 54–5, 57–8, 62

Imari, 10, 88–9, 91–102, 104–16
India, 6, 10, 20–1, 56, 132–3, 165–73, 186, 191, 200–1, 210, 219, 223, 225
Indian Ocean, 120, 123, 126, 167
maritime world, 13, 22
Indian subcontinent, 2, 122
Indonesian Archipelago, 122–3, 134–5

Jakarta, 124, 137
Japan, 4, 7, 10, 12, 15, 17, 24–34, 36–7, 39–40, 63–6, 75, 80, 82–3, 88–91, 94, 98–100, 102, 105, 109–10, 116, 120, 124, 131–4, 140, 143, 147, 192, 203, 212–5, 220, 223, 225
Jingdezhen, 10, 88–98, 100–3, 105–6, 109–16
Ko-sometsuke ware, 93
porcelain/ware, 88–98, 100, 109, 113, 116
joint-stock company, 5–6

kabuki, 64
Kakiemon, 89, 113, 116
Kirkpatrick, Major James Achilles, 172–3

Ko-sometsuke, 93–5, 98–9, 116
Korea, 88
Kotmai Tra Sam Duang, 140, 157
Kraak, 109–11, 116
Kyoto, 37, 64, 67–8, 82, 105

laissez-faire policy, 22
Ligor, 133, 146–7
London, 4, 165, 169

Macao, 8, 16, 18, 28, 55, 57–8, 126, 133
Macartney mission, 53
Madras, 8, 162–72, 175, 182–3, 190, 213
Malacca, 120, 132–3
  Straits, 133–5
Maluku, 126, 134
Manila, 120, 122, 126, 181
Meiji Period, 63
Ming dynasty/period, 22, 64–6, 89–91, 94–5, 97–8, 101–3, 105–6, 109–11
Monsoon Asia, 122, 124, 126, 129
Mughal Empire, 120, 192, 223
Mysore, 177

Nagasaki, 6–10, 12–21, 24–31, 33–40, 63–8, 75–6, 80–3, 90, 124, 126, 131, 145, 192, 213, 215, 220
Nanpin style, 67–8, 70–1, 73, 75–6, 82–4
Narai, King, 143–4, 147, 154–5
Nawab, 171, 187
Netherlands, 49, 90, 111, 125–6, 133–5, 219
Nieuhof, Johan, 121, 125–6, 128–9

Obaku, 64–5, 68, 85

Palmer, William, 162–3, 173
Pasar Ikan, 129, 135
Persia, 8, 10, 13, 19, 132–3, *see also* Safavid Persia
Persian Gulf, 18, 20
Phetracha, King, 144, 153–4
Pondicherry, 8, 170, 175–8, 181, 185, 187, 190–1, 213
port cities, 3–7, 10, 16–7, 22
Prasatthong, King, 142–3, 145–6, 154–5
Pulicat, 132, 213, 219–20, 225

Qing dynasty/government, 16, 19, 22, 52–3, 89–91, 95, 102–3, 105–6, 109–11

Ramayana, 185–6
Ranga Pillai, Ananda, 175–8, 180–2, 184–91
Red Sea, 2, 126, 215

Safavid
  government, 19, 21–2
  Persia, 120, *see also* Persia
sakoku, 17, 35–6
Schouten,
  Joost, 139–40, 142
  Wouter, 128–9
Shah Jahan, 194, 220
Shen Nanpin, 65–8, 70–1, 81, 83–7
Shonzui, 98–101, 116
Siam, 126, 133, 139–44, 146–8, 152–7
Somenishiki, 113–4, 116
South China Sea, 120, 126, 135
Southeast Asia, 2, 4, 110, 120, 139–40, 152, 215, 220
St. Paul's Church, 188, 190
Sumatra, 133–4
Sunda Strait, 126, 134

Surat, 8, 132, 145, 192–203, 207–25
  Fort of, 196, 202, 204–6

Taiwan, 29–30, 126
Tamil, 177, 181, 183–4, 186, 190
  merchants, 175, 181
Tapti River, 193, 195, 207–9
Thaisa, King, 146, 152, 155, 159
Tokugawa government, 10, 14, 18
Tonkin, 30, 36, 126, 133
Treaty of Munster, 119

Valentijn, François, 121, 130–1
VOC, *see* Dutch East India Company

world
  economy, 2
  history, 1–5, 7, 11